THE TRINITY FORUM

ENTREPRENEURS OF LIFE

Faith and the Venture of Purposeful Living

OS GUINNESS

Edited by Ginger Koloszyc
Reader's Guide by Karen Lee-Thorp

NAVPRESS

Bringing Truth to Life
P.O. Box 35001, Colorado Springs, Colorado 80935

OUR GUARANTEE TO YOU

We believe so strongly in the message of our books that we are making this quality guarantee to you. If for any reason you are disappointed with the content of this book, return the title page to us with your name and address and we will refund to you the list price of the book. To help us serve you better, please briefly describe why you were disappointed. Mail your refund request to: NavPress, P.O. Box 35002, Colorado Springs, CO 80935.

Library of Congress Catalog Card Number: 00-067883
ISBN 1-57683-163-9

Cover design by Dan Jamison
Cover illustration of birds by Nanette Hoogslag / Digiatl Vision
Cover illustration of airplane from FPG International
Creative Team: Steve Webb, Karen Lee-Thorp, Darla Hightower, Pat Miller

Portions of the introduction are excerpted from *The Call.* © 1998 by Os Guinness. Word Publishing, Nashville, TN. All rights reserved.

Excerpts from *Harvests of Joy, My Passion, My Life.* © 1998 by Robert Mondavi. Reprinted by permission of Harcourt Inc.

Excerpts from *The Coming of Age* by Simone de Beauvoir. © 1974 by Editions Gallimard. By permission of Rosica Colin Ltd.

Unless otherwise identified, all Scripture quotations in this publication are taken from the *HOLY BIBLE: NEW INTERNATIONAL VERSION*® (NIV®). Copyright © 1973, 1978, 1984 by International Bible Society. Used by permission of Zondervan Publishing House. All rights reserved.

Entrepreneurs of life : faith and the venture of purposeful living / [compiled] by Os Guinness ; edited by Ginger Koloszyc ; reader's guide by Karen Lee-Thorp.
    p. cm. — (The Trinity forum study series)
  Includes bibliographical references.
  ISBN 1-57683-163-9
   1. Christian life. 2. Meaning (Philosophy)—Religious aspects—Christianity. I. Guinness, Os.
II. Koloszyc, Ginger. III. Lee-Thorp, Karen. IV. Series.

BV4509.5 .E397 2001
248.4—dc21

                                                   00-067883

Printed in the United States of America

1 2 3 4 5 6 7 8 9 10 / 05 04 03 02 01

FOR A FREE CATALOG OF
NAVPRESS BOOKS & BIBLE STUDIES,
CALL 1-800-366-7788 (USA)
OR 1-416-499-4615 (CANADA)

THE TRINITY FORUM

Contents

THE TRINITY FORUM

*The Trinity Forum would like to recognize the following people
for their work on this project:*

Project Director: Os Guinness

Selections and Introductions: Os Guinness

Resource Scholars: Steve Garber, Margaret Gardner,
Alonzo L. McDonald

Researchers: Seth Diehl and John Lauber

Editor: Ginger Koloszyc

Copy editor: Peter Edman

NOT SO MUCH A BOOK
AS A WAY OF THINKING

The 'Why' and 'How' of the Trinity Forum Study Series

Thinkers from the time of Socrates to our own day have believed that the unexamined life is not worth living. Today's unique challenge is to lead an examined life in an unexamining age. The sheer pace and pressure of our modern lives can easily crowd out time for reflection. To make matters worse, we live in a war zone against independent thinking. Television jingles, advertising hype, political soundbites, and "dumbed down" discourse of all kinds assault an individual's ability to think for himself or herself. Carefully considered conclusions about life and the best way to live it are too often the casualties.

Into this challenging landscape The Trinity Forum launches its *Study Series*, inviting individuals to think through today's issues carefully and deliberately — in the context of faith — to reach deeper and more firmly established convictions.

About The Trinity Forum

The Trinity Forum was founded in 1991. Its aim: to contribute to the transformation and renewal of society through the transformation and renewal of leaders. Christian in commitment, but open to all who are interested in its vision, it has organized dozens of forums for leaders of all sectors of modern life — from business to education, from fashion to government and the media.

Hundreds of leaders from many faiths across the United States, Canada, and Europe have taken part in these forums.

A distinctive feature of The Trinity Forum is its format. There are no lectures, addresses, or talks of any kind. A curriculum of readings on a given topic is sent out in advance and then explored at the forum in a Socratic-style open discussion led by moderators. This give-and-take challenges the participants to wrestle with the issues themselves and—importantly—to reach their own thought-out conclusions.

By popular demand, The Trinity Forum now offers these curricula to a wider audience, enhanced as the *Trinity Forum Study Series* and designed for individual readers or study groups in homes, churches, and colleges. Each *Study* is intended to help thoughtful people examine the foundational issues through which faith acts upon the public good of modern society. A reader's guide at the back of each book will aid those who want to discuss the material with a group. Those reading the book on their own may also find that the reader's guide will help them focus on the *Study's* big ideas. The reader's guide contains basic principles of small-group leadership, an overview of the *Study's* main ideas, and suggested selections for groups that don't have time to discuss every reading in the *Study*.

Adult in seriousness and tone, yet popular rather than scholarly in style, the *Trinity Forum Study Series* probes each topic through the milestone writings that have shaped its development. This approach will be fresh and exciting to many and, we trust, stimulating to all. It is worth laying out some of the assumptions and convictions that guide this approach, for what is presented here is not so much a book as it is a way of thinking.

Defining Features of the Trinity Forum Study Series

First, the Trinity Forum Study Series *explores the issues of our day in the context of faith.* As stated earlier, The Trinity Forum is Christ-centered in its commitment, but opens its programs to all who share its aims—whether believers, seekers, or skeptics. The same committed but open spirit marks this series of books.

For people of faith, it should be natural to take into account the place of faith when discussing the issues of life, both historically and presently. But it should also be natural for all citizens of Western society, of whatever faith. For no one can understand Western civilization without understanding the Christian faith that, for better or worse, has been its primary shaping force. Yet a striking feature of many of today's thought-leaders and opinion-shapers is their "tone deafness" toward faith of any kind—which means that, unwittingly or otherwise, they do not hear the music by which most people orchestrate their lives.

For example, a national media executive recently admitted his and his colleagues' befuddlement about Americans' deep reliance upon faith. Citing the outpouring of public prayer in response to a tragic school shooting in Kentucky, he confessed, "We simply don't get it." These readings aim to remedy that neglected dimension of understanding, and thereby reintroduce to the modern discussion the perspective of faith that is vital both for making sense of the past and dealing with the present.

Second, the Trinity Forum Study Series *presents the perspective of faith in the context of the sweep of Western civilization, recognizing the vital place of the past in the lives of nations as well as individuals.* A distinctive feature of the modern world is its passion for the present and fascination with the future at the expense of the past. Progress, choice, change, novelty, and the myth of newer-the-truer and latest-is-greatest reign unchallenged, while ideas and convictions from earlier times are boxed-up in the cobwebbed attic of nostalgia and irrelevance. By contrast, Winston Churchill said, "The further backward you can look, the farther forward you can see." For him, as well as the American framers in the eighteenth century and the writers of the Bible before them, remembering is not foremost a matter of nostalgia or historical reverie, and it is far more than mental recall. For all of them, it is a vital key to identity, faith, wisdom, renewal, and the dynamism of a living tradition, for both nations and individuals.

By reintroducing important writings from the past, the *Trinity Forum Study Series* invites readers to a living conversation of ideas and imagination with the great minds of our heritage. Only when we know where we have come from do we know who we are and where we are going.

Third, the Trinity Forum Study Series *presents the perspective of faith in the context of the challenge of other faiths.* If the first feature of this series is likely to offend some unthinking secularists, this one may do the same to unthinking believers. But the truth is, some believers don't appear to know their own faith because they know *only* their own faith. Familiarity breeds inattention. It is true, as essayist Ronald Knox quipped, that comparative religion can make us "comparatively religious." But it is also true that contrast is the mother of clarity.

One important benefit of understanding one's own faith in distinction to others is the ability to communicate ideas and positions persuasively in the public square. Believers properly hold their beliefs on the basis of divine authority. Such beliefs, however, must be conveyed compellingly in a society that does not accept the same authority. An important part of meeting that challenge effectively is the ability to grasp and highlight the differences between faiths.

This series of books, therefore, sets out the perspectives of the Christian faith in the context of the challenge of other faiths. If "all truth is God's truth," and if differences truly make a difference, then such contrasts between one faith and another are not only challenging but illuminating and important for both individuals and society.

Fourth, the Trinity Forum Study Series *is unashamed about the necessity for tough-minded thinking.* Much has been made recently of Christian anti-intellectualism and the scandal of the lack of a Christian mind. As Bertrand Russell put it, "Most Christians would rather die than think — in fact, they do." But failure to think is not confined to any one community or group. Former Secretary of State Henry Kissinger is quoted as saying, "In Washington D.C. there is so little time to think that most people live forever off the intellectual capital from the day they arrive."

In contrast, Abraham Lincoln's greatness was fired in times of thoughtful reflection during the Civil War. Today's profound crises call for similar thoughtful reflection and courage by men and women prepared to break rank with a largely unthinking and conformist age. Just as an earlier generation broke with accepted practices of little exercise and bad eating, restoring a vogue for fitness, so our generation must shake off the lethargy of "dumbed down" discourse and recover the capacity to think tough-mindedly as the issues and our times require.

Fifth, the Trinity Forum Study Series *recognizes that many of the urgent public issues of our day are cultural rather than political.* Much recent discussion of public affairs oscillates uneasily between heavily moral issues (such as abortion) and more strongly political issues (such as campaign finance reform). Yet increasingly, many of the urgent concerns of our day lie in between. They are neither purely moral nor purely political, but integrate elements of both. In other words, many key issues are morally grounded "pre-political" issues, such as the role of "trust" in capitalism, "character" in leadership, "truth" in public discourse, "stewardship" in philanthropy and environmentalism, and "voluntarism" in civil society.

To be sure, it is a symptom of our present crisis that such foundational issues have to be debated at all. But the *Trinity Forum Study Series* addresses these often neglected issues, always presenting them in the context of faith and always addressing them in a nonpartisan manner that befits such cultural discussion.

Finally, the Trinity Forum Study Series *assumes the special need for, and the possibility of, a social and cultural renaissance in our time.* As we consider our present crises with clear-eyed realism, one of the great challenges is to be hopeful with a real basis for hope while always being critical of what is wrong without collapsing into alarmism or despair. To be sure, no freedom, prosperity, or success lasts forever in this life, in either spiritual or secular affairs. But, equally, the grand cycle of birth, growth, and decline is never deterministic, and no source of renewal is more sure and powerful than spiritual revival. The *Study Series* is born of this conviction.

Giving up hope in the worthwhileness of the worthwhile—in God, the good, the true, the just, and the beautiful—is another name for the deadly sin of sloth. Venturing out, under God, to be entrepreneurs of life is another name for faith. Thus, while always uncertain of the outcome of our times, always modest about our own contribution, and always confident in God rather than ourselves, those who present the *Trinity Forum Study Series* desire to encourage people to move out into society with constructive answers and a sense of a confidence born of faith and seasoned by history. In so doing, we seek to sow the seeds for a much-needed renaissance in our own time.

INTRODUCTION—
ENTREPRENEURS OF LIFE

"As you know, I have been very fortunate in my career and I've made a lot of money—far more than I ever dreamed of, far more than I could ever spend, far more than my family needs." The speaker was a prominent businessman at a conference near Oxford University. The strength of his determination and character showed in his face, but a moment's hesitation betrayed deeper emotions hidden behind the outward intensity. A single tear rolled slowly down his well-tanned cheek.

"To be honest, one of my motives for making so much money was simple—to have the money to hire people to do what I don't like doing. But there's one thing I've never been able to hire anyone to do for me: find my own sense of purpose and fulfillment. I'd give anything to discover that."

"But there's one thing I've never been able to hire anyone to do for me: find my own sense of purpose and fulfillment. I'd give anything to discover that."

That issue—purpose and fulfillment—is one of the deepest issues in our modern world. At some point every one of us confronts the question: *How do I find and fulfill the central purpose of my life?* Other questions may come logically prior to and lie even deeper than this one—for example, Who am I? What is the meaning of life itself? But few questions are raised more loudly and more insistently today than the first. As modern people we are all on a search for significance. We desire to make a difference. We long to leave a legacy. We yearn, as Ralph Waldo Emerson put it, "to leave the world a bit better." Our passion is to know that we are fulfilling the purpose for which we are here on earth.

Notions of "the Holy Grail" differ enormously—from an Olympic gold to a Hollywood Oscar to a Nobel Prize to a chairman's executive suite to the White House, 10 Downing Street, or the Palais d'Orsay. So too do notions of "making a difference" and "leaving a legacy." Artists, scientists, and builders often labor to create a unique work that can live forever in their name. Politicians, business people, and administrators usually think of their monuments more in terms of institutions they have created and sustained. Parents, teachers, and counselors, by contrast, view their contribution in terms of lives shaped and matured. But for all the variety, the need for purpose is the same. As Thomas Carlyle wrote, "The man without a purpose is like a ship without a rudder—a waif, a nothing, a no-man."

All other standards of success—wealth, power, position, knowledge, friendships—grow tinny and hollow if we do not satisfy this deeper longing. For some people the hollowness leads to what Henry Thoreau described as "lives of quiet desperation"; for others the emptiness and aimlessness deepen into a stronger despair. In an early draft of Fyodor Dostoyevsky's *The Brothers Karamazov*, the Inquisitor gives a terrifying account of what happens to the human soul when it doubts its purpose: "For the secret of man's being is not only to live . . . but to live for something definite. Without a firm notion of what he is living for, man will not accept life and will rather destroy himself than remain on earth."

Call it the greatest good (*summum bonum*), the ultimate end, the meaning of life, or whatever you choose. But finding and fulfilling our purpose comes up in myriad ways and in all the seasons of our lives:

Teenagers feel it as the world of freedom beyond home and secondary school beckons with a dizzying range of choices.

> *"For the secret of man's being is not only to live . . . but to live for something definite. Without a firm notion of what he is living for, man will not accept life and will rather destroy himself than remain on earth."*
> —FYODOR DOSTOYEVSKY

Are We on Earth for a Purpose?

"yes."

"of course."

"Could you rephrase that question?"

"Sorry, we're just tourists."

Huguette Martel

Graduate students confront it when the excitement of "the world is my oyster" is chilled by the thought that opening up one choice means closing down others.

Those in their early thirties know it when their daily work assumes its own brute reality beyond their earlier considerations of the wishes of their parents, the fashions of their peers, and the allure of salary and career prospects.

People in midlife face it when a mismatch between their gifts and their work reminds them daily that they are square pegs in round holes. Can they see themselves "doing that" for the rest of their lives?

Mothers feel it when their children grow up, and they wonder which high purpose will fill the void in the next stage of their lives.

People in their forties and fifties with enormous success suddenly come up against it when their accomplishments raise questions concerning the social responsibility of their success and, deeper still, the purpose of their lives.

People confront it in all the varying transitions of life—from moving homes to switching jobs to breakdowns in marriage to crises of health. Negotiating these changes feels longer and worse than the changes themselves because transition challenges our sense of personal meaning.

Those in their later years often face it again. What does life add up to? Were the successes real, and were they worth the trade-offs? Having gained a whole world, however huge or tiny, have we sold our souls cheaply and missed the point of it all? As Walker Percy wrote, "You can get all A's and still flunk life."

As Walker Percy wrote, "You can get all A's and still flunk life."

This issue, the question of his own life-purpose, is what drove the Danish thinker Søren Kierkegaard in the nineteenth century. As he realized well, personal purpose is not a matter of philosophy or theory. It is not purely objective, and it is not inherited like a legacy. Many a scientist has an encyclopedic knowledge of the world, many a philosopher can survey vast systems of thought, many a theologian can unpack the profundities of religion, and many a journalist can seemingly speak on any topic raised. But all that is theory and, without a sense of personal purpose, vanity.

Deep in our hearts, we all want to find and fulfill a purpose bigger than ourselves. Only such a larger purpose can inspire us to heights we know we could never reach on our own. For each of us the real purpose is personal and passionate: to know what we are here to do, and why. Kierkegaard wrote in his *Journal:* "The thing is to understand myself, to see what God really wants *me* to do; the thing is to find a truth which is true *for me,* to find the *idea for which I can live and die.*"

"The thing is to understand myself, to see what God really wants me *to do; the thing is to find a truth which is true* for me, *to find the* idea for which I can live and die."*
—Søren Kierkegaard

TOO MUCH TO LIVE WITH, TOO LITTLE TO LIVE FOR

In our own day this question of life purpose is urgent in the highly modern parts of the world, and there is a simple reason why. Three factors have converged to fuel a search for significance without precedent in human history. First, the search for the purpose of life is one of the deepest issues of our experiences as human beings. Second, the expectation that we can all live purposeful lives has been given a gigantic boost by modern society's offer of the

Out of more than a score of great civilizations in human history, modern Western civilization is the very first to have no agreed-on answer to the question of the purpose of life.

maximum opportunity for choice and change in all we do. Third, fulfillment of the search for purpose is thwarted by a stunning fact: Out of more than a score of great civilizations in human history, modern Western civilization is the very first to have no agreed-on answer to the question of the purpose of life. Thus more ignorance, confusion—and longing—surround this topic now than at almost any time in history. The trouble is that, as modern people, we have too much to live with and too little to live for. Some feel they have time but not enough money; others feel they have money but not enough time. But for most of us, in the midst of material plenty, we have spiritual poverty.

The ironies do not stop there. Consider the fact that modern science brings us closer and closer to the extraordinary design in the universe, yet modern people shy away from discovering purpose in individual lives. Or again, consider the fact that there is an emerging consensus on the human "life course"—for example, Daniel Levinson's work on "seasons" or Gail Sheehy's on "passages." But there is no corresponding agreement on the purpose of life that follows this course.

Needless to say, the reason for the confusion lies in the variety of conflicting views offered today—and in the fact that, in the absence of any consensus, many people simply make do by constructing their own sense of purpose as best they can.

VISIONARIES WHO ADD VALUE

This book is for all who long to find and fulfill the purpose of their lives, but who desire to explore the issue carefully. The readings that follow are either milestone writings on the matter, such as the readings from Luther and Eusebius, or are about milestone events in the lives of those responding to a call, such as the abolition of slavery in Great Britain. These readings will examine the main answers offered in today's world, but argue that this purpose can best be found when we discover the specific purpose for which we were created and to which we are called. The great Creator alone creates completely out of nothing—fruitfully and prolifically—and alone knows our reason for being, calling us into a life of purpose. As we human beings rise to the call of our Creator, we become subcreators, entering into our own creativity, artistry, and entrepreneurship as made in his image—thus adding to the rich fruitfulness of the universe. Answering the call of our Creator is therefore "the ultimate why" for living, the highest source of purpose in human existence, because it literally transforms us into "entrepreneurs of life."

All too often the term "creator" is restricted to artists and the term "entrepreneur" to business people, but this restriction is a travesty of our creativity as human beings. As we live life by faith, we are all creators, we are all artists, we are all entrepreneurs, and this is at the very heart of our calling as human beings.

Apart from such a Creator-inspired calling, all hope of discovering purpose (as in the current talk of shifting from "success to significance") will end in disappointment. To be sure, calling is not what it is commonly thought to be. It has to be dug out from under the rubble of ignorance and confusion. And, uncomfortably, it often flies directly in the face of our human inclinations. But nothing short of God's call can ground and fulfill the truest human desire for purpose.

Apart from such a Creator-inspired calling, all hope of discovering purpose (as in the current talk of shifting from "success to significance") will end in disappointment.

One place where the confusion is lifting is the growing understanding that purpose cannot be found in means, only ends. Capitalism, for all its creativity and fruitfulness, falls short when challenged to answer the question "Why?" By itself it is literally meaningless, in that it is only a mechanism, not a source of meaning. So too are politics, science, psychology, management, self-help techniques, and a host of other modern theories. What Tolstoy wrote of science applies to all of them: "Science is meaningless because it gives no answer to our question, the only question important to us, 'what shall we do and how shall we live?'" There is no answer outside a quest for purpose, and no answer to the quest is deeper and more satisfying than answering the call.

One place where the confusion is lifting is the growing understanding that purpose cannot be found in means, only ends.

What is meant by "calling"? Calling is the truth that God calls us to himself so decisively that everything we are, everything we do, and everything we have is invested with a special devotion and dynamism lived out as a response to his summons and service.

And what is meant by "entrepreneur"? The entrepreneur is the person who assumes the responsibility for a creative task, not as an assigned role, a routine function, or an inherited duty, but as a venture of faith, including risk and danger, in order to bring into the world something new and profitable to humankind. Called in this sense, and answering such a call by rising to it in

"Really, I'm fine. It was just a fleeting sense of purpose—I'm sure it will pass."

faith, entrepreneurs of life use their talents and resources to be fruitful and bring added value into the world—quite literally making the invisible visible, the future present, the ideal real, the impossible an achievement, the desired an experience, the status quo dynamic, and the dream a fulfillment.

To be sure, there is much in life we did not choose and cannot change. At the beginning of life none of us decided the date of our birth, the color of our eyes, or the pedigree of our ancestry. And at the end we do not decide the day of our death or the interpretation of our legacy. In between there are a million-and-one circumstances over which we have no control. But we are still, always, essentially people of significance, men and women whose entrepreneurial capacity to exercise dominion, assert influence, and multiply fruitfulness is at the heart of our humanness.

To stress the entrepreneurial must not be confused with the heartless heresy that an individual is valuable only in so far as he or she is profitable. But it is to see, as philosopher Dallas Willard states, that all of us have "a unique eternal calling to count for good in God's great universe."

All of us have "a unique eternal calling to count for good in God's great universe."
—DALLAS WILLARD

The artist Vincent van Gogh captured this expansive view of artistry and entrepreneurship when he wrote to his closest friend, Emile Berhard, just two years before his death. Jesus of Nazareth, he noted, lived "as a greater artist than all other artists, despising marble and clay as well as color, working in living flesh. That is to say, this matchless artist . . . made neither statues nor pictures nor books; he loudly proclaimed that he made . . . living men, immortals."

This truth—calling and its entrepreneurial vision and energy—has been a driving force in many of the greatest "leaps forward" in world history—the construction of the Jewish nation at Mount Sinai, the birth of the Christian movement in Galilee, the sixteenth-century Reformation and its incalculable impetus to the rise of the modern world, and the abolition of slavery and the slave trade in Great Britain, to name a few. Little wonder that the rediscovery of calling should be critical today, not least in satisfying the passion for purpose of millions of questing modern people.

FOR ALL WHO SEEK SIGNIFICANCE

So for whom is this book intended? For all who seek such entrepreneurial purpose. For those who are interested in what the Western tradition says on the matter and how others have lived lives of calling. For all, whether believers or seekers, who are open to the call of the most influential person in history—

Jesus of Nazareth. In particular, it is for those who know that their source of purpose must rise above the highest of self-help humanist hopes and who long for their lives to have integrity, effectiveness, and entrepreneurial potential in the face of all the challenges of the modern world.

Part 1 of these readings sets out the Jewish and Christian view of purpose through calling in contrast to its two most powerful rivals in history—the answers of Eastern thought and Western secularism. The Eastern answer pronounces the search wrong and calls for renunciation and withdrawal, and the Western secularist answer says all purpose is manmade—as Friedrich Nietzsche put it, one must live in such a manner that one can say, "Thus I willed it."

Part 2 examines the lives of two great heroes who demonstrate how individuals can truly make a difference and change their times. One, William Wilberforce, came to know his calling early in life, so that his whole life-task was inspired and shaped by it. The other, Aleksandr Solzhenitsyn, almost stumbled into his calling, but its growing urgency not only gave clarity to his past life, but came to fire his mature stands for truth.

Part 3 explores some of the tests and trials of living life as an entrepreneurial calling—including such stirring stories as Beethoven battling with deafness and Magellan succumbing to hubris after his epic round-the-world journey.

Part 4 begins with Tolstoy's much-loved story of "Two Old Men," which challenges us to appraise our character and priorities in life, and then introduces a questionnaire to press home such a personal appraisal in specific areas.

Part 5 raises the issue of "finishing well" in life's journey and probes this issue with short stories that poignantly raise different aspects of finishing well or not well.

Do you long to discover your own sense of purpose and engage life with an entrepreneurial life-task? You will not find here a one-page executive summary, a how-to manual, a twelve-step program, or a ready-made game plan for figuring out the rest of your life. What you will find may point you toward one of the most powerful and truly awesome truths that has ever arrested the human heart.

Is a sense of calling your ultimate compass in life? In 1941, T. S. Eliot wrote: "Can a lifetime represent a single motive?" If the single motive is simply our own, the answer to Eliot must be no. We are not wise enough, pure enough, or strong enough to aim and sustain such a single motive over a lifetime. That way lies fanaticism or failure.

But if the single motive is the master motive of God's calling, the answer

"Can a lifetime represent a single motive?"
—T. S. Eliot

is yes. In any and all situations, both today and tomorrow's tomorrow, God's call to us is the unchanging and ultimate whence, what, why, and whither of our lives.

"In Ages of Faith," Alexis de Tocqueville observed, "the final aim of life is placed beyond life." That is what calling does. "Follow me," Jesus said two thousand years ago, and he changed the course of history. That is why calling provides the Archimedean point by which faith moves the world. That is why calling is the most comprehensive reorientation and the most profound motivation in human experience—the ultimate Why for living in all history. Calling begins and ends such ages, and lives, of faith, by placing the final aim of life beyond the world, where it was meant to be. Through calling, the entire meaning of our lives lies in the future that is waiting for us. Answering the call is the way to find and fulfill the central, entrepreneurial purpose of your life.

FAITH AS FUTURE-ORIENTED VENTURING

Now faith is being sure of what we hope for and certain of what we do not see. This is what the ancients were commended for. . . .

And without faith it is impossible to please God, because anyone who comes to him must believe that he exists and that he rewards those who earnestly seek him.

By faith Noah, when warned about things not yet seen, in holy fear built an ark to save his family. By his faith he condemned the world and became heir of the righteousness that comes by faith.

By faith Abraham, when called to go to a place he would later receive as his inheritance, obeyed and went, even though he did not know where he was going. By faith he made his home in the promised land like a stranger in a foreign country; he lived in tents, as did Isaac and Jacob, who were heirs with him of the same promise. For he was looking forward to the city with foundations, whose architect and builder is God. . . .

All these people were still living by faith when they died. They did not receive the things promised; they only saw them and welcomed them from a distance. And they admitted that they were aliens and strangers on earth. People who say such things show that they are looking for a country of their own. If they had been thinking of the country they had left, they would have had opportunity to return. Instead, they were longing for a better country—a heavenly one. Therefore God is not ashamed to be called their God, for he has prepared a city for them. . . .

By faith Moses, when he had grown up, refused to be known as the son of Pharaoh's daughter. He chose to be mistreated along with the people of God rather than to enjoy the pleasures of sin for a short time. He regarded disgrace for the sake of Christ as of greater value than the treasures of Egypt, because he was looking ahead to his reward. By faith he left Egypt, not fearing the king's anger; he persevered because he saw him who is invisible. By faith he kept the Passover and the sprinkling of blood, so that the destroyer of the firstborn would not touch the firstborn of Israel.

By faith the people passed through the Red Sea as on dry land; but when the Egyptians tried to do so, they were drowned.

By faith the walls of Jericho fell, after the people had marched around them for seven days.

By faith the prostitute Rahab, because she welcomed the spies, was not killed with those who were disobedient.

And what more shall I say? I do not have time to tell about Gideon, Barak, Samson, Jephthah, David, Samuel and the prophets, who through faith conquered kingdoms, administered justice, and gained what was promised; who shut the mouths of lions, quenched the fury of the flames, and escaped the edge of the sword; whose weakness was turned to strength; and who became powerful in battle and routed foreign armies. Women received back their dead, raised to life again. Others were tortured and refused to be released, so that they might gain a better resurrection. Some faced jeers and flogging, while still others were chained and put in prison. They were stoned; they were sawed in two; they were put to death by the sword. They went about in sheepskins and goatskins, destitute, persecuted and mistreated—the world was not worthy of them. They wandered in deserts and mountains, and in caves and holes in the ground.

These were all commended for their faith, yet none of them received what had been promised. God had planned something better for us so that only together with us would they be made perfect.

—Hebrews 11

ONE
THE ULTIMATE WHY

"*There is but one truly serious philosophical problem, and that is suicide. Judging whether life is worth living amounts to answering the fundamental question of philosophy.*" The famous opening words of Albert Camus's The Myth of Sisyphus *can be put in simpler ways—What is the purpose of my life as an individual human being? Why should I get out of bed in the morning? But Camus is right: The meaning of life is the most urgent human question of all, and the answer to the question of our individual purpose is central to the meaning of life.*

But there are, of course, different accounts of the meaning of life—which is why many people falter in the quest before they ever start. For many people today, the most characteristic response to the modern explosion of beliefs, opinions, and claims is a shrug of the shoulders or the famous teenage reply: "Whatever." Philosophers, we are told, stress relativism, social scientists pluralism, psychologists nonjudgmentalism, and marketers consumerism. So how is any of us to decide between beliefs? And if we believe something strongly, aren't we virtually certain to be dismissed as dogmatic and intolerant?

In the face of such a chorus, people not surprisingly fall back on such clichés of acquiescence as "different strokes for different folks" or "who am I to judge?" Or, more coolly, "whatever."

Ironically, though, the reality of the modern world also underscores the entirely opposite lesson: "Ideas have consequences," "beliefs affect behavior," and "differences make a difference." In fact, when it comes to purpose, fulfillment, and living life as an entrepreneurial venture, varieties of "whatever" are singularly inept. Differences in this area make a huge and highly verifiable difference.

Think of yourself as the product of blind chance or genetic determinism and your "purpose" will be one thing. Think of yourself as a unique person with a unique destiny and it will be quite different. View your individuality as the result of ignorance and illusion and the pursuit of personal fulfillment will only deepen the darkness. View your individuality as something for which you were created and called and your prospects are altogether changed.

As modern people we are awash with data on all aspects of the human course of life—childhood, marriage, divorce, retirement, death, the "empty nest" syndrome, and so on. But such statistics are usually general, abstract, impersonal, and negative—mostly about the breakdowns and pathologies of each stage. They do not tell each of us how best to live with our own sense of purpose in life.

The readings in part 1 explore the three main approaches to the question "Why?" that are available in today's world. Part 1 closes with examples of the wistfulness born of modern confusion. Unquestionably the Jewish and Christian notion of calling has provided the ultimate Why for human living, the most powerful and inspiring vision of life as an entrepreneurial venture. But to see that clearly, we need to see the strong contrast with two competing views—the Eastern and the Western secularist. In passing, we will also note the two philosophies—"chivalry" and "possibility thinking"—that grow from the biblical teaching but have sometimes acted as a secular substitute for it. The conclusion is inescapable: Choices at this level of beliefs decisively determine the possibility and character of any vision of life as an entrepreneurial venture.

Hermann Hesse

Hermann Hesse (1877–1962) was a German novelist and poet who won the Nobel Prize for Literature in 1946. Deeply influenced by the Romantic movement, he wrote widely on psychological and mystical subjects and developed somewhat of a cult following after his death. Born and raised in Germany, he began his career as a bookseller and antiquarian, gaining fame for such works as Steppenwolf *and* The Glass Bead Game. *Hesse's novel* Siddhartha *was published in 1922. Written in the form of a Bildungsroman, or "novel of development," it tells a story of the path to self-fulfillment through the life of Buddha.*

The passage below explores the ascetic stage of Siddhartha's search, which does not lead to final enlightenment. But it shows clearly how in the East, for both Hinduism and Buddhism, individuality is an illusion. Freedom is therefore freedom from individuality, not freedom to be an individual.

Thus the first broad answer to the human quest for individual purpose and fulfillment is: Renounce and Withdraw. Within the Eastern family of faiths, the final reality is viewed as "impersonal and undifferentiated," so there is no final place for the purpose or fulfillment of individuals.

GO EAST, YOUNG MAN

"East is East and West is West, and never the twain shall meet."

—Rudyard Kipling

"Orientation means to know where the Orient is."

—R. D. Laing

"Elementary ecology leads straight to elementary Buddhism."

—Aldous Huxley

A student at Santa Barbara asked theologian Paul Tillich at the end of his life, "Sir, do you pray?" He replied, "No, I meditate."

Siddhartha ❧

Siddhartha had begun to feel the seeds of discontent within him. He had begun to feel that the love of his father and mother, and also the love of his friend Govinda, would not always make him happy, give him peace, satisfy and suffice him. He had begun to suspect that his worthy father and his other teachers, the wise Brahmins, had already passed on to him the bulk and best of their wisdom, that they had already poured the sum total of their knowledge into his waiting vessel; and the vessel was not full, his intellect was not satisfied, his soul was not at peace, his heart was not still. The ablutions were good, but they were water; they did not wash sins away, they did not relieve the distressed heart. The sacrifices and the supplication of the gods were excellent—but were they everything? Did the sacrifices give happiness? And what about the gods? Was it really Prajapati who had created the world? Was it not Atman, He alone, who had created it? Were not the gods forms created like me and you, mortal, transient? Was it therefore good and right, was it a sensible and worthy act to offer sacrifices to the gods? To whom else should one offer sacrifices, to whom else should one pay honor, but to Him, Atman, the Only One? And where was Atman to be found, where did He dwell, where did His eternal heart beat, if not within the Self, in the innermost, in the eternal which each person carried within him? But where was this Self, this innermost? It was not flesh and bone, it was not thought or consciousness. That was what the wise men taught. Where, then, was it? To press towards the Self, towards Atman—was there another way that was worth seeking? Nobody showed the way, nobody knew it—neither his father, nor the teachers and wise men, nor the holy songs. The Brahmins and their holy books knew everything, everything; they had gone into everything—the creation of the world, the origin of speech, food, inhalation, exhalation, the arrangement of the senses, the acts of the gods. They knew a tremendous number of things—but was it worth while knowing all these things if they did not know the one important thing, the only important thing?

And where was Atman to be found, where did He dwell, where did His eternal heart beat, if not within the Self, in the innermost, in the eternal which each person carried within him?

WITH THE SAMANAS

Siddhartha gave his clothes to a poor Brahmin on the road and only retained his loincloth and earth-colored unstitched cloak. He only ate once a day and never cooked food. He fasted fourteen days. He fasted twenty-eight days. The flesh disappeared from his legs and cheeks. Strange dreams were reflected in his enlarged eyes. The nails grew long on his thin fingers and a dry, bristly beard appeared on his chin. His glance became icy when he encountered women; his lips curled with contempt when he passed through a town of well-dressed people. He saw businessmen trading, princes going to the hunt, mourners weeping over their dead, prostitutes offering themselves, doctors attending the sick, priests deciding the day for sowing, lovers making love, mothers soothing their children—and all were not worth a passing glance, everything lied, stank of lies; they were all illusions of sense, happiness and beauty. All were doomed to decay. The world tasted bitter. Life was pain.

Siddhartha had one single goal—to become empty, to become empty of thirst, desire, dreams, pleasure and sorrow—to let the Self die. No longer to be Self, to experience the peace of an emptied heart, to experience pure thought—that was his goal. When all the Self was conquered and dead, when all passions and desires were silent, then the last must awaken, the innermost of Being that is no longer Self—the great secret!

Silently Siddhartha stood in the fierce sun's rays, filled with pain and thirst, and stood until he no longer felt pain and thirst. Silently he stood in the rain, water dripping from his hair on to his freezing shoulders, on to his freezing hips and legs. And the ascetic stood until his shoulders and legs no longer froze, till they were silent, till they were still. Silently he crouched among the thorns. Blood dripped from his smarting skin, ulcers formed, and Siddhartha remained still, motionless, till no more blood flowed, till there was no more pricking, no more smarting.

Siddhartha sat upright and learned to save his breath, to manage with little breathing, to hold his breath. He learned, while breathing in, to quiet his heart-beat, learned to lessen his heartbeats, until there were few and hardly any more.

Instructed by the eldest of the Samanas, Siddhartha practiced self-denial and meditation according to the Samana rules. A heron flew over the bamboo wood and Siddhartha took the heron into his soul, flew over forest and mountains, became a heron, ate fishes, suffered heron hunger, used heron language, died a heron's death. A dead jackal lay on the sandy shore and Siddhartha's soul slipped into its corpse; he became a dead jackal, lay on the shore, swelled, stank, decayed, was dismembered by hyenas, was picked at by vultures, became a skeleton, became dust, mingled with the atmosphere. And Siddhartha's soul returned, died, decayed, turned into dust, experienced the troubled course of the life cycle. He waited with new thirst like a hunter at a chasm where the life cycle ends, where there is an end to causes, where painless eternity begins. He killed his senses, he killed his memory, he slipped out of his Self in a thousand different forms. He was animal, carcass, stone, wood, water, and each time he reawakened. The sun or moon shone, he was again Self, swung into the life cycle, felt thirst, conquered thirst, felt new thirst.

Siddhartha learned a great deal from the Samanas; he learned many ways of losing the Self. He traveled along the path of self-denial through pain, through voluntary suffering and conquering of pain, through hunger, thirst, and fatigue. He traveled the way of self-denial through meditation, through the emptying of the mind of all images. Along these and other paths did he learn to travel. He lost his Self a thousand times and for days on end he dwelt in non-being. But although the paths took him away from Self, in the end they always led back to it. Although Siddhartha fled from the Self a thousand times, dwelt in nothing, dwelt in animal and stone, the return was inevitable; the hour was inevitable when he would again find himself, in sunshine or in moonlight, in shadow or in rain, and was again Self and Siddhartha, again felt the torment of the onerous life cycle.

He lost his Self a thousand times and for days on end he dwelt in non-being. But although the paths took him away from Self, in the end they always led back to it.

From Herman Hesse, *Siddhartha*, translated by Hilda Rosner. (New York: New Directions Publishing Corp., 1951), pp. 5-6, 13-14. Reprinted by permission of New Directions Publishing Corporation and Laurence Pollinger Limited.

FREEDOM IS FREEDOM *FROM* INDIVIDUALITY

"Brahman alone is real, the phenomenal world is unreal, or mere illusion."

—Shankara, ninth-century Hindu sage and philosopher

"Who are you? Who am I? Whence have I come? Who is my mother? Who is my father? Think of all this as having no substance, leave it all as the stuff of dreams."

—Shankara

Shankara used to tell the story of a pupil who kept asking his master about the nature of Brahman or God or the Absolute Self. Each time the question came, the teacher would turn a deaf ear, until finally he turned impatiently on his pupil and said, "I am teaching you but you do not follow. The Self is silence."

Humanity must be cut from "the dark forest of delusion."

—Lord Krishna, in the Bhagavad-Gita

"I am nowhere a somewhatness for anyone."

—Buddhagosa,
describing the fourfold emptiness

"If you want to get the plain truth,
be not concerned with right and wrong.
The conflict between right and wrong
Is the sickness of the mind."

—Yun-Men, Zen master

The goal of Zen is not incarnation but "excarnation."

—D. T. Suzuki

Humans are "God's temporary self-forgetfulness."

—Radakrishnan,
philosopher and President of India

"God entranced himself and forgot the way back, so that now he feels himself to be man, playing—
guiltily—at being God."

—Alan Watts

"A real merging of the limited in the ocean of universal life involves complete surrender of separative
existence in all its forms."

—Meher Baba

"'And if he left off dreaming about you, where do you suppose you'd be?'
    "'Where I am now, of course,' said Alice.
    "'Not you!' Tweedledee retorted contemptuously. 'You'd be nowhere. Why, you're only a sort of
thing in his dream! If that there King was to wake,' added Tweedledum, 'you'd go out—bang!—just
like a candle!'"

—Alice talks to Tweedledee and Tweedledum
about dreams in Lewis Carroll's Through the Looking Glass

"'Everything is good.'
    "'Everything?'
    "'Everything. Man is unhappy because he doesn't know he's happy. That's the only reason. The man
who discovers that will become happy that very minute. That stepdaughter will die, the little girl will
remain—and everything is good. I suddenly discovered that.'

"'So it's good, too, that people die of hunger and also that someone may abuse or rape that little girl?'

"'It's good. And if someone breaks open that man's skull for the girl, that's good too. And if someone doesn't break his skull, it's equally good. Everything's good.'"

—Kirilov argues with Stavrogin in Fyodor Dostoyevsky's *The Possessed*

"[W]e might think of a human person . . . as being a wave that rises and falls, or a bubble that forms and bursts, on the immortal sea's surface. . . . But, if that is what we are, we have to live and die without ever knowing in what relation we stand to the Ultimate Reality that is the source and destination of our being in our ephemeral human life on earth. Are we accidents that have no meaning in terms of this reality from which, as persons, we are temporarily differentiated? Or are we truants, who have alienated ourselves from the source of our being by a perverse *tour de force* that we cannot sustain beyond the brief span of a human life's trajectory?"

—Arnold Toynbee, *Man's Concern with Death*

"The particular name and form of any deity are limitations which we in our weakness impose on the all-pervading Spirit which is really nameless and formless. The Supreme Being is a person only in relation to ourselves and our needs. . . . The highest theism is only a sort of glorified anthropomorphism but *we cannot do without it.*"

—modern Indian philosopher D. S. Sharma

"If God is One, what is bad?"

—Charles Manson

"[I]t was within a Western Christian setting that our technological civilization came to birth, and this was no accident, for Christianity is both this-worldly and other-worldly."

—R. C. Zaehner, Spalding Professor of Eastern Religions and Ethics, Oxford University

"In practice it means that neither religion [Hinduism and Buddhism] in its classical formulation pays the slightest attention to what goes on in the world today."

—R. C. Zaehner

QUESTIONS FOR THOUGHT AND DISCUSSION

1. In the opening paragraph, what are some of the issues troubling Siddhartha?

2. How would you describe Atman? Why does Siddhartha see he is more worthy of sacrifices and honor than the other gods? Where does he dwell? What does Siddhartha see as the challenge in reaching Atman? What is the "one important thing"?

3. In the first paragraph of "With the Samanas," what is Siddhartha's approach to life? How does he see everyday events? What is his assessment of life overall?

4. What does Hesse mean that "Siddhartha had one single goal—to become empty, to become empty of thirst, desire, dreams, pleasure and sorrow—to let the Self die"? How does Siddhartha go about trying to achieve this goal? What does he hope to discover? Why does Hesse say Siddhartha feels "the torment of the onerous life cycle"?

5. Read the quotes from R. C. Zaehner in the box, "Freedom Is Freedom *from* Individuality." Do you think an Eastern Buddhist setting could have produced our scientific and technological civilization? Why or why not?

6. How would you describe this Eastern approach to life? According to this worldview, what is the meaning of life, its purpose?

7. How would this way of thinking affect the way one sees personal identity, occupation, and relationships? What would be the consequences of this view for such notions as human rights and democracy? For life itself?

Ayn Rand

Ayn Rand (1905–1982) was a Russian-born American thinker and writer whose novels are polemical and melodramatic vehicles for her ideas. She was the founder of the "objectivist" school of philosophy, and won fame for the novels she wrote illustrating and embodying its practical outworking, most notably The Fountainhead *(1943) and* Atlas Shrugged *(1957). These books, prime examples of Western secularist thought, were widely appreciated for their defense of capitalism and their attacks on government and all outside controls that inhibit self-interested individuals. The central tenet of objectivism is that selfishness and self-assertion are the highest good to which human beings can attain. After Rand's death, her disciple Nathaniel Brandon established an institute to carry on her legacy and promote objectivism as a philosophy.*

The central tenet of objectivism is that selfishness and self-assertion are the highest good to which human beings can attain.

The following passage comes from Atlas Shrugged, *Rand's most famous work, in which titans of industry, led by a shadowy and elusive figure named John Galt, abandon their enterprises to chaos and ruin in a "reverse strike." Their object is to drive home the point that the society that has so long reviled them for their wealth and success needs them for its very survival. In the process Rand repeatedly underscores the contrast between "the prime movers" and "the parasites," the "creators" and the "second-handers." The former "must worship Man"—which means "his own highest potentiality"—but must not make the mistake of worshiping "Mankind."*

The irony, of course, is that the practical outworking of Rand's self-reliant and self-assertive philosophy—as illustrated by the strike—is equivalent to the Eastern ideal of renouncing and withdrawing. In this passage, Francisco d'Anconia, a mining industrialist who has joined John Galt in his "strike," tries to convince Dagny Taggart, a railroad industrialist, to join them as well.

Atlas Shrugged was a best seller read by people who would rarely crack a philosophy text. But essentially it is Nietzscheanism in a pinstriped suit with a Russian accent. Thus the second broad answer to the human quest for purpose and fulfillment is: Do it yourself. Within the Western secularist family of faiths (including humanism, materialism, and naturalism) the final reality is viewed as only matter, so the answer to the human quest for purpose and fulfillment is for human beings not only to create their purpose but themselves.

Thus the second broad answer to the human quest for purpose and fulfillment is: Do it yourself.

I, MYSELF, AND ME

"My personal life is a postscript to my novels; it consists of the sentence: *'And I mean it.'* I have always lived by the philosophy I present in my books."

—Ayn Rand, 1957

"My philosophy, in essence, is the concept of man as a heroic being, with his own happiness as the moral purpose of his life, with productive achievement as his noblest activity, and reason as his only absolute."

—Ayn Rand, 1957

"'Francisco, what's the most depraved type of human being?'

" 'The man without a purpose.' "

—Ayn Rand, *Atlas Shrugged*

"Dagny, there's nothing of any importance in life—except how well you do your work. Nothing. Only that. Whatever else you are, will come from that. It's the only measure of human value. All the codes of ethics they'll try to ram down your throat are just so much paper money put out by swindlers to fleece people of their virtues. The code of competence is the only system of morality that's on a gold standard. When you grow up, you'll know what I mean."

—Francisco d'Anconia, *Atlas Shrugged*

"'Mr. Rearden,' said Francisco, his voice solemnly calm, 'if you saw Atlas, the giant who holds the world on his shoulders, if you saw that he stood, blood running down his chest, his knees buckling, his arms trembling but still trying to hold the world aloft with the last of this strength, and the greater his effort the heavier the world bore down on his shoulders—what would you tell him to do?'

"'I . . . don't know. What . . . could he do? What would *you* tell him?'

"'To shrug.' "

—*Atlas Shrugged*

"I believed that one person owes a duty to another with no payment for it in return. I believed that it was my duty to love a woman who gave me nothing, who betrayed everything I lived for, who demanded her happiness at the price of mine. I believed that love is some static gift which, once granted, need no longer be deserved—just as they believe that wealth is a static possession which can be seized and held without further effort. I believed that love is a gratuity, not a reward to be earned—just as they believe it is their right to demand an unearned wealth. And just as they believe that their need is a claim on my energy, so I believed that her unhappiness was a claim on my life."

—Henry Rearden,
Atlas Shrugged

"Love of our brothers? That's when we learned to hate our brothers for the first time in our lives. We began to hate them for everything they swallowed, for every small pleasure they enjoyed, for one man's new shirt, for another's wife's hat, for an outing with their family, for a paint job on their house—it was taken from us, it was paid for by our privations, our denials, our hunger."

—foreman,
explaining the start of the strike, *Atlas Shrugged*

"The door of the structure was a straight, smooth sheet of stainless steel, softly lustrous and bluish in the sun. Above it, cut in the granite, as the only feature of the building's rectangular austerity, there stood an inscription:
    'I SWEAR BY MY LIFE AND MY LOVE OF IT THAT I WILL NEVER LIVE FOR THE SAKE OF ANOTHER MAN, NOR ASK ANOTHER MAN TO LIVE FOR MINE.'"

—description of the entrance to John Galt's home, *Atlas Shrugged*

"Man's life is the *standard* of morality, but your own life is its *purpose*. If existence on earth is your goal, you must choose your actions and values by the standard of that which is proper to man—for the purpose of preserving, fulfilling, and enjoying the irreplaceable value which is your life."

—John Galt, *Atlas Shrugged*

"Pride is the recognition of the fact that you are your own highest value and, like all of man's values, it has to be earned—that of any achievements open to you, the one that makes all others possible is the creation of your own character—that your character, your actions, your desires, your emotions are the products of the premises held by your mind."

—John Galt, *Atlas Shrugged*

"Do you ask what moral obligation I owe to my fellow men? None—except the obligation I owe to myself, to material objects and to all of existence: rationality."

—John Galt, *Atlas Shrugged*

Atlas Shrugged ◈

"Yes, Dagny, it was our own guilt."
    "Because we didn't work hard enough?"
    "Because we worked too hard—and charged too little."
    "What do you mean?"
    "We never demanded the one payment that the world owed us—and we

let our best reward go to the worst of men. The error was made centuries ago, it was made by Sebastián d'Anconia, by Nat Taggart, by every man who fed the world and received no thanks in return. You don't know what is right any longer? Dagny, this is not a battle over material goods. It's a moral crisis, the greatest the world has ever faced and the last. Our age is the climax of centuries of evil. We must put an end to it, once and for all, or perish—we, the men of the mind. It was our own guilt. We produced the wealth of the world—but we let our enemies write its moral code."

"But we never accepted their code. We lived by our own standards."

"Yes—and paid ransoms for it! Ransoms in matter and in spirit—in money, which our enemies received, but did not deserve, and in honor, which we deserved, but did not receive. *That* was our guilt—that we were willing to pay. We kept mankind alive, yet we allowed men to despise us and to worship our destroyers. We allowed them to worship incompetence and brutality, the recipients and the dispensers of the unearned. By accepting punishment, not for any sins, but for our virtues, we betrayed our code and made theirs possible. Dagny, theirs is the morality of kidnappers. They use your love of virtue as a hostage. They know that you'll bear anything in order to work and produce, because you know that achievement is man's highest moral purpose, that he can't exist without it, and your love of virtue is your love of life. They count on you to assume any burden. They count on you to feel that no effort is too great in the service of your love. Dagny, your enemies are destroying you by means of your own power. Your generosity and your endurance are their only tools. Your unrequited rectitude is the only hold they have upon you. They know it. You don't. The day when you'll discover it is the only thing they dread. You must learn to understand them. You won't be free of them, until you do. But when you do, you'll reach such a stage of rightful anger that you'll blast every rail of Taggart Transcontinental, rather than let it serve them!"

"But to leave it to them!" she moaned. "To abandon it . . . To abandon Taggart Transcontinental . . . when it's . . . it's almost like a living person . . . "

"It was. It isn't any longer. Leave it to them. It won't do them any good. Let it go. We don't need it. We can rebuild it. They can't. We'll survive without it. They won't."

"But *we*, brought down to renouncing and giving up!"

"Dagny, we who've been called 'materialists' by the killers of the human spirit, we're the only ones who know how little value or meaning there is in material objects as such, because we're the ones who create their value

> *"We produced the wealth of the world—but we let our enemies write its moral code."*
> —FRANCISCO D'ANCONIA

> *"But we, brought down to renouncing and giving up!"*
> —DAGNY TAGGART

and meaning. We can afford to give them up, for a short while, in order to redeem something much more precious. We are the soul, of which railroads, copper mines, steel mills, and oil wells are the body—and they are living entities that beat day and night, like our hearts, in the sacred function of supporting human life, but only so long as they remain our body, only so long as they remain the expression, the reward and property of achievement. Without us, they are corpses and their sole product is poison, not wealth or food, the poison of disintegration that turns men into hordes of scavengers. Dagny, learn to understand the nature of your own power and you'll understand the paradox you now see around you. *You* do not have to depend on any material possessions, they depend on you, you create them, you own the one and only tool of production. Wherever you are, you will always be able to produce. But the looters—by their own stated theory—are in desperate, permanent, congenital need and at the blind mercy of matter. Why don't you take them at their word? They need railroads, factories, mines, motors, which they cannot make or run. Of what use will your railroad be to them without you? Who held it together? Who kept it alive? Who saved it, time and time again? Was it your brother James? Who fed him? Who fed the looters? Who produced their weapons? Who gave them the means to enslave you? The impossible spectacle of shabby little incompetents holding control over the products of genius—who made it possible? Who supported your enemies, who forged your chains, who destroyed your achievement?"

The motion that threw her upright was like a silent cry. He shot to his feet with the stored abruptness of a spring uncoiling, his voice driving on in merciless triumph:

"You're beginning to see, aren't you? Dagny! Leave them the carcass of that railroad, leave them all the rusted rails and rotted ties and gutted engines—but don't leave them your mind! Don't leave them your mind! The fate of the world rests on that decision!"

From Ayn Rand, *Atlas Shrugged* (New York: Penguin Books, 1985), pp. 572–573. All efforts have been made to contact the copyright holder.

'THUS I WILLED IT'

"In the pride of your heart you say 'I am a god' . . . but you are a man and no god, though you think you are as wise as a god."

—Ezekiel, prophesying against Tyre

"Man is the measure of all things."

—Protagoras

The "Supreme Maker" speaks to man:

"We have made you a creature neither of heaven nor of earth, neither mortal nor immortal, in order that you may, as the free and proud shaper of your own being, fashion yourself in the form you may prefer."

—Giovanni Pico Della Mirandola, *Oration on the Dignity of Man*

"[I]f we will, we can."

—Giovanni Pico Della Mirandola, *Oration on the Dignity of Man*

"A man can do all things if he will."

—Leon Battista Alberti

"Glory to man in the highest! For man is the Master of things."

—Algernon Swinburne

A man can achieve almost anything "by the exercise of his own free powers of action and self-denial."

—Samuel Smiles, *Self-Help*, 1859

"We see the future of man as one of his own making."

—H. J. Müller

"For everyone now strives most of all to separate his person, wishing to experience the fullness of life within himself, and yet what comes of all his efforts is not the fullness of life but full suicide, for instead of the fullness of self-definition, they fall into complete isolation. For all men in our age are separated into units, each seeks seclusion in his own hole, each withdraws from the others, hides himself, and hides what he has, and ends by pushing himself away from people and pushing people away from himself. He accumulates wealth in solitude, thinking: how strong, how secure I am now; and does not see, madman as he is, that the more he accumulates, the more he sinks into suicidal impotence. For he is accustomed to relying only on himself, he has separated his unit from the whole, he has accustomed his soul to not believing in people's help, in people or in mankind, and now only trembles lest his money and his acquired privileges perish. Everywhere now the human mind has begun laughably not to understand that a man's true security lies not in his own solitary effort, but in the general wholeness of humanity."

—Elder Zosima in Fyodor Dostoyevsky's *The Brothers Karamazov*

"We, however, want to become those we are—human beings who are new, unique, incomparable, who give themselves laws, who create themselves."

—Friedrich Nietzsche, *The Gay Science*

"To redeem those who have lived in the past and to turn every 'it was' into a 'thus I willed it'—that alone I should call redemption."

—Friedrich Nietzsche,
Ecce Homo

"That which is creative must create itself."

—John Keats

"Today, in twentieth-century man, the evolutionary process is at last becoming aware of itself."

—Sir Julian Huxley

"Brief and powerless is man's life; on him and all his race the slow, sure doom falls pitiless and dark. Blind to good and evil, reckless of destruction, omnipotent matter rolls on its relentless way; for man, condemned today to lose his dearest, tomorrow himself to pass through the gate of darkness, it remains only to cherish, ere yet the blow fall, the lofty thoughts that ennoble his little day; disdaining the coward terrors of the slave of Fate, to worship at the shrines that his own hands have built; undismayed by the empire of chance, to preserve a mind free from the wanton tyranny that rules his outward life; proudly defiant of the irresistible forces that tolerate, for a moment, his knowledge and his condemnation, to sustain alone, a weary but unyielding Atlas, the world that his own ideals have fashioned despite the trampling march of unconscious power."

—Bertrand Russell,
"A Free Man's Worship"

"You're a reporter. You want to know what I think about Charlie Kane. Well, I suppose he had some private sort of greatness, but he kept it to himself. He never gave himself away. He never gave anything away. He just left you a tip.

"He had a generous mind. I don't suppose anybody ever had so many opinions. But he never believed in anything except Charlie Kane, he never had a conviction except Charlie Kane in his life. I suppose he died without one."

—from Orson Welles' *Citizen Kane*, 1941

"All men's problems were created by man and can be solved by man."

—John F. Kennedy

"To be a man means to reach toward being God."

—John Paul Sartre

"For what is a man, what has he got?
If not himself, then he has naught.
To say the things he truly feels;
And not the words of one who kneels.
The record shows I took the blows—
And did it my way!"

—Frank Sinatra, "My Way"

"La vie est plus belle quand on l'écrit soi-même."

—Guerlain ad for Champs-Elysées perfume
("Life is more beautiful when you write your own script")

QUESTIONS FOR THOUGHT AND DISCUSSION

1. In the first full paragraph, Francisco says there is a "moral crisis." What does he mean? What is the "moral code" that was erected by his enemies?

2. What does Francisco mean in saying he and the other "materialists" have "paid ransoms" for living by their own standards? How does he say the materialists betrayed their own moral code? Why does he argue that the world owes them?

3. Why does he tell Dagny, "theirs is the morality of kidnappers. They use your love of virtue as a hostage"? What does he mean? How is "man's highest moral purpose" being used against her?

4. What would be the effects of "the strike"? What would the strike cost them? What do the entrepreneurs hope to achieve by striking? How does this behavior echo the "renounce and withdraw" worldview of the East?

5. What is the important element of truth in this argument? What sorts of people, in terms of class, age, and type, is it most likely to appeal to?

6. What happens when these ideas are lived out in practice—say, not just in economics, but in family relationships? Do you know of any people like this or examples of this way of thinking?

George Steiner

George Steiner (born 1929) is among the most eminent and distinguished scholars and writers in the world today. Born in Paris and educated at the Universities of Chicago, Harvard, and Oxford, he has worked on the editorial staff of The Economist and served as Fellow of Churchill College, Cambridge and professor of English and Comparative Literature at the University of Geneva.

Quite different from his more scholarly works, The Portage to San Cristóbal of A. H. (1981) is a serious novel that became a searing international best seller. It also created a storm of controversy because it was written by a Jew, yet appeared to allow Hitler to exonerate himself. Hitler's views portrayed here, it must be said, are not pure fiction; they are based on historical research into Hitler's youth.

The A. H. of the title is Adolf Hitler. Far from dead by suicide in a Berlin bunker, Hitler as portrayed by Steiner is ninety years old and alive in the Amazon jungle—for Israeli Nazi-hunters, the ultimate quarry. Yet also far from an obvious monster, his Hitler is a shriveled old man who says little to his captors until the last chapter. Suddenly the novel crackles into life as Hitler gives his defiant rationale for Nazism.

Unlike other religions, the Jewish and Christian faiths hold that the link between God and human beings is a call in the form of words.

This reading contains the second of Hitler's three arguments for Nazism, including his stunning appreciation-cum-attack on the notion of God's calling. As Moses said to the Israelites at Sinai, "Then the LORD spoke to you out of the fire. You heard the sound of words but saw no form; there was only a voice" (Deuteronomy 4:12). Unlike other religions, the Jewish and Christian faiths hold that the link between God and human beings is a call in the form of words. Agree with this understanding of calling or not, this story asserts the decisive impact of a Jewish and Christian truth on world history and Western civilization.

Individuality is therefore the glory of human beings made in the image of God, but can be found only in God as the source—and emphatically on his terms.

Steiner's shocking story aptly introduces the answer to the quest for purpose and fulfillment given by the biblical family of faiths—Jewish and Christian. Within this view the final reality in the universe is both personal and infinite. Individuality is therefore the glory of human beings made in the image of God, but can be found only in God as the source—and emphatically on his terms.

The Portage to San Cristóbal of A. H. ✎

There had to be a solution, a final solution. For what is the Jew if he is not a long cancer of unrest? Gentlemen, I beg your attention, I demand it. Was there ever a crueler invention, a contrivance more calculated to harrow human existence, than that of an omnipotent, all-seeing, yet invisible, impalpable, inconceivable God? Gentlemen, I pray you, consider the case, consider it closely. The pagan earth was crowded with small deities, malicious or consoling, winged or potbellied, in leaf and branch, in rock and river. Giving companionship to man, pinching his bottom or caressing him, but of his measure. Delighting in honey cakes and roast meat. Gods after our own image and necessities. And even the great deities, the Olympians, would come down in mortal visitation, to do war and lechery. Mightier than we, I grant you, but tangible and taking on the skin of things. The Jew emptied the world by setting his God apart, immeasurably apart from man's senses. No image. No concrete embodiment. No imagining even. A blank emptier than the desert. Yet with a terrible nearness. Spying on our every misdeed, searching out the heart of our heart for motive. . . .

And the Jew mocks those who have pictures of their god. *His* God is purer than any other. The very thought of Him exceeds the powers of the human mind. We are as blown dust to His immensity. But because we are His creatures, we must be better than ourselves, love our neighbor, be continent, give of what we have to the beggar. Because His inconceivable, unimaginable presence envelops us, we must obey every jot of the Law. We must bottle up our rages and desires, chastise the flesh and walk bent in the rain. You call me a

The Jew emptied the world by setting his God apart, immeasurably apart from man's senses.

The Jew invented conscience and left man a guilty serf.

tyrant, an enslaver. What tyranny, what enslavement has been more oppressive, has branded the skin and soul of man more deeply than the sick fantasies of the Jew? You are not God-killers, but *God-makers*. And that is infinitely worse. The Jew invented conscience and left man a guilty serf.

But that was only the first piece of blackmail. There was worse to come. The white-faced Nazarene. Gentlemen, I find it difficult to contain myself. But the facts must speak for themselves. What did that epileptic rabbi ask of man? That he renounce the world, that he leave mother and father behind, that he offer the other cheek when slapped, that he render good for evil, that he love his neighbor as himself, no, far better, for self-love is an evil thing to be overcome. Oh grand castration! Note the cunning of it. Demand of human beings more than they can give, demand that they give up their stained, selfish humanity in the name of a higher ideal, and you will make of them cripples, hypocrites, mendicants for salvation. The Nazarene said that his kingdom, his purities were not of this world. Lies, honeyed lies. It was here on earth that he founded his slave church. It was men and women, creatures of flesh, he abandoned to the blackmail of hell, of eternal punishment. What were our camps compared with *that*? Ask of man more than he is, hold before his tired eyes an image of altruism, of compassion, of self-denial which only the saint or the madman can touch, and you stretch him on the rack. Till his soul bursts. What can be crueler than the Jew's addiction to the ideal?

It was men and women, creatures of flesh, he abandoned to the blackmail of hell, of eternal punishment. What were our camps compared with that?

What can be crueler than the Jew's addiction to the ideal?

First the invisible but all-seeing, the unattainable but all-demanding God of Sinai. Second the terrible sweetness of Christ. Had the Jew not done enough to sicken man? No, gentlemen, there is a third act to our story.

"Sacrifice yourself for the good of your fellow man. Relinquish your possessions so that there may be equality for all. Hammer yourself hard as steel, strangle emotion, loyalty, mercy, gratitude. Denounce parent or lover. So that justice may be achieved on earth. So that history be fulfilled and society be purged of all imperfection." . . . The Jew had grown impatient, his dreams had gone rancid. Let the kingdom of justice come here and now, next Monday morning. Let us have a secular messiah instead. But with a long beard and his bowels full of vengeance.

Three times the Jew has pressed on us the blackmail of transcendence. Three times he has infected our blood and brains with the bacillus of perfection. Go to your rest and the voice of the Jew cries out in the night: "Wake up! God's eye is upon you. Has He not made you in His image? Lose your life so that you may gain it. Sacrifice yourself to the truth, to justice, to the good of mankind." That cry had been in our ears too long, gentlemen, far too long. Men had grown sick of it, sick to death. When I turned on the Jew, no one came to his rescue. No one. France, England, Russia, even Jew-ridden America did nothing. They were glad that the exterminator had come. Oh they did not say openly, I allow you that. But secretly they rejoiced. We had to find, to burn out the virus of utopia before the whole of our Western civilization sickened. To return to man as he is, selfish, greedy, shortsighted, but warm and housed, so marvelously housed, in his own stench. "We were chosen to be the conscience of man" said the Jew. And I answered him, yes, I, gentlemen, who now stand before you: "You are not man's conscience, Jew. You are only his bad conscience. And we shall vomit you so we may live and have peace." A final solution. How could there be any other?

From George Steiner, *The Portage to San Cristóbal of A. H.* (New York: Simon and Schuster, 1981), pp. 182–190. Copyright © 1979, 1981 by George Steiner. Reprinted by permission of George Borchardt, Inc. for the author. All rights reserved by the author.

QUESTIONS FOR THOUGHT AND DISCUSSION

1. How would you characterize the three ways the Jew has "pressed on us the blackmail of transcendence" that Hitler cites?

2. In the first two paragraphs, Hitler describes the first form of "blackmail" — the Jew's understanding of God. How does the Jewish God compare to the deities on "pagan earth"? What does he mean by "the Jew emptied the world by setting his God apart"?

3. How have the Jews raised the bar for humanity by their allegiance to God? Why does Hitler consider this a tyranny and enslavement? How would this be different than a world of pagan deities? What is Hitler saying in the statement, "The Jew invented conscience and left man a guilty serf"?

4. The second form of "blackmail" was the arrival of the "white-faced Nazarene" — Jesus. How did Jesus make things worse for humanity, according to Hitler? What does he expect of his followers? How did Hitler interpret these teachings?

5. The third form of "blackmail" was a secular utopia — Rabbi Marx's communism. Despite the absence of God, how do the Jews continue in the same vein of demanding perfection, in Hitler's view?

6. How is God's calling involved in the Jewish "cancer of unrest"?

7. What does Hitler's crazed logic show us of the cultural impact of Judaism, the Christian faith, and Marxism? To what extent do you agree or disagree?

Dietrich Bonhoeffer

Dietrich Bonhoeffer (1906–1945) was a great German theologian and writer, eventually martyred for his participation in an unsuccessful plot to kill Hitler. Born in Breslau, Germany, he and his twin sister grew up in academic surroundings as the children of a professor of psychiatry. In 1930 Bonhoeffer was appointed lecturer in systematic theology, and in 1933 he denounced Hitler and his ideas on the radio. Two years later, after a period spent in London as pastor of the German Church, he was forbidden to teach and banned from Berlin by the Nazis.

Bonhoeffer was lecturing in the United States when war broke out. Many of his friends thought he was foolish not to stay. He chose, however, to return to Germany and lead a double life—working as a pastor while taking part in the underground resistance movement. He was arrested in April 1943 because of suspected participation in a plot to kill Hitler (the ignition for the time bomb failed; Hitler's plane landed safely). Two years later, after a series of imprisonments including Buchenwald, the concentration camp, he was hanged at Flossenbürg.

Bonhoeffer is best known for his books, especially The Cost of Discipleship *and* Letters and Papers from Prison. *In this passage from the former, which expounds Jesus of Nazareth's call of his disciples, he captures stunningly how two simple words— "Follow me"—changed the world.*

TWO WORDS THAT CHANGED THE WORLD

"As Jesus walked beside the Sea of Galilee, he saw Simon and his brother Andrew casting a net into the lake, for they were fishermen.

"'Come, follow me,' Jesus said, 'and I will make you fishers of men.'

"At once they left their nets and followed him.

"When he had gone a little farther, he saw James son of Zebedee and his brother John in a boat, preparing their nets. Without delay he called them, and they left their father Zebedee in the boat with the hired men and followed him."

—Mark 1:16-20

"Once again Jesus went out beside the lake. A large crowd came to him, and he began to teach them. As he walked along, he saw Levi son of Alphaeus sitting at the tax collector's booth. 'Follow me,' Jesus told him, and Levi got up and followed him.

> "While Jesus was having dinner at Levi's house, many tax collectors and 'sinners' were eating with him and his disciples, for there were many who followed him."
>
> —Mark 2:13-15
>
> "When Christ calls a man, he bids him come and die."
>
> —Dietrich Bonhoeffer,
> *The Cost of Discipleship*
>
> "The tree has to die before it can be made into a cross."
>
> —W. B. Yeats,
> *Autobiographies*

The Cost of Discipleship ❧

And as he passed by he saw Levi, the son of Alphaeus, sitting at the place of toll, and he saith unto him, Follow me. And he arose and followed him. (Mark 2.14)

The call goes forth, and is at once followed by the response of obedience. The response of the disciples is an act of obedience, not a confession of faith in Jesus. How could the call immediately evoke obedience? The story is a stumbling-block for the natural reason, and it is no wonder that frantic attempts have been made to separate the two events. By hook or by crook a bridge must be found between them. Something must have happened in between, some psychological or historical event. Thus we get the stupid question: Surely the publican must have known Jesus before, and that previous acquaintance explains his readiness to hear the Master's call. Unfortunately our text is ruthlessly silent on this point, and in fact it regards the immediate sequence of call and response as a matter of crucial importance. It displays not the slightest interest in the psychological reasons for a man's religious decisions. And why? For the simple reason that the cause behind the immediate following of call by response is Jesus Christ himself. It is Jesus who calls, and because it is Jesus, Levi follows at once. This encounter is a testimony to the absolute, direct, and unaccountable authority of Jesus. There is no need of any preliminaries, and no other consequence but obedience to the call. Because Jesus is the Christ, he has the authority to call and to demand obedience to his word. Jesus summons men to follow him not as a teacher or a pattern of the good

The response of the disciples is an act of obedience, not a confession of faith in Jesus.

This encounter is a testimony to the absolute, direct, and unaccountable authority of Jesus.

life, but as the Christ, the Son of God. In this short text Jesus Christ and his claim are proclaimed to men. Not a word of praise is given to the disciple for his decision for Christ. We are not expected to contemplate the disciple, but only him who calls, and his absolute authority. According to our text, there is no road to faith or discipleship, no other road—only obedience to the call of Jesus.

And what does the text inform us about the content of discipleship? Follow me, run along behind me! That is all. To follow in his steps is something which is void of all content. It gives us no intelligible programme for a way of life, no goal or ideal to strive after. It is not a cause which human calculation might deem worthy of our devotion, even the devotion of ourselves. What happens? At the call, Levi leaves all that he has—but not because he thinks that he might be doing something worth while, but simply for the sake of the call. Otherwise he cannot follow in the steps of Jesus. This act on Levi's part has not the slightest value in itself, it is quite devoid of significance and unworthy of consideration. The disciple simply burns his boats and goes ahead. He is called out, and has to forsake his old life in order that he may "exist" in the strictest sense of the word. The old life is left behind, and completely surrendered. The disciple is dragged out of his relative security into a life of absolute insecurity (that is, in truth, into the absolute security and safety of the fellowship of Jesus), from a life which is observable and calculable (it is, in fact, quite incalculable) into a life where everything is unobservable and fortuitous (that is, into one which is necessary and calculable), out of the realm of finite (which is in truth the infinite) into the realm of infinite possibilities (which is the one liberating reality). Again it is no universal law. Rather is it the exact opposite of all legality. It is nothing else than bondage to Jesus Christ alone, completely breaking through every programme, every ideal, every set of laws. No other significance is possible, since Jesus is the only significance. Beside Jesus nothing has any significance. He alone matters.

When we are called to follow Christ, we are summoned to an exclusive attachment to his person. The grace of his call bursts all the bonds of legalism. It is a gracious call, a gracious commandment. It transcends the difference between the law and the gospel. Christ calls, the disciple follows: that is grace and commandment in one. "I will walk at liberty, for I seek thy commandments" (Ps. 119.45). . . .

Discipleship without Jesus Christ is a way of our own choosing. It may be the ideal way. It may even lead to martyrdom, but it is devoid of all promise. Jesus will certainly reject it.

And they went to another village. And as they went in the way, a certain man said unto him, I will follow thee withersoever thou goest.
And Jesus said unto him, The foxes have holes, and the birds of
heaven have nests, but the Son of man hath not where to lay his head.
And he said unto another, Follow me. But he said, Lord, suffer me first
to go and bury my father. But he said unto him, Leave the dead to
bury their dead, but go thou and publish abroad the kingdom of God.
And another said, I will follow thee, Lord; but suffer me first to bid
farewell to them that are at my house. But Jesus said unto him, No
man, having put his hand unto the plough, and looking back, is fit for
the kingdom of God. (Luke 9.57–62)

The first disciple offers to follow Jesus without waiting to be called. Jesus
damps his ardour by warning him that he does not know what he is doing.
In fact he is quite incapable of knowing. That is the meaning of Jesus'
answer—he shows the would-be disciple what life with him involves. We
hear the words of One who is on his way to the cross, whose whole life is
summed up in the Apostles' Creed by the word "suffered." No man can
choose such a life for himself. No man can call himself to such a destiny, says
Jesus, and his word stays unanswered. The gulf between a voluntary offer to
follow and genuine discipleship is clear.

No man can choose such a life for himself. No man can call himself to such a destiny, says Jesus.

But where Jesus calls, he bridges the widest gulf. The second would-be disciple wants to bury his father before he starts to follow. He is held bound by
the trammels of the law. He knows what he wants and what he must do. Let
him first fulfill the law, and then let him follow. A definite legal ordinance acts
as a barrier between Jesus and the man he has called. But the call of Jesus is
stronger than the barrier. At this critical moment nothing on earth, however
sacred, must be allowed to come between Jesus and the man he has called—
not even the law itself. Now, if never before, the law must be broken for the
sake of Jesus; it forfeits all its rights if it acts as a barrier to discipleship.
Therefore Jesus emerges at this point as the opponent of the law, and com-
mands a man to follow him. Only the Christ can speak in this fashion. He
alone has the last word. His would-be follower cannot kick against the pricks.
This call, this grace, is irresistible.

Now, if never before, the law must be broken for the sake of Jesus; it forfeits all its rights if it acts as a barrier to discipleship.

The third would-be disciple, like the first, thinks that following Christ
means that he must make the offer on his own initiative, as if it were a career
he had mapped out for himself. There is, however, a difference between the first
would-be disciple and the third, for the third is bold enough to stipulate his

own terms. Unfortunately, however, he lands himself in a hopeless inconsistency, for although he is ready enough to throw in his lot with Jesus, he succeeds in putting up a barrier between himself and the Master. "Suffer me first." He wants to follow, but feels obliged to insist on his own terms. Discipleship to him is a possibility which can only be realized when certain conditions have been fulfilled. This is to reduce discipleship to the level of the human understanding. First you must do this and then you must do that. There is a right time for everything. The disciple places himself at the Master's disposal, but at the same time retains the right to dictate his own terms. But then discipleship is no longer discipleship, but a programme of our own to be arranged to suit ourselves, and to be judged in accordance with the standards of a rational ethic. The trouble about this third would-be disciple is that at the very moment he expresses his willingness to follow, he ceases to want to follow at all. By making his offer on his own terms, he alters the whole position, for discipleship can tolerate no conditions which might come between Jesus and our obedience to him. Hence the third disciple finds himself at loggerheads not only with Jesus, but also with himself. His desires conflict not only with what Jesus wants, but also with what he wants himself. He judges himself, and decides against himself, and all this by saying, "suffer me first." The answer of Jesus graphically proves to him that he is at variance with himself and that excludes discipleship. "No man, having put his hand to the plough and looking back, is fit for the kingdom of God."

By making his offer on his own terms, he alters the whole position, for discipleship can tolerate no conditions which might come between Jesus and our obedience to him.

From Dietrich Bonhoeffer, *The Cost of Discipleship,* translated by R. H. Fuller, revised by Irmgard Booth. (New York: Simon and Schuster, 1995), pp. 57–62. Copyright © 1959 SCM Press, Ltd. Reprinted with the permission of Scribner, a division of Simon & Schuster, and of SCM Press.

WHOSE FOOL ARE YOU?

"Brethren, the tears of Christ overwhelm me with shame and fear and sorrow. I was playing out of doors in the street, while sentence of death was being passed upon me in the privacy of the royal council-chamber. But the King's only-begotten Son heard of it. And what did he do? He went forth from the palace, put off his diadem, covered himself with sackcloth, strewed ashes on his head, bared his feet, and wept and lamented because his poor slave was condemned to death. I meet him unexpectedly in this sad condition. I am astonished at the woeful change in him and inquire the cause. He tells me the whole story. What am I to do now? Shall I continue to play and make a mockery of his tears? Surely I am insane and devoid of reason if I do not follow him and unite my tears with his."

—Bernard of Clairveaux

"When a man has a toothache the world says, 'Poor man'; when a man's wife is unfaithful to him the world says, 'Poor man'; when a man is in financial embarrassment the world says, 'Poor man'—when it pleased God in the form of a lowly servant to suffer in this world the world says, 'Poor man'; when an Apostle with a divine commission has the honor to suffer for the truth the world says, 'Poor man'—poor world!"

—Søren Kierkegaard, *Journal*

QUESTIONS FOR THOUGHT AND DISCUSSION

1. What is the response of Levi to the call of Jesus of Nazareth? Why does Bonhoeffer make the point that this is not a "confession of faith"? What is it that Levi is responding to? Why is Jesus able to demand instant obedience?

2. What is "the content of discipleship"? What does that mean for the disciple—for what he leaves behind and what he can expect of the future?

3. In contrast to Levi's response of obedience to Jesus, Bonhoeffer examines in a passage from Luke three disciples who try to fashion discipleship to their own liking. What does he say about such "discipleship without Jesus"?

4. Why does Jesus not accept the first disciple's offer? What does Bonhoeffer mean by "No man can choose such a life for himself. No man can call himself to such a destiny"? Why do you think this is so? How would you characterize the volunteer disciple?

5. What are the circumstances surrounding the second disciple? Do you think his request is unreasonable? What is behind the request? What do Jesus' demands say of the power of his call on the lives of his disciples? What does Bonhoeffer say? In what areas of our lives can we allow "the law"—or doing what is expected of us—to become a barrier to our call?

6. How would you characterize the third disciple? Why, according to Bonhoeffer, do his stipulations preclude his becoming a disciple? How can our expectations limit Jesus' call on our lives? Is it possible to negotiate the terms of our call?

7. How do you understand this uncompromising, brooks-no-refusal call of Jesus? What do you think it meant to Bonhoeffer in the context of Nazi Germany?

8. In looking back over the passage, what would you say is the difference between a "confession of faith" and "discipleship"? How does this way of following Jesus differ from the way most people "become Christians" today?

❧ *Eusebius* ❧

Eusebius (about 260–340) was the Bishop of Caesarea and the "father of church history." A prolific but rather unpolished writer, he is our principal source for the history of the Christian faith from the apostolic age down to his own day. He is a particularly valuable witness because he lived through such historic experiences as the Diocletian persecution (A.D. 303–310), the "conversion" of Constantine (A.D. 312), and the Council of Nicea (A.D. 325), which gave us the Nicene Creed.

His main work is his Ecclesiastical History, *but the following reading is from a shorter treatise,* Demonstration of the Gospel, *which attempts to "prove" the Christian faith from the Old Testament. The passage illuminates the rise of a two-tier view of calling: the spiritual life of contemplation is set against the secular life of action. With the partial exception of the traditional Benedictine view of praying and working ("ora et labora"), this unfortunate view dominated the medieval world until the time of the Reformation, undermining the sense that calling is for all, regardless of one's occupation. It is still alive today in such notions as "full-time Christian service" that sets ministers and other "religious specialists" apart from laypeople.*

That the Christian Life Is of Two Characters ❧

While on the other the side of the teaching which they considered was suitable to men still in the world of passion and needing treatment, they accommodated to the weakness of the majority, and handed over to them to keep sometimes in writing, and sometimes by unwritten ordinances to be observed by them.

The one wrote on lifeless tables, the Other wrote the perfect commandments of the new covenant on living minds. And His disciples, accommodating their teaching to the minds of the people, according to the Master's will, delivered on the one hand to those who were able to receive it, the teaching given by the perfect master to those who rose above human nature. While on the other the side of the teaching which they considered was suitable to men still in the world of passion and needing treatment, they accommodated to the weakness of the majority, and handed over to them to keep sometimes in writing, and sometimes by unwritten ordinances to be observed by them.

Two ways of life were thus given by the law of Christ to His Church. The one is above nature, and beyond common human living; it admits not marriage, child-bearing, property nor the possession of wealth, but wholly and permanently separate from the common customary life of mankind, it devotes itself to the service of God alone in its wealth of heavenly love! And they who enter on this course, appear to die to the life of mortals, to bear with them nothing earthly but their body, and in mind and spirit to have passed to heaven. Like some celestial beings they gaze upon human life, performing the duty of a priesthood to Almighty God for the whole race, not with sacrifices of bulls and blood, nor with libations and unguents, nor with smoke and consuming fire and destruction of bodily things, but with right principles of true holiness, and of a soul purified in disposition, and above all with virtuous deeds and words; with such they propitiate the Divinity, and celebrate their priestly rites for themselves and their race. Such then is the perfect form of the Christian life.

And the other, more humble, more human, permits men to join in pure nuptials and to produce children, to undertake government, to give orders to soldiers fighting for right; it allows them to have minds for farming, for trade, and the other more secular interests as well as for religion: and it is for them that times of retreat and instruction, and days for hearing sacred things are set apart. And a kind of secondary grade of piety is attributed to them, giving just such help as such lives require, so that all men, whether Greeks or barbarians, have their part in the coming of salvation, and profit by the teaching of the Gospel.

And a kind of secondary grade of piety is attributed to them, giving just such help as such lives require, so that all men, whether Greeks or barbarians, have their part in the coming of salvation, and profit by the teaching of the Gospel.

From *Demonstration of the Gospel*, Book I, Chapter 8.

QUESTIONS FOR THOUGHT AND DISCUSSION

1. What are the two ways of life and the fundamental contrast Eusebius portrays between them?

2. In the opening paragraph, Eusebius charges that Jesus' disciples "accommodat[e] their teaching to the minds of the people." What is he saying? In what two groups does Eusebius divide people? How does he say the teaching that is given these groups is different?

3. In explaining the first group in greater detail, Eusebius uses such phrases as "above nature," "beyond common human living," "nothing earthly," and "like some celestial beings." What value does he place on these people and this way of life? How are they to live? How are they to interact with other people and society? What are their responsibilities to the larger group and to God?

4. How is the second, "more humble, more human" group able to achieve "a kind of secondary grade of piety"? What is their daily life like? When do they receive religious teaching? How does the value of this group compare to the first?

5. Do you know examples of the same contrast expressed and continued today?

6. How does this line of thinking exclude "calling" in the lives of those working outside church?

7. How would this affect the way we'd see everyday life? Christian service? For those on both sides of the divide, what are the potential pitfalls in making this division?

8. Do you know passages from Scripture that might seemingly confirm Eusebius's view? What about those that would refute it?

Martin Luther

Martin Luther (1483–1546) was the leader of the German Reformation and thus the pioneer of Protestantism. Born in Saxony, the son of a miner, he was a vicar in the Augustinian order before his revolt against church excesses, expressed in his celebrated nailing of the 95 Theses to the door of the Schlosskirche in Wittenberg in 1517.

The Babylonian Captivity is one of three writings published in 1520 that marked his break with Rome. (He was excommunicated in 1521.) The "captivity" in question is the church's denial to the laity of their spiritual rights. Most of the pamphlet is a discussion of the sacraments, but the following passage heralds the recovery of the biblical view of calling. In one blow, Luther undermines the medieval universe with its sacred/secular, contemplation/action, higher/lower distinctions. The challenge is for "everyone everywhere in everything" so to act by faith that God is glorified. Ironically, papal encyclicals today are closer to Luther's teaching than many modern Protestants are.

The Babylonian Captivity

Speaking now in behalf of the church's liberty and the glory of baptism, I feel myself in duty bound to set forth publicly the counsel I have learned under the Spirit's guidance. I therefore counsel those in high places in the churches, first of all, to abolish all those vows and religious orders, or at least not to approve and extol them. If they will not do this, then I counsel all men who would be assured of their salvation to abstain from all vows, above all from the major and lifelong vows. I give this counsel especially to teenagers and young people. This I do, first because this manner of life has no witness or warrant in the Scriptures, as I have said, but is puffed up solely by the bulls (and they truly are "bulls") of human popes. Second, because it greatly tends to hypocrisy, by reason of its outward show and unusual character, which engender conceit and a contempt of the common Christian life. And if there were no other reason for abolishing these vows, this one would be reason enough, namely, that through them faith and baptism are slighted and works are exalted, which cannot be done without harmful results. For in the religious orders there is scarcely one in many thousands who is not more concerned about his works than about faith, and on the basis of this madness, they claim superiority over each other, as being "stricter" or "laxer," as they call it.

Therefore I advise no one to enter any religious order or the priesthood, indeed, I advise everyone against it—unless he is forearmed with this knowledge and understands that the works of monks and priests, however holy and arduous they may be, do not differ one whit in the sight of God from the works of the rustic laborer in the field or the woman going about her household tasks, but that all works are measured before God by faith alone, as Jer. 5 [:3] says: "O Lord, do not thy eyes look for faith?" and Ecclus. 32 [:23]: "In all thy works believe with faith in thy heart, for this is to keep the commandments of God."

Indeed, the menial housework of a manservant or maidservant is often more acceptable to God than all the fastings and other works of a monk or priest, because the monk or priest lacks faith.

Indeed, the menial housework of a manservant or maidservant is often more acceptable to God than all the fastings and other works of a monk or priest, because the monk or priest lacks faith. Since, therefore, vows nowadays seem to tend only to the glorification of works and to pride, it is to be feared that there is nowhere less of faith and of the church than among the priests, monks, and bishops. These men are in truth heathen or hypocrites. They imagine themselves to be the church, or the heart of the church, the "spiritual" estate and the leaders of the church, when they are everything else but that. This is indeed "the people of the captivity," among whom all things freely given to us in baptism are held captive, while the few poor "people of the earth" who are left behind, such as married folk, appear vile in their eyes.

From Martin Luther, *Three Treatises* (Minneapolis: Fortress Press, 1970). Used by permission of Augsburg Fortress.

QUESTIONS FOR THOUGHT AND DISCUSSION

1. What are the two reasons Luther gives in speaking out against taking vows and religious orders? He argues that "through them faith and baptism are slighted and works are exalted." How so?
2. In contrast to the teaching of Eusebius, how does Luther measure the work of the average person against the work of the religious worker? On what does he base his reasons?
3. How does the principle of "faith alone" have radical social consequences?
4. What do you imagine were the reactions of (a) church leaders and (b) ordinary people to this Reformation teaching?

5. What were the consequences of such teaching for the status of lay-people, for the dignity of work, and for the sense of "calling" in life?

CALLING'S LOOK-ALIKE 1: "CHIVALRY"

"Long enough hast thou borne the belt, the sword, and the spurs! The time has now come for you to change the belt for a rope, the sword for the Cross of Jesus Christ, the spurs for the dust and dirt of the road! Follow me and I will make you a knight in the army of Christ!"

—St. Francis of Assisi, to a young knight who wanted to join him

"The age of chivalry is never past, so long as there is a wrong left unaddressed on the earth, or a man or a woman left to say 'I will redress that wrong, or spend my life in the attempt.'"

—Charles Kingsley, sermon before Queen Victoria, 1865

"I had rather regenerate England with football elevens [teams] than with average members of Parliament."

—Edward Bowen, Harrow schoolmaster, 1884

Soccer was "a grand game for developing a lad physically and also morally, for he learns to play with good temper and unselfishness, to play in his place and 'play the game,' and these are the best of training for any game of life."

—Robert Baden-Powell, founder of the Boy Scouts, 1908

"For when the One Great Scorer comes
To write against your name
He marks—not that you won or lost—
But how you played the game."

—Grantland Rice, "Alumnus football," 1920

❧ *John Cotton* ❧

John Cotton (1584–1652) was an eminent seventeenth-century minister and the architect of New England congregationalism. Born in Derby, England, he was educated at Trinity and Emmanuel Colleges, Cambridge, where he was deeply influenced by the great Puritan thinkers William Perkins and Richard Sibbes. In 1630, after twenty years as a minister in Boston, Lincolnshire, he preached his famous farewell sermon "God's Promise to his Plantation" to the passengers of the Arbella. In 1633 he departed for the New World himself and became teacher of the First Church of Boston, Massachusetts.

Cotton's great evangelical preaching and writing gave him enormous authority. According to Roger Williams, most colonists "could hardly believe that God would suffer Mr. Cotton to err."

The following passage on Christian calling is a clear statement of the Puritan conviction about purposeful living that has put its stamp on the character of America. Later secularized and distorted in such themes as "manifest destiny" and "the American Dream," America's characteristic sense of purpose and mission was originally rooted in Puritan teaching on calling. The distinctive Puritan understanding is captured here in Cotton's juxtaposition of "diligence in worldly businesses, and deadness to the world."

PURITAN PROPULSION

"I think I can see the whole destiny of America contained in the first Puritan who landed on those shores, as that of the whole human race in the first man."

—Alexis de Tocqueville, *Democracy in America*

"The earning of money within the modern economic order is, so long as it is done legally, the result and the expression of virtue and proficiency in a calling. . . . And in truth this peculiar idea, so familiar to us today, but in reality so little a matter of course, of one's duty in a calling, is what is most characteristic of the social ethic of capitalistic culture, and is in a sense the fundamental basis of it."

—Max Weber, *The Protestant Ethic and the Spirit of Capitalism*

Puritanism was "the innermost propulsion of the United States."

—Perry Miller, *The Errand into the Wilderness*

"Puritanism was a cutting edge which hewed liberty, democracy, humanitarianism, and universal education out of the black forest of feudal Europe and the American wilderness."

—Samuel Eliot Morison

"The modern Western beliefs in progress, in the rights of man, and the duty of conforming political action to moral ideals, whatever they may owe to other influences, derive ultimately from the moral ideals of Puritanism and its faith in the possibility of the realization of the Holy Community on earth by the efforts of the elect."

—Christopher Dawson

"It was a spiritual wind that drove the Americans irresistibly ahead from the beginning. What was behind their compulsion to improve a man's lot was an all-pervading religious sense of duty, the submission to a God-given imperative, to a God-given code of personal behavior, the willing acceptance of all the necessary sacrifices, including death in battle. Few foreigners understand this, even today."

—Luigi Barzini, *The Europeans*

Christian Calling

We are now to speak of living by faith in our outward and temporal life. Now, our outward and temporal life is twofold, which we live in the flesh: it is either a civil or a natural life; for both these lives we live, and they are different the one from the other. Civil life is that whereby we live as members of this or that city or town or commonwealth, in this or that particular vocation and calling.

Natural life I call that by which we do live this bodily life. I mean, by which we live a life of sense, by which we eat and drink, and by which we go through all conditions, from our birth to our grave, by which we live and move and have our being. And now both these a justified person lives by faith.

To begin with the former: A true believing Christian, a justified person, he lives in his vocation by his faith. Not only my spiritual life but even my civil life in this world, all the life I live, is by the faith of the Son of God: He exempts no life from the agency of His faith; whether he lives as a Christian man, or as a member of this or that church or commonwealth, he doth it all by the faith of the Son of God. Now, for opening of this point, let me show you what are those several acts of faith which it puts forth about our occasions and vocations,

Not only my spiritual life but even my civil life in this world, all the life I live, is by the faith of the Son of God.

that so we may live in God's sight therein:

First: faith draws the heart of a Christian to live in some warrantable calling. As soon as ever a man begins to look towards God and the ways of His grace, he will not rest till he find out some warrantable calling and employment. . . . (1. It hath a care that it be a warrantable calling, wherein we may not only aim at our own, but at the public good. That is a warrantable calling. . . . 2. Another thing to make a calling warrantable, is, when God gives a man gifts for it, that he is acquainted with the mystery of it and hath gifts of body and mind suitable to it. . . . 3. That which makes a calling warrantable is, when it is attained unto by warrantable and direct means, when a man enterprises not a calling but in the use of such means as he may see God's providence leading him to it. . . .)

Secondly: another work of faith about a man's vocation and calling, when faith hath made choice of a warrantable calling, then he depends upon God for the quickening and sharpening of his gifts in that calling, and yet depends not upon his gifts for the going through his calling but upon God that gave him those gifts; yea, he depends on God for the use of them in his calling. Faith saith not, give me such a calling and turn me loose to it; but faith looks up to heaven for skill and ability. Though strong and able, yet it looks at all its abilities but as a dead work, as like braided wares in a shop, as such as will be lost and rust unless God refresh and renew breath in them. And then if God do breathe in his gifts, he depends not upon them for the acting his work but upon God's blessing in the use of his gifts. Though he have never so much skill and strength, he looks at it as a dead work unless God breathe in him; and he looks not at his gifts as breathed only on by God, as able to do the work, unless also he be followed by God's blessing. . . .

Thirdly: we live by faith in our vocations, in that faith, in serving God, serves men, and in serving men, serves God. The Apostle sweetly describes it in the calling of servants (Eph. 6:5–8): "Not with eye service as man-pleasers, but as the servants of Christ, doing the will of God from the heart with good will, as unto the Lord, and not unto men, not so much man or only man, but chiefly the Lord," so that this is the work of every Christian man in his calling. Even then when he serves man, he serves the Lord; he doth the work set before him, and he doth it sincerely and faithfully so as he may give account for it; and he doth it heavenly and spiritually: "He uses the world as if he used it not" (1 Cor. 7:31). This is not the thing his heart is set upon; he looks for greater matters than these things can reach him, he doth not so much look at the world as at heaven. And therefore—that which follows upon this—he doth it all comfortably, though he meet with little encouragements from man, though the more faithful service he doth, the less he is accepted; whereas an unbelieving heart would be discontented that he can find no acceptance, but all he doth is taken in the worst part. . . .

Fourthly: another act of faith about a man's vocation is this: It encourageth a man in his calling to the most homeliest and difficultest and most dangerous things his calling can lead and expose himself to. If faith apprehend this or that to be the way of my calling, it encourages me to it, though it be never so homely and difficult and dangerous. Take you a carnal, proud heart, and if his calling lead him to some homely business, he can by no means embrace it; such homely employments a carnal heart knows not how to submit unto. But now faith having put us into a calling, if it require some homely employment, it encourages us to it. He considers, "It is my calling," and therefore he goes about it freely; and though never so homely, he doth it as a work of his calling (Luke 15:19): "Make me one of thy hire servants." A man of his rank and breeding was not wonted to hired servile work, but the same faith that made him desirous to be in a calling made him stoop to any work his calling led him to; there is no work too hard or too homely for him, for faith is conscious that it hath done the most base drudgery for Satan. No lust of pride or what else so insolent but our base hearts could be content to serve the Devil and nature in it; and therefore what drudgery can be too homely for me to do for God? . . .

Fifthly: another act of faith by which a Christian man lives in his vocation is that faith casts all the failings and burthens of his calling upon the Lord: that is the proper work of faith; it rolls and casts all upon Him.

Now there are three sorts of burthens that befall a man in his calling:

1. Care about the success of it; and for this faith casts its care upon God. . . .
2. A second burthen is fear of danger that may befall us therein from the hand of man. . . .
3. Another burthen is the burthen of injuries which befalls a man in his calling. . . .

Sixthly: faith hath another act about a man's vocation, and that is, it takes all successes that befall him in his calling with moderation; he equally bears good and evil successes as God shall dispense them to him. Faith frames the heart to moderation; be they good or evil, it rests satisfied in God's gracious dispensation: "I have learned in what estate soever I am, therewith to be content" (Phil. 4:11,12). This he had learned to do: if God prosper him, he had learned not to be puffed up; and if he should be exposed to want, he could do it without murmuring. It is the same act of unbelief that makes a man murmur in crosses which puffs him up in prosperity. Now faith is like a poise: it keeps the heart in an equal frame; whether matters fall out well or ill, faith takes them much what alike; faith moderates the frame of a man's spirit on both sides.

Seventhly: the last work which faith puts forth about a man's calling is this: faith with boldness resigns up his calling into the hands of God or man; whenever God calls a man to lay down his calling when his work is finished, herein the sons of God far exceed the sons of men. Another man when his calling comes to be removed from him, he is much ashamed and much afraid; but if a Christian man be to forgo his calling, he lays it down with comfort and boldness in the sight of God and man. . . .

A man that in his calling hath sought himself and never looked farther than himself, he never comes to lay down his calling, but he thinks it is to his utter undoing. A swine that never did good office to his owner till he comes to lie on the hurdle, he then cries out; but a sheep, who hath many times before yielded profit, though you take him and cut his throat, yet he is as a lamb dumb before the shearer. So a carnal man that never served any man but himself, call him to distress in it and he murmurs and cries out at it; but take you a Christian man that is wonted to serve God in serving of men, when he hath been faithful and useful in his calling, he never lays it down but with some measure of freedom and boldness of spirit. . . .

This is the comfort of a Christian: when he comes to lay down his calling, he cannot only with comfort look God in the face but all the sons of men. There is never a Christian that lives by faith in his calling but he is able to challenge all the world for any wrong done to them; we have wronged and defrauded no man (Acts 20:26; 2 Cor. 12). We have done most there, where we are least accepted; that is the happiness of a Christian: those who have been the most weary of him have had the least cause.

So a carnal man that never served any man but himself, call him to distress in it and he murmurs and cries out at it; but take you a Christian man that is wonted to serve God in serving of men, when he hath been faithful and useful in his calling, he never lays it down but with some measure of freedom and boldness of spirit.

From John Cotton, "The Life of Faith," in *The Way of Life, or, God's Way and Course, In Bringing the Soule into, Keeping It in and Carrying It on, in the Ways of Life and Peace* (London: Printed by M. F. for L. Fawne, and S. Gellibrand, at the Brasen Serpent in Paul's Church-Yard, 1641), pp. 436–448.

THE ELIXIR

Teach me, my God and King,
In all things Thee to see,
And what I do in anything
To do it as for Thee.

A man that looks on glass,
On it may stay his eye;
Or it he pleaseth, through it pass,
And then the heav'n espy.

All may of Thee partake:
Nothing can be so mean,
Which with his tincture—"for Thy sake"—
Will not grow bright and clean.

A servant with this clause
Makes drudgery divine:
Who sweeps a room as for Thy laws,
Makes that and th' action fine.

This is the famous stone
That turneth all to gold;
For that which God doth touch and own
Cannot for less be told.

—George Herbert, 1633

QUESTIONS FOR THOUGHT AND DISCUSSION

1. What constitutes the "twofold" life, as described by John Cotton? Is this the same as Eusebius's view? How is it different?

2. According to Cotton, what undergirds the "civil life" for the Christian?

3. What are the characteristics of a "warrantable calling"? How do these criteria compare with how we choose jobs today?

4. There is considerable talk about "giftedness" today. Compare and contrast Cotton's view with this way of thinking.

5. What does it mean for Cotton to have God as our only audience? Beyond piety, what does this mean practically in, say, attitudes to success or failure?

6. How does faith affect one's attitude toward menial tasks? Challenges? Failures? Successes? How is this so?

7. In Cotton's final point, how is it that a person can lay down a call as easily as pick it up? What does this mean for the understanding of unemployment or retirement?

8. Of John Cotton's seven main points, which did you find the most striking or helpful?

9. Taking this passage as typical of early Puritan themes, where do you see their stamp on American character and where do you think Americans have changed beyond all recognition?

CALLING'S LOOK ALIKE 2: "THE POWER OF POSITIVE THINKING"

"If you believe, you will receive whatever you ask for in prayer."

—Matthew 21:21

"God is a twenty-four hour station. All you need to do is to plug in."

—Nineteenth-century evangelist

"There is enough power in *you* to blow the city of New York to rubble."

—Norman Vincent Peale

To be a success, people need "a winning belief system . . . I'm going to give it the label 'God.'"

—Peter Lowe, motivational speaker, 1999

"Paul I find appealing, but Peale I find appalling."

—Adlai Stevenson

Marilyn Ferguson

Marilyn Ferguson (born 1938) was a writer and public speaker living in Los Angeles. Widely identified as a leader of the New Age movement, she is best known as the author of the best-selling Aquarian Conspiracy. The following reading comes from her chapter on "values and vocation" in which—admirably—she explores the need to "make a life, not just a living." But on what basis? She uses the word calling to give a sense of meaning and higher purpose to work. But in her view there is no personal God who is doing the calling. So the call is simply "the summons of that which needs doing."

This short passage from Ferguson is the first of three contemporary readings that all reflect Western society's present confusion over work and calling, purpose, and fulfillment.

The Aquarian Conspiracy

In the new paradigm [of New Age philosophy], work is a vehicle for transformation. Through work we are fully engaged in life. Work can be what Milton Mayerhoff called "the appropriate other," that which requires us, which makes us care. In responding to vocation—the call, the summons of that which needs doing—we create and discover meaning, unique to each of us and always changing.

That famous transition, the mid-life crisis, may be due in part to the cumulative effect of decades of denial, the sudden thrust into consciousness of pain that can no longer be sedated. One sensitive observer of the phenomenon said that it manifests as "either a cry or a call"—a cry of disappointment or the stirring call to new purpose—to vocation—experienced by one who has been engaged in introspective, transformative processes for some time.

However intently the person with a vocation may pursue his purpose, he should not be confused with a "workaholic." The workaholic, like an alcoholic, is indiscriminate in his compulsion. He attempts to find meaning by working. The individual with a vocation, on the other hand, finds meaningful work. A vocation is not a job. It is an ongoing transformative relationship.

In responding to vocation—the call, the summons of that which needs doing—we create and discover meaning, unique to each of us and always changing.

QUESTIONS FOR THOUGHT AND DISCUSSION

1. Ferguson wants to reintroduce dignity into work through calling. But not having a Caller, how does she define calling? How adequate do you think her definition is?

2. What does Ferguson say lies behind the mid-life crisis phenomenon? How does it manifest itself as "a cry or a call"? Does her definition of calling resolve the crisis? Why or why not?

3. How does Ferguson define the drivenness of workaholism? Again, does her definition solve or worsen the problem in your view? Within a biblical framework, what would be the difference between "called" and "driven"?

4. Where else today do you see a similar sleight of hand as people use the word "calling" without any Caller to give it meaning?

Ernest Becker

Ernest Becker (1924–1974) is one of the twentieth century's best writers on psychology and the human sciences. The following passage is from his Pulitzer prize-winning book, The Denial of Death, *published in 1973, the year before his untimely death. He is referring to a passage in Søren Kierkegaard's small classic,* Fear and Trembling.

The Denial of Death ⟨⟩

One can only talk about an ideal human character from the perspective of absolute transcendence. . . .

Kierkegaard had his own formula for what it means to be a man. He put it forth in those superb pages wherein he describes what he calls "the knight of faith." This figure is the man who lives in faith, who has given over the meaning of life to his Creator, and who lives centered on the energies of his Maker. He accepts whatever happens in this visible dimension without complaint, lives his life as a duty, faces his death without a qualm. No pettiness is so petty that it threatens his meanings; no task is too frightening to be beyond his courage. He is fully in the world on its terms and wholly beyond the world in his trust in the invisible dimension. It is very much the old Pietistic ideal that was lived by Kant's parents. The great strength of such an ideal is that it allows one to be open, generous, courageous, to touch others' lives and enrich them and open them in turn. As the knight of faith has no fear-of-life-and-death trip to lay onto others, he does not cause them to shrink back upon themselves, he does not coerce or manipulate them. The knight of faith, then, represents what we might call an ideal of mental health, the continuing openness of life out of the death throes of dread.

Put in these abstract terms the ideal of the knight of faith is surely one of the most beautiful and challenging ideals ever put forth by man. It is contained in most religions in one form or another, although no one, I think, has described it at length with such talent as Kierkegaard. Like all ideals it is a creative illusion, meant to lead men on, and leading men on is not the easiest thing. . . .

One cannot give the gifts of the knight of faith without first being dubbed a knight by some Higher Majesty.

From Ernest Becker, *The Denial of Death* (New York: The Free Press, 1973). Reprinted with permission of The Free Press, a division of Simon & Schuster Inc.

QUESTIONS FOR THOUGHT AND DISCUSSION

1. Do you agree with Becker that the possibility of ideal human character requires a perspective of transcendence? Explain your view?
2. What are the marks of the "knight of faith"? How is his life a response to God's calling?
3. How does the "this worldly/otherworldly" aspect of the knight of faith affect the way he interacts with people and sees life?
4. For Becker, who dismisses all faith as a projection, the figure of the knight of faith is only a "creative illusion." What does that mean for his view of human character?
5. Do you know people, who live life as a calling, who could fit Becker's beautiful description of the "knight of faith"?

Václav Havel

Václav Havel (born 1936) is President of the Czech Republic and one of Europe's foremost playwrights and essayists. Founder and leader of the Charter 77 dissident movement, he was prominent in the Eastern European revolution of 1989 and became the first president of free Czechoslovakia.

Born the son of a civil engineer, Havel was thwarted in gaining higher education for political reasons. Joining a Prague theatre as a stagehand in the 1950s, he worked his way up and became a distinguished playwright. His international stature also derives from his long involvement in the human rights movement and his authorship of many essays on the nature of totalitarianism, including his famous "Open Letter to Dr. Husak." He is a winner of Europe's prestigious Erasmus Award.

Havel was twice sentenced to prison (once for four and one-half years), and while there was allowed to write to his wife, Olga, once a week. He used the occasion for profound reflections on life and modern society. The following excerpts are from two of 144 letters written between 1979 and 1983. Significantly, he explores the notion of responsibility and, writing as an atheist, he works his way to the threshold of faith in a personal God as the only way of grounding responsibility.

THE BITTEREST PILL?

"Man's complete lack of responsibility for his behavior and for his nature, is the bitterest drop which the man of knowledge must swallow if he had been in the habit of seeing responsibility and duty as humanity's claim to nobility."

—Friedrich Nietzsche

"[T]he task of breeding an animal entitled to make promises."
—Friedrich Nietzsche, defining the search for human responsibility

Letters to Olga

July 17, 1982
Dear Olga,
For many years now, whenever I have thought about responsibility or discussed it with someone, a trivial illustration has come to mind: at night, I board

the rear car of a tram to go one stop. The car is empty, and since the fare is paid by dropping a crown into a box, not even a conductor is present (this self-service system, as far as I know, is no longer used on Prague streetcars). So I have the option of throwing the fare into the box or not: if I don't, no one will see me, or ever find out; no witnesses will ever be able to testify to my misdemeanor. So I'm faced with a great dilemma, regardless of how much money I happen to have with me: to pay or not to pay? From the point of view of my existence in the world, it clearly makes sense not to pay, since putting a crown in the box amounts to throwing it down the drain. Still, it troubles me; I hesitate, think about it; in fact I might even be said to agonize over it. Why? What, after all, is compelling me to pay? Certainly not fear of the consequences if I don't—for my misdemeanor will never be discovered, nor will I ever be brought to trial. It is not even a desire to demonstrate my sense of civic duty, for there is no one either to condemn me for cheating or commend me for paying. My friends, fellow citizens, the public, society, the transport commission, and the state itself are all, at this moment, sound asleep, quite outside my dilemma, and any instrumental regard for their opinion would be obvious nonsense. The conflict is entirely my own, and my concern, or lack of it, for opinion is simply not a factor. But more than that: in this dispute, not even the extent of my concern, or lack of it, for the general good is germane: clearly, my night ride in the streetcar will cost society what it will cost whether I pay or not, and clearly it is of no concern to the transport commission whether my crown shows up in their ledgers or not. Why, then, does something urge me to pay? Or conversely, why does the thought of not paying make me feel guilty?

What, after all, is compelling me to pay?

Let us examine, then, the structure of this drama:—I think everyone must realize, from his own experience, that what is going on here is a dialogue. A dialogue between my "I," as the subject of its own freedom (I can pay or not), of its ability to reflect (I give thought to what I should do), and of its choice (I will pay or I won't) and something that is outside this "I," separated from it and not identical with it. This "partner," however, is not standing beside me; I can't see it, nor can I quit its sight: its eyes and its voice follow me everywhere; I can neither escape it nor outwit it; it knows everything. Is it my so-called "inner voice," my "superego," my "conscience"? Certainly, if I hear it calling me to responsibility, I hear this call within me, in my mind and my heart; it is my own experience, profoundly so, though different from the experiences mediated to me by my senses. This, however, does nothing to alter the fact that the voice addresses me and enters into conversation with me, in other words, it comes to my "I"—which I trust is not schizoid—from the outside.

I think everyone must realize, from his own experience, that what is going on here is a dialogue.

Who, then, is in fact conversing with me? Obviously someone I hold in higher regard than the transport commission, than my best friends (this would come out when the voice would take issue with their opinions), and higher, in some regards, than myself, that is, myself as subject of my existence-in-the-world and the carrier of my "existential" interests (one of which is the rather natural effort to save a crown). Someone who "knows everything" (and is therefore omniscient), is everywhere (and therefore omnipresent) and remembers everything; someone who, though infinitely understanding is entirely incorruptible; who is, for me, the highest and utterly unequivocal authority in all moral questions and who is thus Law itself; someone eternal, who through himself makes me eternal as well, so that I cannot imagine the arrival of a moment when everything will come to an end, thus terminating my dependence on him as well; someone to whom I relate entirely and for whom, ultimately, I would do everything. At the same time, this "someone" addresses me directly and personally (not merely as an anonymous public passenger, as the transport commission does).

But who is it? God? . . .

[In another letter two weeks later, he confesses his anguish over a misstep with the Communist prosecutor.]

July 31, 1982
Dear Olga,

. . . But to return to my story: I have my failure to thank for the fact that for the first time in my life I stood — if I may be allowed such a comparison — directly in the study of the Lord God himself: never before had I looked into his face or heard his reproachful voice from such proximity, never had I stood before him in such profound embarrassment, so humiliated and confused, never before had I been so deeply ashamed or felt so powerfully how unseemly anything I could say in my own defense would be.

. . . By casting doubt on my sense of responsibility, the shock I experienced, of course, cast doubt on my identity as well. Everything I was, for myself and for others, suddenly found itself open to question. I had to assume that those around me were justified in asking — and I had to ask with them — who I really was. Was I still the same person my entire previous history had defined me as, or was I now someone else, someone who, in extreme circumstances, knuckles under and who is not — as the previous one was — entirely reliable?

. . . But that, too, was immensely useful: it enabled me not only to understand (it's something that everyone knows theoretically) but to experience, in a directly physical way, the fact that one's identity is never in one's possession as something given, completed and unquestionable, as an entity among entities, as something one can husband like anything else, that one can use, depend on, draw on, and, every so often, give a new coat of paint. I had to learn the hard way that the opposite is true: one can, at any time—in the space of a few minutes—deny one's entire history and turn it upside down: all it takes is a moment of inattention, of self-indulgent relaxation, of careless trust that one is what one is, and must be so always. . . . Human identity, simply put, is not a "place of existence" where one sits things out, but a constant encounter with the question of how to be, and how to exist in the world.

One can, at any time— in the space of a few minutes—deny one's entire history and turn it upside down: all it takes is a moment of inattention, of self-indulgent relaxation, of careless trust that one is what one is, and must be so always.

From Václav Havel, *Letters to Olga: June 1979–September 1982* (London: Faber and Faber, 1988), letters 137, 139. Reprinted by permission of Faber and Faber and the author.

WHERE THE BUCK STOPS, THERE STAND I

"We possess nothing in this world other than the power to say I."

—Simone Weil

"The secret of man is the secret of his responsibility."

—Václav Havel

"All the shrewdness of 'man' seeks one thing: to be able to live without responsibility."

—Søren Kierkegaard

Faith's significance for society "ought to be to do everything to make every man eternally responsible for every hour he lives."

—Søren Kierkegaard

"Who stands fast? Only the man whose final standard is not his reason, his principles, his conscience, his freedom, or his virtue, but who is ready to sacrifice all this when he is called to obedient and responsible action in faith and in exclusive allegiance to God—the responsible man, who tries to make his whole life an answer to the question and call of God. Where are these responsible people?"

—Dietrich Bonhoeffer, *Ethics*

QUESTIONS FOR THOUGHT AND DISCUSSION

1. In Havel's streetcar illustration, what are some of the reasons he says "it clearly makes sense not to pay"? Do you find his points convincing? Why then does he feel guilty at the thought of not paying?

2. Havel says "I think everyone must realize, from his own experience, that what is going on here is a dialogue." Have you experienced such a dialogue about responsibility? What were the circumstances and the outcome?

3. Why does Havel say "the partner" is outside himself? How is he able to hear his voice?

4. In the paragraph starting "Who, then, is in fact conversing with me?", what are some of the observations he makes?

5. What is the significance of the transition he makes from "inner voice" to "someone eternal" and the possibility of God? How would that affect his response to the "call to responsibility"? Why does Havel believe we need a "partner" for our sense of responsibility that goes beyond conscience and duty?

6. What do you think Havel means when he says his dialogue led him to stand "directly in the study of the Lord God himself"? What is the connection between the streetcar illustration and his real experience of failure? How did his failure "cast doubt on [his] identity"?

7. What does he mean in saying, "Human identity, simply put, is not a 'place of existence' where one sits things out, but a constant encounter with the question of how to be, and how to exist in the world"? What does this have to do with the idea of the calling of God?

TWO
MAKING A DIFFERENCE

"PHILOSOPHERS HAVE INTERPRETED THE WORLD IN VARIOUS WAYS. THE POINT IS TO CHANGE *it."* *The collapse of Marxism has rightly discredited the teachings of Karl Marx, but this observation is one of his maxims that deserves to survive. We need to move from mere observation to action. The same point, of course, has been made in many more homespun ways. "When all is said and done, much more will have been said than done." It is important to "walk the talk" and so on.*

The point bears emphasis because there is a yawning gap today between the many people who long for their lives to "make a difference" and the few who move into action and do something. Reasons for this gap are not hard to find. Most are not new. But there are distinct modern pressures that reinforce the problem of inaction. Some come from ideas that undercut the notion of individual significance. Others come from the scale and speed of modern life that dwarf us as individuals and often leave us with a sense of impotence, even futility.

No two antidotes to this lethargy are stronger than a sense of calling and a knowledge of what others have achieved. Needless to say, faithfulness, not success, is the first requirement for followers of Christ. There are times when the impact of our lives on others around us or the force of our faithfulness to our calling won't be fully realized in our lifetime. But the pages of history abound with men and women whose faithfulness—and vision, courage, sacrifice, and endurance—has inspired them in tasks whose ripples touch our own day.

Few individuals in history have challenged greater evils and accomplished greater success than William Wilberforce and Aleksandr Solzhenitsyn. We live in a day when few people read biographies and various "mass" forces undermine the significance of great leaders. These readings therefore show us examples of entrepreneurial leadership that are inspiring and challenging.

There are distinct modern pressures that reinforce the problem of inaction.

73

Arthur M. Schlesinger Jr.

Arthur M. Schlesinger Jr. (born 1917) is an eminent American historian and man of ideas. A graduate of Harvard and Cambridge, he was a professor of history at Harvard before becoming special assistant to President Kennedy from 1961–63. He won the Pulitzer Prize for The Age of Jackson *in 1946 and for* A Thousand Days *in 1966. He lives in New York and is the Albert Schweitzer Professor in the Humanities at the City University of New York.*

The reading below is from his 1986 book, The Cycles of American History. *In the face of contrary positions, such as determinism, it sets out boldly the conviction that individuals make a difference in history.*

NO RIPPLES?

"Man is a stone thrown into the pond that causes no ripples."

—Zen saying

"Unlike egoism, the drive to significance is a simple extension of the creative impulse of God that gave us being. . . . We were built to count, as water is made to run downhill. We are placed in a specific context to count in ways no one else does. That is our destiny.

"Our hunger for significance is a signal of who we are and why we are here."

—Dallas Willard, *The Divine Conspiracy*

Democracy and Leadership

Leadership—the capacity to inspire and mobilize masses of people— is a public transaction with history.

Leadership is really what makes the world go round. Love no doubt smoothes the passage; but love is a private transaction between consenting adults. Leadership—the capacity to inspire and mobilize masses of people—is a public transaction with history. I borrow the title of this essay, a little warily, from Irving Babbitt, a shrewd scholar of eccentrically conservative tendencies who deserves to be better remembered than he is. In his book of 1924, *Democracy and Leadership*, Babbitt argued that leaders, good or bad, there will always be and that democracy becomes a menace to civilization when it seeks to evade this truth. Numerical majorities are no substitute for leadership. Salvation lies in leaders who can reestablish the inner check on unbridled human impulse: self-reform, not social reform. I do not know why Babbitt's traditionalism has not been rediscovered in the age of Reagan. Perhaps it is because Babbitt detested greedy capitalists as much as he did sentimental liberals. His diagnosis of the democratic malady smells of the library lamp rather than of the smoke-filled room; and he could have learned much about the world of power from Machiavelli, whom he both disliked and misunderstood. Yet Babbitt was ever-lastingly right in his conviction that democracy will stand or fall on the quality of its leadership.

Now the very concept of leadership implies the proposition that individuals make a difference to history. This proposition has never been universally accepted. From classical times to the present, eminent thinkers have regarded individuals as no more than pawns of larger forces, whether the gods and goddesses of Mount Olympus or latter-day divinities of Race, Class, Nation, Progress, the Dialectic, the General Will, the Spirit of the Age, History itself. Against such mighty deities the individual is deemed impotent, his sense of freedom and significance mere vanity and delusion.

So runs the thesis of historical determinism. Tolstoy's great novel *War and Peace* offers a famous statement of the case. Why, Tolstoy asked, did masses of men in the Napoleonic wars, denying their human feelings and their common sense, move back and forth across Europe, slaughtering their fellows along the way? "The war," Tolstoy answered, "was bound to happen simply because it was bound to happen." All history determined it. As for leaders, they were in Tolstoy's view the most deluded figures of all. Great men "are but the labels that serve to give a name to an end and, like labels, they have the least possible connection with the event." The greater the leader, "the more conspicuous the inevitability and the predestination of every act he commits." The leader, said Tolstoy, is "the slave of history."

Determinism takes many forms. Marxism is the determinism of class, Nazism the determinism of race; Spengler and Toynbee are determinists of growth and decay. There is even a determinism of the free market. But however much determinists differ in the explanation of causes, they unite in the conclusion that the individual will is irrelevant as a factor in history. Determinism, as William James put it, "professes that those parts of the universe already laid down absolutely appoint and decree what the other parts shall be. The future has no ambiguous possibilities hidden in its womb." History is fixed from eternity, an iron block in which there can be no equivocation or shadow of turning.

Determinism may or may not be true, but it unquestionably violates our deepest human instincts. It abolishes the idea of human freedom by discrediting the presumption of choice that underlies every word we speak and every decision we make. It abolishes the idea of human responsibility by depriving the individual of accountability for his acts. No one can live consistently by any deterministic creed. The communist and fascist states prove this themselves by their extreme susceptibility to the cult of the great leader. If we were to take determinism seriously, as Isaiah Berlin wrote in his brilliant essay "Historical Inevitability," then the changes "in the whole of our language, our moral terminology, our attitudes toward one another, our views of history, of society, and of everything else will be too profound to be even adumbrated"; it would be like living in a world without time or with seventeen-dimensional space.

Apply determinism to specific historical episodes, and the results are self-convicting. According to the hard determinist view, no individual makes a difference. As slaves of history, we are all interchangeable parts. If Napoleon had not led those armies across Europe, slaughtering as they went, someone else would have done so. James, rebutting Herbert Spencer's onslaught on the "great man" theory of history, asked whether Spencer really believed "the convergence of sociological pressures to have so impinged on Stratford-upon-Avon about the 26th of April, 1564, that a W. Shakespeare, with all his mental peculiarities, had to be born there." And did Spencer believe "that if the aforesaid W. Shakespeare had died of cholera infantum, another mother at Stratford-upon-Avon would needs have engendered a duplicate copy of him, to restore the sociologic equilibrium?" James was kidding the determinists, but he did not greatly exaggerate their position. "In default of a Napoleon," said Engels, "another would have filled his place, that is established by the fact that whenever a man was necessary, he has always been found." Shakespeare too? The principle is the same.

In December 1931 a British politician crossing Park Avenue in New York City between Seventy-sixth and Seventy-seventh streets around ten-thirty at night looked in the wrong direction and was knocked down by an automobile—a moment, he later recalled, of a man aghast, a world aglare: "I do not understand why I was not broken like an eggshell or squashed like a gooseberry." Fourteen months later an American politician, sitting in an open car in Miami, Florida, was fired on by an assassin; the man beside him was killed. Those who believe with Spencer and Engels that individuals make no difference because substitutes are "sure to be found" (Engels) might well ponder whether the next two decades would really have been the same had the automobile killed Winston Churchill in 1931 and the bullet killed Franklin Roosevelt in 1933. Would Neville Chamberlain or Lord Halifax have rallied Britain in 1940? Would John N. Garner have produced the New Deal and the Four Freedoms? Suppose, in addition, that Lenin had died of typhus in Siberia in 1895 and Hitler had been killed on the western front in 1916. What would the twentieth century have looked like now?

Leadership may alter history for better or for worse. Leaders have been responsible for the most horrible crimes and the most extravagant follies that have disgraced the human race. They also have been vital in urging humanity on toward individual freedom, social justice and religious and racial tolerance. For better or for worse, they make a difference. "The notion that a people can run itself and its affairs anonymously," said James, "is now well known to be the silliest of absurdities. Mankind does nothing save through initiatives on the part of inventors, great or small, and imitation by the rest of us—these are the sole factors in human progress. Individuals of genius show the way, and set the patterns, which common people then adopt and follow."

James did not suppose that genius was omnipotent. There is a necessary equation between the person and the times. Not every man fits every hour. Genius may come too early or too late. In the tenth century John Stuart Mill would have died an unknown. The nineteenth century would have sent Peter the Hermit to a lunatic asylum. Cromwell and Napoleon needed their revolutions, Grant his Civil War. Genius must be adapted to "the receptivities of the moment." Nor, James should have added, is all social change the work of individuals of genius. Modes of production, of distribution, of communication, set the scene and have their independent dynamism. Still, without leadership, there would be little movement in history.

Those who believe with Spencer and Engels that individuals make no difference because substitutes are "sure to be found" (Engels) might well ponder whether the next two decades would really have been the same had the automobile killed Winston Churchill in 1931 and the bullet killed Franklin Roosevelt in 1933.

Mankind does nothing save through initiatives on the part of inventors, great or small, and imitation by the rest of us—these are the sole factors in human progress.

From Arthur M. Schlesinger Jr., *The Cycles of American History* (Houghton Mifflin Co., 1986), © 1986 by Arthur M. Schlesinger Jr. Reprinted with permission of Houghton Mifflin Company.

QUESTIONS FOR THOUGHT AND DISCUSSION

1. What do you think of Schlesinger's definition of leadership and the weight he gives it? Why does this understanding of leadership require that individuals matter?
2. Most people would instinctively agree with Schlesinger that "individuals make a difference to history," but far fewer really live that way and

many do not have a basis for knowing why individuals truly count.
Why do you think this is so?

3. How does historical determinism "[violate] our deepest human
   instincts"? What are some examples that he gives of using determinism
   to explain historical events? Why do they seem far-fetched?

4. Why, in your own thinking, does individuality count?

5. Do you agree that "Not every man fits every hour"? What do you think
   this means for our goals and expectations in life?

6. What are the assumptions in "calling" that underscore individual
   significance?

William Wilberforce

William Wilberforce (1759–1833) was a British parliamentarian and philan-thropist, best known as the leader of the movement that abolished slavery, and arguably the most successful reformer in history. Born in Hull, he attended Cambridge where he became a close friend of William Pitt, the youngest prime minister in British history. His life was turned around by his conversion ("the great change") in 1785, and clergymen John Wesley and John Newton encouraged him early in his reforming endeavors.

At one stage in his life, Wilberforce was an active par-ticipant in an astonishing sixty-nine different public initia-tives, ranging from directly spiritual projects—he was the founder of the world's first Bible Society—to more secular initia-tives, including helping to found the Sierra Leone Colony for freed slaves, the Royal Society for the Prevention of Cruelty to Animals, the Royal Institute of Science, and the National Gallery. His crowning achievements were the abolition of the slave trade in 1807 and of slavery in the British Empire in 1833—just days before his death. His book, A Practical View of Christianity, was a best seller for fifty years.

Historian G. M. Trevelyan described abolition as "one of the turning points in the history of the world." Wilberforce's achievements were therefore historic, but they were neither easy nor quick—suppression of the slave trade alone took twenty years and full emancipation nearly fifty years. The following readings are a collage of Wilberforce's own words, along with those of his contemporaries and later historians. They underscore what one of his biographers noted—that a mod-ern person can change modern times, but he or she cannot do it alone.

The following readings without other citation are taken from the biography written by his son, Samuel Wilberforce, who served as Bishop of Oxford and Winchester—the Life of William Wilberforce *(London: John Murray, 1843, revised 1868).*

Wrestling with His Growing Sense of Calling 🐎

Wilberforce's first inclination after his conversion to faith in Christ was to leave the world of politics and be ordained as a minister—mistakenly believing, as many do, that spiritual things are higher than secular things. Fortunately, friends counseled him to stay and discover his calling in public life. John Newton and Thomas Scott, for example, were two ministers who wisely persuaded him to serve in Parliament and not become a minister.

A NEAR MISS

"But the cause of Mr Wilberforce is the cause of justice, humanity, and piety, as well as of Britain. I feel a sort of self-congratulation, at present, that above twenty years ago I withstood with all my energy Mr _____'s counsel, who advised Mr Wilberforce to retire from public life. Had that counsel been followed, the slave trade might have been continued to future generations."

—REV. THOMAS SCOTT, IN A LETTER OF JUNE 1807

"My anguish of soul for some months was indescribable, nor do I suppose it has often been exceeded. Almost the first person to whom I unfolded the state of my heart was [the poet William] Cowper's friend—good old John Newton—whom I had often heard preach when I lived with my Uncle William and Aunt Hannah [as a boy]. . . . [Newton] entered most kindly and affectionately into my case, and told me he well remembered me, and never ceased to pray for me. . . . [I]n the interviews I had with him, [he] advised me to avoid at present making many religious acquaintances, and to keep up my connection with Pitt, and to continue in Parliament."

—FROM AN AUTOBIOGRAPHICAL MANUSCRIPT
DICTATED TO JOHN HARFORD

From John Harford, *Recollections of William Wilberforce* (London: Longman, Green, Longman, Roberts & Green, 1864).

ADVICE FROM HIS FRIEND, PRIME MINISTER WILLIAM PITT (THE YOUNGER)

The passage below is the advice of his great friend Prime Minister William Pitt (the younger), who had earlier written to him and referred to Wilberforce's "constant call for Something out of the Common Way." His urging here came as a turning point for Wilberforce.

"Wilberforce, why don't you give notice of a motion on the subject of the slave trade? You have already taken great pains to collect evidence, and are therefore entitled to the credit which doing so will insure you. Do not lose time, or the ground may be occupied by another."

—BENEATH AN OAK TREE ON THE VALE OF KESTON, MAY 1787

WILBERFORCE'S MOMENT OF DECISION

Wilberforce's decision to take up the cause of abolition was triggered by various events, including Pitt's advice, his own research, and his deep sense of calling.

"So enormous, so dreadful, so irremediable did the Trade's wickedness appear that my own mind was completely made up for Abolition. Let the consequences be what they would, I from this time determined that I would never rest until I had effected its abolition."

—SPEECH TO THE HOUSE OF COMMONS AFTER
RESEARCH INTO SLAVERY, 1787

Written a few months after the above speech, this famous journal entry represents one of the most audacious statements of life purpose in history. Notice, too, the date, which sets the decision against the backdrop of revolutionary ferment in Europe.

"God Almighty has set before me two great objects, the suppression of the Slave Trade and the reformation of manners."

—WRITTEN IN HIS JOURNAL, SUNDAY, OCTOBER 28, 1787

From the very first speeches onward, Wilberforce brought to the issue the passion and moral urgency that such a calling inspired.

"Sir, the nature and all the circumstances of the Trade are now laid open to us. We can no longer plead ignorance. We cannot evade it. We may spurn it. We may kick it out of the way. But we cannot turn aside so as to avoid seeing it. For it is brought now so directly before our eyes that this House must decide and must justify to all the world and to its own conscience, the rectitude of the grounds of its decision. . . . Let not Parliament be the only body that is insensible to the principles of natural justice. Let us make reparation to Africa, as far as we can, by establishing trade upon true commercial principles, and we shall soon find the rectitude of our conduct rewarded by the benefits of a regular and growing commerce."

—CONCLUSION TO WILBERFORCE'S FIRST (AND UNSUCCESSFUL)
MOTION AGAINST SLAVERY, MAY 1788

FOR A LEADER, PUBLIC RESPONSIBILITY WAS CHRISTIAN RESPONSIBILITY

Wilberforce's journal entry here is in clear and settled contrast to his first inclinations to leave public life.

"My walk, I am sensible, is a public one. My business is in the world; and I must mix in assemblies of men, or quit the post which Providence seems to have assigned me. . . . My shame is not occasioned by my thinking that I am too studiously diligent in the business of life; on the contrary, I then feel that I am serving God best when from proper motives I am most actively engaged in it."

—WRITTEN IN HIS JOURNAL, 1788

HIS DECISION WAS TAKEN WITH THE FORCE OF A CALL

"The first years that I was in Parliament," he has said, "I did nothing to any good purpose; my own distinction was my object." But now he acted upon new principles; he regarded his powers of mind, his eloquence in speech, his influence with Mr. Pitt, his general popularity, as talents lent to him by God, for the due use of which he must render an account. . . . In this spirit he approached the strife, and let it never be forgotten, that it was a belief in God's call which armed him for his championship of the liberty of the oppressed.

Recognition of the Daunting Challenges ❦

Championing abolition was a dangerous business. The slave trade occupied a position in the British economy (as a percentage of gross national product) equivalent to that of the defense industry in the United States today. At one stage, Wilberforce was the most vilified man in England. He was even threatened and attacked physically, for example, by slave-trading captains whose reputations and livelihood were menaced by the campaign against slavery.

LETTER FROM JOHN WESLEY

The following letter, written in a faltering hand, is one of John Wesley's last messages. The next day, February 25, he sank into a coma and never recovered, dying on March 2. Wilberforce marked the letter "Wesley's last words."

February 24, 1791

Dear Sir,

Unless God has raised you up for this very thing, you will be worn out by the opposition of men and devils. But if God be for you, who can be against you?

Unless the divine power has raised you to be as Athanasius contra mundum [Athanasius against the world], I see not how you can go through your glorious enterprise in opposing that execrable villainy, which is the scandal of religion, of England, and of human nature. Unless God has raised you up for this very thing, you will be worn out by the opposition of men and devils. But if God be for you, who can be against you? Are all of them together stronger than God? O be not weary of well doing! Go on, in the name of God and in the power of his might, till even American slavery (the vilest that ever saw the sun) shall vanish away before it. . . .

That he who has guided you from youth up may continue to strengthen you in this and all things is the prayer of, dear sir,

Your affectionate servant,
John Wesley

In *Letters,* ed. John Telford (Epworth Press, 1931), VIII, 265.

LETTER FROM JOHN NEWTON

Newton was a converted slave trader who had become an Anglican rector and renowned hymn writer (including "Amazing Grace"). He had a decisive influence on the young Wilberforce. He urged him not to leave Parliament and encouraged him to take up the championing of abolition, despite its dangers.

Paul's Cray, Kent, July 21, 1796

My very dear Sir,
It is true that you live in the midst of difficulties and snares, and you need a double guard of watchfulness and prayer. But since you know both your need of help, and where to look for it, I may say to you as Darius to Daniel, "Thy God whom thou servest continually is able to preserve and deliver you." Daniel, likewise, was a public man, and in critical circumstances; but he trusted in the Lord, was faithful in his department, and therefore, though he had enemies, they could not prevail against him.

Indeed the great point for our comfort in life is to have a well grounded persuasion that we are, where, all things considered, we ought to be. Then it is no great matter whether we are in public or in private life, in a city or a village, in a palace or a cottage. . . .

I am your very affectionate, and much obliged,
John Newton

From *The Correspondence of William Wilberforce*, Vol. I, ed. Robert Isaac Wilberforce and Samuel Wilberforce (1840).

WILBERFORCE *CONTRA MUNDUM*

I will not allow the rights of the plantation owners to be infringed "while I have an arm to fight in their defense or a tongue to launch my voice against the damnable doctrine of Wilberforce and his hypocritical allies."

—Admiral Lord Nelson, writing from his flagship *Victory*

"Surely the Enthusiastic rage of Mr. Wilberforce and his friends cannot prevail in a matter of such consequence to the Colonies and the Mother Country."

—agent of the slave owners in Antigua

"I shall expect to read of you being carbonadoed by West Indian planters, barbecued by African merchants and eaten by Guinea captains, but do not be daunted, for—I will write your epitaph!"

—letter to Wilberforce from a friend

The Importance of Community in the Abolition Cause

Partnership, community, and the power of moral influence were critical to the success of Wilberforce and his colleagues, who were known as the "Clapham Circle" or "the Saints." One of their maxims was "Always seek a neighbor before you seek a home." Their conversations were so stimulating and so constant that it was said of them: they were "like a meeting that never adjourned."

PEOPLE OF CHARACTER AND INTEGRITY

In Parliament, too, the Clapham Sect were in a minority. The whole of Wilberforce's following, including a much wider circle than the Clapham Sect itself, never numbered more than twenty or thirty. The influence they exercised was again because of the intensity of their passion. They carried into their political life the same standards that governed them elsewhere. Henry Thornton began his parliamentary career by refusing to pay the bribe of one guinea a vote, which was then a matter of course. And his attitude was the considered attitude of the group. Even Babington, with less prestige than Wilberforce or Thornton, remained in Parliament for twenty years without bribery. The whole group presented to the House of Commons of their day the impressive spectacle of men who put principle before party or profit, "who looked to the facts of the case and not to the wishes of the minister, and who before going into the lobby required to be obliged with a reason instead of with a job."

Nominally they may have been Tory, as were Wilberforce and Stephen, or Whig, as were Babington and Smith; actually they were independent. To advance their causes and to uphold their principles they would support any government, or with equal resolution oppose any government—even though their action might deal a painful blow to their party and their friends. Wilberforce's diary has this typical comment (1807): ". . . Babington, and I, and Grant, and Henry Thornton too, all settle down into trying the new ministry, and treating them as their measures shall deserve."

It was said that the only times Pitt could not sleep were at the time of the naval mutiny at the Nore and at the first serious opposition of Wilberforce. Later it was charged that Wilberforce's speech in support of the censure of Lord Melville concerning the finances of the Admiralty contributed to Pitt's death. When Wilberforce retired from leadership of the anti-slavery party he impressed on his successor "the importance of keeping this great cause in possession of its old honorable distinction of being one in which all party differences were extinguished."

In consequence the "Saints" gained a unique moral ascendancy over the House of Commons.

Confidence and respect, and, (what in the House of Commons is their unvarying accompaniment,) power, were gradually, and to a great extent involuntarily, accorded to this group of members. They were not addicted to crotchets, nor to the obtrusive and unseasonable assertion of conscientious scruples. The occasions on which they made proof of independence and impartiality were such as justified, and dignified, their temporary renunciation of party ties. They interfered with decisive effect in the debates on the great scandals of Lord Melville and the Duke of York, and in more than one financial or commercial controversy that deeply concerned the national interests. . . .

Where moral questions were concerned they became a sort of barometer by which doubtful men came to their decisions. ". . . they commanded the ear of the House, and exerted on its proceedings an influence, the secret of which those who have studied the Parliamentary history of the period find it only too easy to understand." And they left an impression on the House of Commons which did not end with their passing. Sir G. O. Trevelyan gave his opinion that among the most permanent of their legacies is "their undoubted share in the improvement of our political integrity."

From Ernest Marshall Howse, *Saints in Politics: The 'Clapham Sect' and the Growth of Freedom* (Toronto: University of Toronto Press, 1952). Reprinted by permission of by University of Toronto Press.

NETWORKING

The Claphamites lived in great intimacy. They would wander into one another's houses and gardens and always find themselves welcome. There seemed to be a general assumption that a friend could come in at any time. They would also call on one another unexpectedly in the country and expect and receive the same welcome. They liked to spend their holidays with other members of the Sect, often in a series of prolonged visits to one another's houses. The Grants, Thornton, Eliot, and Wilberforce were so close to one another that although each of their houses on Henry Thornton's property had its own garden allotted to it there was no attempt to make any demarcation and they all treated the garden as a form of common property. It was perhaps natural that, living so closely together, the Clapham Sect should marry into one another's families and they did so to an almost incestuous degree. Wilberforce was first cousin to the Thornton and Smith brothers; Stephen married Wilberforce's sister, Gisborne Babington's, Babington Macaulay's, Charles Eliot Venn's. Macaulay, the supply of sisters having been exhausted, married one of Hannah More's pupils. The relationships of the next generation were even more complicated.

This seal of England's Slave Emancipation Society became a rallying symbol of the Abolition campaign when issued as a cameo medallion by William and Josiah Wedgewood. A similar image, used on a coin issued in the United States in the 1830s, shows a woman in chains and the phrase, "Am I not a Woman and a Sister?"

Living in such proximity to one's friends was both pleasant and useful. Wilberforce always found "the very prospect [of returning to Clapham] mends, fixing and solemnizing my mind." The enthusiasm for one another's good causes with which the group became infected led to the birth of a mass of societies for the relief of every class of unfortunate from Russian sufferers to Irish serving women. Wilberforce has been compared to a Prime Minister of a cabinet of philanthropists, in which each of his ministers held a particular portfolio, Stephen and Macaulay the Slave Trade, Lord Teignmouth the Bible Society, Thornton the Exchequer, Grant India, Macaulay and Hannah More public relations. Milner, Venn, and Simeon were his spiritual consultants, and he looked perhaps more to Babington than anyone else for general advice.

Even if one excludes the contribution made by those who did not live in Clapham, it is safe to say that never in the history of the Church did the inhabitants of a single parish have such an effect on the world. For the Clapham Sect's good works were not limited to England and Africa. They intervened on behalf of the convicts of Australia, the victims of the Napoleonic wars, the Greeks struggling for freedom, the Haitians, the North American Indians, the Hottentots, and the slaves. They distributed bibles and sent out missionaries to every corner of the world. They have been criticized for concentrating so much of their energies on religious campaigns, though it would be unrealistic to expect such religious men to do anything else. But the drive behind their campaigns was so great that their temporal achievements were enough to put any other group to shame. If they had never succeeded in anything else, their share in either of the great victories of Abolition and Emancipation would have guaranteed their place in history.

From Robin Furneaux, *William Wilberforce* (London: Hamish Hamilton, 1974), pp. 118–119. Copyright © 1974 by Robin Furneaux. By permission of Gillon Aitken Associates Ltd.

Success Came on His Deathbed

On Friday, July 26, 1833, the Bill for the Abolition of Slavery passed its second reading in the House of Commons. It was a government measure now and its success was assured. Wilberforce lapsed into a coma soon after hearing news of his great success, and died three days later on Monday, July 29, 1833, aged seventy-three. The amount of money cited—phenomenal in those days—is the sum with which the planters were to be compensated; it represented about half the market value of their slaves.

"Thank God, that I should have lived to witness a day in which England is willing to give twenty millions sterling for the Abolition of Slavery."

—WILBERFORCE, ON HEARING NEWS OF THE SUCCESS OF ABOLITION, 1833

Prerequisites of an Effective Reformer

Political and public style is critical to any reform movement opposing evil and stirring controversy. Means that do not serve ends become an obstacle to success. Wilberforce's generation saw this as the challenge of "doing the Lord's work in the Lord's way." In this passage Sir Reginald Coupland, one of Wilberforce's contemporaries, reflects on the ideal fit between Wilberforce's gifts and the challenges of his task. His comments have many applications to today's political movements.

DID SOMEONE SAY "FANATIC"?

"There is such a constant hilarity in every look and motion, such a sweetness in all his tones, such a benignity in all his thoughts, words, and actions, that . . . you can feel nothing but love and admiration for a creature of so happy and blessed a nature."

—poet Robert Southey, of Wilberforce

"It is necessary to watch him as he is blessed with a very sufficient quantity of that Enthusiastic Spirit, which is so far from yielding that it grows more vigorous from blows."

—agent of the slave owners in Jamaica

If the country must first be schooled and roused the second step must be to break through the apathy of Parliament. . . . And for this a politician is needed, and a politician endowed with very rare gifts indeed.

He must possess, in the first place, the virtues of a fanatic without his vices.

He must possess, in the first place, the virtues of a fanatic without his vices. He must be palpably single-minded and unself-seeking. He must be strong enough to face opposition and ridicule, staunch enough to endure obstruction and delay. In season and out of season, he must thrust his cause on Parliament's attention. Yet, somehow or other, Parliament must not be bored. He must not be regarded as the tiresome victim of an *idée fixe*, well-meaning possibly, but an intolerable nuisance. Somehow or other he must be persistent, yet not unpopular.

Secondly, he must possess the intellectual power to grasp an intricate subject, the clarity of mind to deal with a great mass of detailed evidence, the eloquence to expound it lucidly and effectively. He must be able to speak from the same brief a score of times without surfeiting his audience with a hash of stale meat. And he must have a natural delicacy of feeling. He will have terrible things to say; they will form an important part of his case; but in the choice of them and in the manner in which he says them he must avoid the besetting sin of the professional humanitarian. He must never be morbid. He must not seem to take a pleasure in dwelling on the unsavory vices of his fellow men. He must not pile up the horrors and revel in atrocious detail. He must shock, but not nauseate, the imagination of his hearers.

Finally, he must be a man of recognized position in society and politics. It must be impossible to deride him in London drawing-rooms as an obscure crank, a wild man from beyond the pale. And he must have, or by some means must obtain a footing in Downing Street. For without at least some shadow of support from Government his task might well prove desperate.

Sir Reginald Coupland, quoted in *Shaftesbury: The Great Reformer* by Georgina Battiscombe (Boston: Houghton Mifflin, 1974), pp. 83–84.

Epilogue from God's Politician

One of the commonest illusions of our day is that the individual is helpless, unable to do anything to alter events around him. Seeing the allegedly powerful so often at a loss, the ordinary man concludes that external forces are too strong for him and lapses into the "helplessness syndrome."

This syndrome is particularly cruel because it drains the meaning out of life. Without vision the people perish, sunk in a slough of comfort, frustration, or self-concern. Much of the mindless violence of our time stems from this sense that nothing constructive can be done.

Much of the mindless violence of our time stems from this sense that nothing constructive can be done.

The helplessness syndrome is at first sight a strange malady to affect mankind in the midst of a technological revolution which is said to make all things possible. One would expect people to be living in a fever of hope and opportunity. Surveys however show that fewer and fewer people think that the individual matters. Many of our most potentially creative people seem to think with the celebrated British painter Francis Bacon that "man now realizes that he is an accident, a completely futile being" or with Kenneth Tynan who bewailed our "new and grievous plight, awaiting death in a universe without God, ungoverned by reason and devoid of purpose."

Christianity has always officially contradicted this view and proclaimed the infinite worth and potential of the individual. "I can do all things," wrote St. Paul, "through Him who strengthens me." But in reality the helplessness syndrome has deeply eroded such faith in many Christians.

Many, perhaps a majority, feel with the Member of the House of Lords who replied to a recent survey, that "the business of surviving and enjoying our leisure is all we are prepared to do." The more committed seem often to resort to one of two false alternatives: either to retreat into a ghetto of personal belief from which the affairs of the world are excluded or to adopt an almost entirely political stance which sees no need of conversion.

"Wilberforce," writes Pollock, "proved that a man can change his times but that he cannot do it alone." He needed, in fact, a living God to change, remotivate, guide, and strengthen him. He also needed a band of like-minded men and women to plan and work with him, and to help keep his aims and motives clear. Together they created the leadership which was required—and the nationwide ground-swell which made that leadership effective.

"Wilberforce," writes Pollock, "proved that a man can change his times but that he cannot do it alone."

Some will say that such things could happen in the Britain of the eighteenth and nineteenth centuries, but are impossible in twentieth-century societies. Organizations are so vast and forces so impersonal, they argue, that the individual can no longer initiate significant change.

This, in my experience, is untrue. God is no less powerful today than formerly and men still have the capacity, if they will, to find his plan for themselves and events around them. Hundreds of people are initiating changes in conditions, large and small, all the time, and I personally have been privileged to see many such changes, some even on an international scale. The world today is waiting to see which countries will produce bands of committed people who will tackle together the seemingly insuperable problem of the coming age, as Wilberforce and his friends tackled the deadlocked situations of their times.

From Garth Lean, *God's Politician* (Colorado Springs: Helmers & Howard Publishers, 1980). Reprinted by permission of Helmers & Howard Publishers.

THE WASHINGTON OF HUMANITY

"When Mr. Wilberforce passes through the crowd on the day of the opening of parliament, every one contemplates this little old man, worn with age, his head sunk upon his shoulders, as a sacred relic; as the Washington of humanity."

—Count Pecchio

"I have not allowed myself to forget that the abolition of the Slave-trade by Great Britain, was agitated a hundred years before it was a final success. . . . School-boys know that Wilberforce . . . helped that cause forward . . . who can now name a single man who labored to retard it?"

—Abraham Lincoln, in *Speeches and Writings, 1832–1858*

"He could not have done what he did if he had desired office. With his talents and position he would probably have been Pitt's successor as prime minister had he preferred Party to mankind. His sacrifice of one kind of fame and power gave him another and nobler title to remembrance."

—G.M. Trevelyan, *English Social History*

QUESTIONS FOR THOUGHT AND DISCUSSION

1. Read the letter by Rev. Thomas Scott ("A Near Miss"). From what you read in part 1, what might have been the thinking behind the advice that, upon conversion, Wilberforce should "retire from public life" and become a minister? What would have happened if Wilberforce had followed it? What strains of such teaching still survive today?

2. John Newton counsels the freshly converted Wilberforce to "avoid at present making many religious acquaintances" and keep up his former friendships and previous job. Why do you think he advises this? What tends to happen when new converts don't follow such advice?

3. Pitt's advice to Wilberforce was a turning point in his taking up the cause of slavery. What do you think were Pitt's motives?

4. Read Wilberforce's mission statement on "two great objects." Which of the two do you think was the bigger and harder? Why?

5. Read the letter from John Wesley. What is Wesley saying? What must this have meant to Wilberforce as "the last words" of the grand old man?

6. In the section entitled "People of Character and Integrity," what are the secrets of the moral power of the Clapham Circle? What would have been the costs of such a stand?

7. In the section called "Networking," what dimensions of life did the Claphamites share? What do you make of the range of causes they were involved in?

8. In the section, "Prerequisites of an Effective Reformer," Coupland makes a big point of the difference between a reformer and a fanatic. Why is this important? What made Wilberforce such a passionate reformer but not a fanatic?

9. In the sixth paragraph of the "Epilogue from *God's Politician*," Lean summarizes the lessons of Wilberforce's life and influence. Which do you think are most important for us today? How many people do you know who have similar visions today? Do you?

Aleksandr Solzhenitsyn

Aleksandr I. Solzhenitsyn (born 1918) is a writer, novelist, Nobel laureate, and a living legend in the twentieth century. Born in Kislovodsk, Russia, he was educated in mathematics and physics and served in World War II, but was imprisoned from 1945–1953 for negative comments on Stalin's conduct of the war.

After surviving Stalin's infamous Soviet Corrective Labor Camps, the Gulag, Solzhenitsyn turned his pen into a sword and his books into military divisions. He became not only a Nobel Prize winner but a one-man resistance movement against Communist totalitarianism. Running a personal blockade of terror and enforced silence from the authorities and the secret police, his writings have given life to suppressed realities of the past and names to countless unnamed victims. He has thus reinvested distorted events with the weight of truth and justice. Behind all the courage of his stand is his unshakable commitment to truth and conscience—and a deeply mystical sense of calling. Unlike Wilberforce, whose calling to a life-task came when he was a young man, Solzhenitsyn's sense of calling grew only slowly and is clearer from the perspective of hindsight.

TRUTH IS FREEDOM

"One word of truth outweighs the whole world."

—Aleksandr Solzhenitsyn

"Truth prevails for those who live in truth."

—motto of Czechoslovakia's
Charter 77 movement

"'The truth prevails for those who live in truth' is the saving message that might well be inscribed on the 'Moses baskets' of every nation's babies."

—Václav Havel, *Living in Truth*

The Writer Underground ❧

Underground is where you expect to find revolutionaries. But not writers.

For the writer intent on truth, life never was, never is (and never will be!) easy: his like have suffered every imaginable harassment—defamation, duels, a shattered family life, financial ruin or lifelong unrelieved poverty, the madhouse, jail. . . .

I drifted into literature unthinkingly, without really knowing what I needed from it, or what I could do for it. I just felt depressed because it was so difficult, I thought, to find fresh subjects for stories. I hate to think what sort of writer I would have become (for I would have gone on writing) if I had not been *put inside*.

I hate to think what sort of writer I would have become (for I would have gone on writing) if I had not been put inside.

Once arrested, once I had spent two years in prisons and camps, depressed now by the mountainous overabundance of subjects, I accepted as effortlessly as the air I breathed, accepted with all the other unchallengeable realities before my eyes, the knowledge that not only would no one ever publish me, but a single line could cost me my life. Without hesitation, without inner debate, I entered into the inheritance of every modern Russian writer intent on the truth: I must write simply to ensure that it was not all forgotten, that posterity might someday come to know of it. Publication in my own lifetime I must shut out of my mind, out of my dreams.

I put away my idle dream. And in its place there was only the surety that my work would not be in vain, that it would someday smite the heads I had in my sights, and that those who received its invisible emanations would understand. I no more rebelled against lifelong silence than against the lifelong impossibility of freeing my feet from the pull of gravity. As I finished one piece after another, at first in camps, then in exile, then after rehabilitation, first verses, then plays, and later prose works too, I had only one desire: to keep all these things out of sight and myself with them.

In the camp this meant committing my verse—many thousands of lines— to memory. To help me with this I improvised decimal counting beads and, in transit prisons, broke up matchsticks and used the fragments as tallies. As I approached the end of my sentence I grew more confident of my powers of memory, and began writing down and memorizing prose—dialogue at first, but then, bit by bit, whole densely written passages. My memory found room for them! It worked. But more and more of my time—in the end as much as one week every month—went into the regular repetition of all I had memorized.

Then came exile, and right at the beginning of my exile, cancer. In autumn 1953 it looked very much as though I had only a few months to live. In December the doctors—comrades in exile—confirmed that I had at most three weeks left. . . .

All that I had memorized in the camps ran the risk of extinction together with the head that held it.

This was a dreadful moment in my life: to die on the threshold of freedom, to see all I had written, all that gave meaning to my life thus far, about to perish with me. The peculiarities of the Soviet postal censorship made it impossible for me to cry out for help: Come quickly, take what I have written, save it! You can't very well appeal to strangers anyway. My friends were all in camps themselves. My mother was dead. My wife had married again. All the same, I sent for her to say goodbye, thinking that she might take my manuscripts away with her, but she did not come. . . .

In those last few weeks that the doctors had promised me I could not escape from my work in school, but in the evening and at night, kept awake by pain, I hurriedly copied things out in tiny handwriting, rolled them, several pages at a time, into tight cylinders and squeezed these into a champagne bottle. I buried the bottle in my garden—and set off for Tashkent to meet the new year (1954) and to die.

Since then, all the life that has been given back to me has not been mine in the full sense: it is built around a purpose.

I did not die, however. With a hopelessly neglected and acutely malignant tumor, this was a divine miracle; I could see no other explanation. Since then, all the life that has been given back to me has not been mine in the full sense: it is built around a purpose. . . .

AN URGENT MISSION

My plan was an immensely ambitious one; in another ten years' time I should be ready to face the world with all that I had written, and I should not mind if I perished in the flames of that literary explosion—but now, just one slip of the foot, one careless move, and my whole plan, my whole life's work had come to grief. And it was not only my life's work but the dying wish of the millions whose last whisper, last moan, had been cut short on some hut floor in some prison camp. I had not carried out their behests, I had betrayed them, had shown myself unworthy of them. It had been given to me, almost alone, to crawl to safety; the hopes once held in all those skulls buried now in common graves in the camps had been set on me—and I collapsed, and their hopes had slipped from my hands.

From dawn to dusk the correction and copying of *Gulag* went forward; I could scarcely keep the pages moving fast enough. Then the typewriter started breaking down every day, and I had either to solder it myself or take it to be repaired. This was the most frightening moment of all: we had the only original manuscript and all the typed copies of *Gulag* there with us. If the KGB suddenly descended, the many-throated groan, the dying whisper of millions, the unspoken testament of those who had perished, would all be in their hands, and I would never be able to reconstruct it all, my brain would never be capable of it again.

I could have enjoyed myself so much, breathing the fresh air, resting, stretching my cramped limbs, but my duty to the dead permitted no such self-indulgence. They are dead. You are alive: Do your duty. The world must know *all about it.*

You are alive: Do your duty.

They could take my children hostage—posing as "gangsters," of course. (They did not know that we had thought of this and made a superhuman decision: our children were no dearer to us than the memory of the millions done to death, and nothing could make us stop that book.)

THE WORD AS WEAPON

It is infinitely difficult to begin when mere words must move a great block of inert matter. But there is no other way if none of the material is strength on your side. And a shout in the mountains has been known to start an avalanche.

Books are like divisions or army corps: at times they must dig themselves in, hold their fire, lie low; at times they just cross bridges in the dark and noiselessly; at times, concealing their preparations to the last dribble of loose earth, they must rush into a concerted offensive from the least expected quarter at the least expected moment. While the author is like a commander in chief, here throwing in a unit, there moving up another to wait its turn.

CALLING AND CONSCIENCE

Later the true significance of what had happened would inevitably become clear to me, and I would be numb with surprise. I have done many things in my life that conflicted with the great aims I had set myself—and something has always set me on the true path again. I have become so used to this, come to rely on it so much, that the only task I need to set myself is to interpret as clearly and quickly as I can each major event in my life. (V. V. Ivanov came to the same conclusion, though life supplied him with quite different material to think about. He puts it like this: "Many lives have a mystical sense, but not everyone reads it aright. More often than not it is given to us in cryptic form, and when we fail to decipher it, we despair because our lives seem meaningless. The secret of a great life is often a man's success in deciphering the mysterious symbols vouchsafed to him, understanding them and so learning to walk in the true path.")

I was disgusted with myself. The most terrible danger of all is that you may do violence to your conscience, sully your honor. No threat of physical destruction can compare with it.

In retrospect, almost all my life since the day I was first arrested had been the same: just for *that* particular week, *that* month, *that* season, *that* year, there had always been some reason for not writing—it was inconvenient or dangerous or I was too busy—always some need to postpone it. If I had given in to common sense, once, twice, ten times, my achievement as a writer would have been incomparably smaller. But I had gone on writing—as a bricklayer, in overcrowded prison huts, in transit jails without so much as a pencil, when I was dying of cancer, in an exile's hovel after a double teaching shift. I had let nothing—dangers, hindrances, the need for rest—interrupt my writing, and only because of that could I say at fifty-five that I now had no more than twenty years of work to get through, and had put the rest behind me.

The one worrying thing was that I might not be given time to carry out the whole scheme. I felt as though I was about to fill a space in the world that was meant for me and had long awaited me, a mold, as it were, made for me alone, but discerned by me only this very moment. I was a molten substance, impatient, unendurably impatient, to pour into my mold, to fill it full, without air bubbles or cracks, before I cooled and stiffened.

Once again, my vision and my calculations are probably faulty. There are many things which I cannot see even at close quarters, many things in which the Hand of the Highest will correct me. But this casts no cloud over my feelings. It makes me happier, more secure, to think that I do not have to plan and manage everything for myself, that I am only a sword made sharp to smite the unclean forces, an enchanted sword to cleave and disperse them.

Grant, O Lord, that I may not break as I strike! Let me not fall from Thy hand!

> *"The secret of a great life is often a man's success in deciphering the mysterious symbols vouchsafed to him, understanding them and so learning to walk in the true path."*
> —V. V. IVANOV

> *It makes me happier, more secure, to think that I do not have to plan and manage everything for myself, that I am only a sword made sharp to smite the unclean forces, an enchanted sword to cleave and disperse them.*

CONCLUSION

How simply it is all ending. The calf has butted and butted the oak. The pygmy would stand up to Leviathan. Till the world press fulminated: ". . . the only Russian whom the regime fears! He is undermining Marxism—and he walks around central Moscow a free man!"

I have never doubted that the truth would be restored to my people. I believe that we shall repent, that we shall be spiritually cleansed, that the Russian nation will be reborn.

From Aleksandr I. Solzhenitsyn, *The Oak and the Calf*. Copyright © 1975 by Aleksandr I. Solzhenitsyn. English translation copyright © 1979, 1980 by Harper & Row, Publishers, Inc. Reprinted by permission of HarperCollins Publishers.

VIEW FROM THE STERN

"If we are permitted to finish the work He gave us to do, it matters little how much we suffer in doing it. In fact, the suffering is part of the work. . . . But surely it is also part of the work to tell the world what we have suffered & how we have been hindered, in order that the world may be able to spare others. To act otherwise is to treat the world as an incorrigible child which cannot listen or a criminal which will not listen."

—Florence Nightingale, in her diary, 1857

"For what a mighty task your husband was chosen: all the trouble the Lord took with him, the infinite detours, the intricate zigzag curves, all suddenly find their explanation in one hour. . . . Everything acquires its meaning in retrospect, which was hidden. Mami and Papi, the brothers and sisters, the little sons, Kreisau and its troubles . . . it has all at last become comprehensible in a single hour."

—Helmuth James von Moltke, in his last letter to his wife Freya before his execution by the Nazis, 1945

"The gradual *reading* of one's own life, seeing a pattern emerge, is a great illumination at our age."

—C. S. Lewis, age 58, in a letter to a friend

QUESTIONS FOR THOUGHT AND DISCUSSION

1. How does Solzhenitsyn believe being "put inside" affected his early attitudes to a writing career?

2. How do you understand his apparently paradoxical confidence that "no one would ever publish me" but there was "the surety that my work would not be in vain"?

3. Review his heroic efforts at writing—writing whole books in his head, memorizing thousands of lines, exile, cancer, desertion, and so on. What was motivating him? What was the effect of the "divine miracle" of surviving cancer?

4. In the section "An Urgent Mission," a new note enters: "the dying wish of the millions." How does this affect him? Do you have any similar passion or burden in your life?

5. What was Solzhenitsyn's decision about his children? How does this compare with the common modern maxim that "work" never come above "family"? Which of the two is closer to the teaching of Jesus?

6. Clearly Solzhenitsyn has a high view of the power of words ("a shout in the mountain has been known to start an avalanche"). What lies behind this conviction? Do we have a similar view in the West? What has changed our attitudes to words? How can we counter this situation?

7. Solzhenitsyn quotes V.V. Ivanov: "Many lives have a mystical sense, but not everyone reads it aright. . . " In retrospect, how does Solzhenitsyn apply this understanding of life direction to his own experience? What do you think of this mystical understanding of calling?

8. His strongest statement of his calling is in the paragraph beginning "The one worrying thing. . . " What are the components of this extraordinary statement?

9. Do you have an equivalent, if less dramatic, sense of purpose in your life?

10. Wilberforce came to his sense of calling early (at the age of 28) and lived all his life in the light of it. Solzhenitsyn came to the same blazing conviction late and then could look back and decipher all God's signs leading up to it. Which of the two do you most identify with in this respect? Or does your experience differ from both?

TALENTS THAT MAKE MORE TALENTS

"Again, it will be like a man going on a journey, who called his servants and entrusted his property to them. To one he gave five talents of money, to another two talents, and to another one talent, each according to his ability. Then he went on his journey. The man who had received the five talents went at once and put his money to work and gained five more. So also, the one with the two talents gained two more. But the man who had received the one talent went off, dug a hole in the ground and hid his master's money.

"After a long time the master of those servants returned and settled accounts with them. The man who had received the five talents brought the other five. 'Master,' he said, 'you entrusted me with five talents. See, I have gained five more.'

"His master replied, 'Well done, good and faithful servant! You have been faithful with a few things; I will put you in charge of many things. Come and share your master's happiness!'

"The man with the two talents also came. 'Master,' he said, 'you entrusted me with two talents; see, I have gained two more.'

"His master replied, 'Well done, good and faithful servant! You have been faithful with a few things; I will put you in charge of many things. Come and share your master's happiness!'

"Then the man who had received the one talent came. 'Master,' he said, 'I knew that you are a hard man, harvesting where you have not sown and gathering where you have not scattered seed. So I was afraid and went out and hid your talent in the ground. See, here is what belongs to you.'

"His master replied, 'You wicked, lazy servant! So you knew that I harvest where I have not sown and gather where I have not scattered seed? Well then, you should have put my money on deposit with the bankers, so that when I returned I would have received it back with interest.

"'Take the talent from him and give it to the one who has the ten talents. For everyone who has will be given more, and he will have an abundance. Whoever does not have, even what he has will be taken from him. And throw that worthless servant outside, into the darkness, where there will be weeping and gnashing of teeth.'"

—Jesus, describing the kingdom of the heavens, Matthew 25:14-30

THREE
THE TRIALS AND TRIUMPHS OF QUESTING

THERE IS AN IRONY TO MODERN LIFE. WITH CHOICE AND CHANGE AT ITS HEART, MODERN *life is inherently dynamic and subversive of tradition. Yet many modern people have lost the dynamism of the traditional sense of life as a journey and a quest, with its accompanying sense of life's vicissitudes—its ups and downs, progress and setbacks, trials and triumphs, seasons and phases. For too many, life is expected to be like a cruise in a luxury car—all plush comfort, climate control, state-of-the-art engineered progress, and global positioning to ensure an on-time arrival.*

This theme of quest-with-conflict is at the heart of human experience and of its most enduring stories. From the Gilgamesh story in the ancient Near East, to Homer's Odyssey in classical Greece, to John Bunyan's Pilgrim's Progress in seventeenth-century England, to George Lucas's Star Wars today, and on to the real-life stories of many of us, venturing is never a tale of untroubled progress but of questing and conflict. It is the story of steps forward and steps back, of wounds given and wounds received. Of heights scaled and potholes hit. Of heroic feats and comic pratfalls. Of heartwarming relationships and bitter betrayals. Of stories to be told and retold and incidents too shabby to admit.

Faith provides no immunity from the raggedness of such challenges. In fact, no holy book is less holy than the Bible when it comes to describing the lives of its heroes and saints—including liars, cheats, adulterers, and murderers. The entrepreneurial vision of faith even intensifies the challenge. It expands the horizon, raises the stakes, deepens the possibilities of redemption, and invests each moment of the quest with a significance that transcends all other commitments and loyalties.

In this section we explore some of the trials and triumphs of the venture of faith. For centuries stories of growing up, breaking away, and winning spurs have been carried by the literature of chivalry and "romance." In the twentieth century their timeless inner drama about "the discovery of identity" was covered more and

This theme of quest-with-conflict is at the heart of human experience and of its most enduring stories.

The entrepreneurial vision of faith even intensifies the challenge. It expands the horizon, raises the stakes, deepens the possibilities of redemption, and invests each moment of the quest with a significance that transcends all other commitments and loyalties.

103

more by psychology. But the greatest stories have always been of real people in real life. These readings therefore illustrate vital aspects of the quest-with-conflict of entrepreneurial living. Modern life, as Spanish philosopher José Ortega y Gasset said, is fired at us point-blank. Stories such as these are an inspiration, a comfort, a challenge, and an encouragement as we undergo the passages and confront the challenges of our lives.

Yehudi Menuhin

Yehudi Menuhin (1916–1999) was a world-famous violinist, conductor, and ambassador for humanitarian causes. Growing up in San Francisco, he achieved fame as a soloist at the age of seven. "Now I know there is a God in heaven," exclaimed Albert Einstein after hearing him play. After World War II he made his home in England and Switzerland, and became a world figure, founding music festivals and music schools, and promoting such diverse causes as yoga, environmentalism, and world peace. His difficult personal background—scolded by his mother, beaten by his father, and unhappily married the first time—was in strong contrast with his public saintliness and the bliss of his second marriage.

Menuhin's story raises the issue of a second important contrast between the Jewish and Christian stress on the uniqueness of calling and other views of individual fate—for example, Eastern notions of karma or the "acorn theory" of growth, which holds that each person is born with an innate image and character that is given and overseen by an individual life-guardian, or daemon.

In the biblical understanding, "called to be" is far more than simply "constituted to be." "Who am I?" and "What am I about?" are not simply a matter of reading back early recollections that announce our later destiny. As we respond to his call, God leads forward. We become what we are constituted to be by creation. But we also become what we are not yet, and can only become by re-creation as called people.

We become what we are constituted to be by creation. But we also become what we are not yet, and can only become by re-creation as called people.

FATED TO BE

"When all the souls had chosen their lives, they went before Lachesis. And she sent with each, as the guardian of his life and the fulfiller of his choice, the daemon that he had chosen, and this divinity led the soul first to Clotho, under her hand and her turning of the spindle to ratify the destiny of his lot and choice, and after contact with her, the daemon again led the soul to the spinning of Atropos to make the web of its destiny irreversible, and then without a backward look it passed beneath the throne of Necessity."

—Plato, *Republic X*

"Coming into this particular body, and being born of these particular parents, and in such a place, and in general what we call external circumstances. That all happenings form a unity and are spun together is signified by the Fates."

—Plotinus

"In the final analysis, we count for something only because of 'the essential' we embody, and if we do not embody that, life is wasted."

—C. G. Jung

"Moira? the unfinished shape of our fate, the line drawn round it. It is the task the gods allot us, and the share of glory they allow; the limits we must not pass; and our appointed end. Moira is all of these."

—Mary Renault,
The King Must Die

"I don't develop; I am."

—Pablo Picasso

Unfinished Journey *&*

Looking back on the eighty years I have lived, I am struck most of all by the straightforwardness of the pattern. Everything that I am, or think, or do, almost everything that has happened to me, seems traceable to its origins with the simple clarity of geometrical proof. It is a curious, even a faintly disconcerting sensation to find oneself fulfilling what seems to have been a destiny. One wants to protest that initiative is not an illusion, that one could have influenced events quite otherwise; and such claims are surely unreasonable. Take by way of analogy the composition of music. Laboriously the composer feels his way through the notes of his symphony to the last triumphant bar, only to discover that their choice and sequence were inevitable all along. The inevitability does not rob him of achievement, however, for only hindsight can preclude all other notes and only he could father these. So it is with my life. Once traveled, the route is clear, but prescience did not divine it and I am at least in part accountable for the turns it took.

Once traveled, the route is clear, but prescience did not divine it and I am at least in part accountable for the turns it took.

    I cannot of course claim sole responsibility for its direction. For one thing, a *leitmotif* of my history has been the happy accident which demands from me a not more energetic act of will than compliance (although compliance has generally exacted a handsome expenditure of energy). For another, I know myself to be the offspring of the past. Much of my life's design was laid before I was born, and I sometimes feel that I have brought to consummation not just my own yearnings but also those of my parents, and yet perhaps at their expense. . . .

Perched high on the Curran Theatre cliff on concert afternoons, I let my gaze slide past the conductor, whose part in the delightful goings-on below rather defeated my comprehension, to focus on the concertmaster, Louis Persinger. Once in a while he would have a solo passage. I learned to wait for those moments when the sweet, lovely sound of the violin floated up to the gallery, thrilling, caressing, and more entrancing than any other. During one such performance I asked my parents if I might have a violin for my fourth birthday and Louis Persinger to teach me to play it.

If this narrative has taken its time to relate a detail which earlier accounts have furnished straight away, it is to undo the impression that I was shapeless protoplasm one day and myself the next, that musical gift comes to light with the *éclat* of the transformation scene in a pantomime. The finger I pointed at Louis Persinger could base its choice on four years that had given me what as many years of college rarely give the graduate: a sense of vocation. Is this particular sense native to childhood itself? I wonder. Have the fortunate simply rescued from an otherwise lost age of innocence the conviction of unlimited possibility, the instinct for real worth, which make it easier for children to identify with great soloists or simple souls than with able middlemen? Certainly, looking at children from an adult perspective, I have long believed that the grown-up world consistently underrates the young, finding marvels in ambition and achievement where none exists. At the age of four I was too young to know that the violin would exact a price commensurate with the grace it conferred—the grace of flying, of occupying an absolute vantage point, of enjoying such dominion over nerve, bone and muscle as could render the body an ecstatic absentee. But I did know, instinctively, that to play was to be.

Quite simply I wanted to be Persinger, and with equal straightforwardness proposed the means of bringing this enviable situation about. I don't think my parents found my request far-fetched—Aba's childhood had set a precedent, after all—but they may have found it more whimsical than urgent, and hesitated to invest any of their small resources in what might prove to be a child's caprice. As events were to show, they retailed my plea to friends and relations, in the manner of fond parents everywhere, and as a consequence I acquired in turn a toy fiddle and a real one.

I shall never forget the disappointment of that imitation violin. Made of metal, with metal strings, cold to the touch, with a sound as horribly tinny as its construction, this travesty of my longings enraged me for, as far as I recall, the first time in my life. The setting of its presentation and my ungracious reception of it was a large, beautiful park on a hill at the top of Steiner Street, a park whose lawns

Have the fortunate simply rescued from an otherwise lost age of innocence the conviction of unlimited possibility, the instinct for real worth, which make it easier for children to identify with great soloists or simple souls than with able middlemen?

and thickets were to become very familiar to my sisters and myself a couple of years later. Seated with Aba and Imma on a bench was a fellow teacher from Aba's school who there and then gave me his present. The poor man must have been taken aback when, getting no response from the toy, I burst into sobs, threw it on the ground and would have nothing more to do with it. I am sorry that my first patron in the matter of violins should have been so dustily rewarded for his kindness. I could not know that for myself gratification was only postponed.

From Yehudi Menuhin, *Unfinished Journey: Twenty Years Later* (New York: Fromm International Publishing Corporation, 1997), pp. 1, 20–21. Reprinted by permission of the publisher.

DO WHAT YOU ARE

"Aquinas was still generally known only as one obscure and obstinately unresponsive pupil, among many more brilliant and promising pupils, when the great Albert broke silence with his famous cry and prophecy; 'You call him a Dumb Ox; I tell you this Dumb Ox shall bellow so loud that his bellowings will fill the world.'"

—G. K. Chesterton, *St. Thomas Aquinas*

"What am I that I am not in harmony with all this, that their life is not good enough for me? Oh God, what am I? The thoughts & feelings that I have now I can remember since I was 6 years old. It was not I that made them. Oh God, how did they come? Are they the natural cross of my father and mother? What are they? A profession, a trade, a necessary occupation, something to fill & employ all my faculties, I have always felt essential to me, I have always longed for, consciously or not . . . The first thought I can remember & the last was nursing work & in the absence of this, education work, but more education of the bad than of the young."

—Florence Nightingale, a personal note in 1850,
before her parents relented and allowed her to go into nursing

"As king fishers catch fire, dragonflies draw flame;
As tumbled over rim in roundy wells
Stones ring; like each tucked string tells, each hung bell's
Bow swung finds tongue to fling out broad its name;
Each mortal thing does one thing and the same:
Deals out that being indoors each one dwells;
Selves—goes itself; myself it speaks and spells,
Crying What I do is me: for that I came."

—Gerard Manley Hopkins

"I thought I was in heaven. I made separate pieces; arms, heads, feet, then attacked the entire figure. I understood the ensemble at one blow; I modeled it with as much care as I do today. I was in ecstasy."

—Auguste Rodin as a 15-year-old,
on moving from drawing to sculpture

"I must, I *must*, before I die, find *some* way to say the essential thing that is in me, that I have never said yet. . . . I want to stand at the rim of the world, and peer into the darkness beyond, and see a little more than others have seen of the strange shapes of mystery that inhabit that unknown night. . . . I want to bring back into the world of men some little bit of new wisdom."

—Bertrand Russell, to a friend after describing his plans for the future

"Jennie, I believe God made me for a purpose, but he also made me fast. And when I run, I feel his pleasure."

—Eric Liddell, in *Chariots of Fire*,
explaining to his sister, who is worried that his running is distracting him
from his calling as a missionary to China, why he feels he has to run

"Is that what they call a vocation, what you do with joy as if you had fire in your heart, the devil in your body?"

—dancer Josephine Baker

"I felt as if I were walking with destiny, and that all my past life had been but a preparation for this hour and for this trial."

—Winston Churchill,
reflecting on the night he was asked by King George VI
to form a government and lead Britain against the Nazis

"Maybe twice in my life I reached what I wanted to. Once we were playing 'These Foolish Things' and at the end the band stops and I play a little cadenza. That cadenza—*no one* can do it better. Let's say it's five bars. That's a very good thing to have done in a lifetime. An artist should be judged by his best, just as an athlete. Pick out my one or two best things and say, 'That's what we did: all the rest was rehearsal.'"

—clarinetist Artie Shaw, to an interviewer

"You must take this money. You should give up journalism. The only wrong act that matters is not doing one's best work."

—Lady Isabella Gregory to W. B. Yeats,
leaving him a gift of £20 to encourage him to become a poet

"Do you think now that Tennyson should have been given that peerage?"
"One's only doubt is if he should have accepted it: it was a finer thing to be Alfred Tennyson."

—W. B. Yeats's father and a friend

"What matters, therefore, is not the meaning of life in general but rather the specific meaning of a person's life at a given moment. To put the question in general terms would be comparable to the question posed to a chess champion: 'Tell me, Master, what is the best move in the world?' There simply is no such thing as the best or even a good move apart from a particular situation in a game and the particular personality of one's opponent. The same holds for human existence. One should not search for an abstract meaning of life. Everyone has his own specific vocation or mission in life to carry out, a concrete assignment which demands fulfillment. Therein he cannot be replaced, nor can his life be repeated. Thus, everyone's task is as unique as is his specific opportunity to implement it."

—Viktor E. Frankl, "The Meaning of Life"

"There is always one moment in childhood when the door opens and lets the future in."

—Graham Greene, *The Power and the Glory*

"Neither in environment nor in heredity can I find the exact instrument that fashioned me, the anonymous roller that passed upon my life a certain intricate watermark whose unique design becomes visible when the lamp of art is made to shine through life's foolscap."

—Vladimir Nabokov, *Speak, Memory*

"I do not believe that man's life necessarily has a definite purpose; but if I think of my life and the aims I have until now set for myself, I recognize only one of them is well defined and conscious, and it is precisely this, to bear witness, to make my voice heard by the German people."

—Holocaust survivor Primo Levi

"When I sing, I feel, oh, I feel, well, like when you're first in love. . . . I feel chills, weird feelings slipping all over my body, it's a supreme emotional and physical experience."

—rock star Janis Joplin

"God, I'm glad I'm not me."

—Bob Dylan, rejecting his
stereotype as a sixties icon

"I feel blessed.

"So many men and women search and search but never find their passion, their calling, the sense of mission that would ignite their hearts and fill their lives with meaning and joy. . . .

"For some people in the Napa Valley, wine was just a business, an agreeable way to earn a living. Not for me. Wine for me had always been something much larger and it still is. Wine to me is passion. It's family and friends. It's warmth of heart and generosity of spirit. Wine is art. It's culture. It's the essence of civilization and the Art of Living."

—Robert Mondavi, *Harvests of Joy*

"Find a job you love and you'll never have to work a day in your life."

—Robert Mondavi's third secret of success

QUESTIONS FOR THOUGHT AND DISCUSSION

1. How old was Menuhin when he developed his "sense of vocation" described in the fourth paragraph? He asks, "Is this particular sense native to childhood itself?" What do you think? What do you think of his belief that "the grown-up world consistently underrates the young, finding marvels in ambition and achievement where none exists"?

2. What do you suppose it was like to grow up with a talent like Menuhin's and the intuition that "to play was to be"?

3. Menuhin says, "Quite simply I wanted to be Persinger." What does that say of the importance of exposure and role models in hearing and responding to a calling?

4. Other than disappointment, what impact did the "imitation violin" have on him? Why?

5. How does the biblical view of "called to be" differ from the acorn theory's view of "constituted to be"? Which, if either, do you subscribe to?

6. Returning to the opening two paragraphs, as Menuhin looks back at his life, he says "Everything that I am . . . seems traceable to its origins . . . seems to have been a destiny." Why is this so? Do you think this feeling of destiny is only for those who become outstanding in their fields?

7. Menuhin says, "Much of my life's design was laid before I was born." What is he saying in the so-called "acorn theory" of development? What are the main features of this theory as you see them in the box, "Fated to Be"?

❈ François de Fénelon ❈

François de Salignac de La Mothe-Fénelon (1651–1715) was a French priest, the-ologian, and author whose influential writing was at times quite controversial. Born to an aristocratic but impoverished family in Périgord, Fénelon was ordained a priest in 1675 and became Archbishop of Cambrai in 1695. His various ministries included teaching women and ex-Huguenots newly converted to Catholicism, sup-porting liberal education for the former in his treatise, On the Education of Girls *(1687). His letters of spiritual counsel are still highly valued today.*

In 1689, Fénelon was appointed tutor to the Duke of Burgundy, the grandson of Louis XIV, whom he taught for ten years, preparing the young duke for the crown he stood to inherit. For his royal charge, Fénelon wrote a number of works, including Fables, Dialogues of the Dead, *and* Telemachus, *with the aim of train-ing up a moderate and enlightened successor to his extravagant and despotic grandfather, Louis XIV. The Sun King, however, preferred the absolutist counsel of Fénelon's famous rival bishop, J. B. Bossuet. Louis saw* Telemachus *as an attack on his court and immediately dismissed Fénelon as tutor on its publication. Any hopes of this early training changing the governing of France in the future were dashed by the premature death of the Duke of Burgundy in 1712.*

Fénelon himself died just three years later, banished by the court, condemned by Rome, and exiled in his own diocese. Though Telemachus *contributed to Fénelon's downfall, it was spectacularly successful and became the most-read lit-erary work in eighteenth-century France, after the Bible. Had the Bourbons followed Fénelon, not Bossuet, there would have been no French revolution, and the history of the world would not have been the same.*

"Mentoring" has often become an empty cliché today. It survives best in the robust practice of coaching in sports, but its deepest roots lie in the models of tutor-ing and apprenticeship demonstrated by Socrates and Plato and, supremely, Jesus and his disciples. The central idea? The deepest things in life cannot be taught in words (or books, lectures, seminars, and sermons). They must be learned in expe-rience under the authority of a Master.

Fénelon's is the most systematic development of this notion, though there are oddities in his version. He is a Christian, but his Mentor is the pre-Christian god-dess Minerva in male disguise. Therefore the content of the counsel and the omniscient source from which it springs are hardly a model for today. But the role

The deepest things in life cannot be taught in words (or books, lectures, seminars, and sermons). They must be learned in experience under the authority of a Master.

of Mentor in this crucial stage of Odysseus' son Telemachus is both touching, telling, and instructive.

Telemachus *is the story of the moral and political education of a young man by a wise and virtuous tutor. In Homer's* Odyssey, *Telemachus is the son of Odysseus (or Ulysses, the Roman name used in this translation), the wisest of the Greek heroes of the Trojan War. Telemachus providentially vanishes between Books 5 and 15 of the* Odyssey. *Fénelon's* Telemachus *is an imaginative filling in of those ten books.*

WHY I WROTE IT

As for *Télémaque*, it is a fabulous narration in the form of an heroic poem like those of Homer and Virgil, into which I have put the main instructions which are suitable for a young prince whose birth destines him to rule . . . In these adventures I have put all the truths necessary to government, and all the faults that one can find in sovereign power.

—François Fénelon in a letter to Father LeTellier

WE MUST GRADUATE

One repays a teacher badly if one remains only a pupil.

—Friedrich Nietzsche, *Ecce Homo*

Telemachus ✒

During the voyage, Telemachus said to Mentor: " . . . I am fully persuaded that the most important point in government is to discern well the different characters of men, and to employ them according to their talents: but how such discernment is to be acquired, is what I am at a loss to know."

Mentor thus replied: "To know men you must not only study them, but keep their company and deal with them. Kings ought to converse with their subjects, make them speak, consult them, and test them by inferior employments, of which they should exact an account, in order to discover whether they are qualified for higher functions. How was it, my dear Telemachus, that you learned in Ithaca to know the nature of horses? Was it not by seeing them often, and having their excellencies and defects pointed out to you by persons of experience and skill? Just in the same manner, in order to know men, you must talk about their good and bad qualities with other wise and virtuous men, who have long studied their characters; thus you will insensibly become acquainted with them, and be able to judge what you have to expect from their qualifications. What was it that taught you to distinguish between good and bad poets? Was it not the frequent reading of them, and talking of them with those who had a taste for poetry? What was it that made you a judge of music? Was it not your diligent attention to the performances of good musicians? How can any prince hope to govern a nation well, if he is ignorant of human nature? And how can he avoid being ignorant of it, unless he lives with men? It is not living with them to see them in public, where nothing is said on either side, but unimportant trifles, or the language of art and premeditation; it is a matter of visiting them in private, to trace all the secret springs that move their hearts; to probe them on every side; and even relieve their wants, in order to discover their maxims. But to be able to form a sound judgment of men, you must begin with knowing what they ought to be; you must know in what true and solid merit consists, so that you may be capable of distinguishing between those who are possessed of it, and those who do not have it.

How can any prince hope to govern a nation well, if he is ignorant of human nature?

"People are continually talking of virtue and merit, without having any clear ideas of them. In the mouths of most men they are only fine words without any determinate meaning. . . .

"Learn then, my dear Telemachus, learn to know mankind; examine them, make them talk of one another, and prove them by little and little: but repose no blind confidence in any. . . . "

[At the end of the book, Mentor discloses that he is the goddess Minerva in disguise and addresses Telemachus one last time.]

At last Minerva addressed him thus: "Son of Ulysses, hear me once more, and for the last time. I never took so many pains to instruct any mortal as you. I have led you by the hand through shipwrecks, unknown lands, bloody wars, and all the disasters that the heart of man can encounter. I have shown you by facts, of which you were a witness, the consequences of the true and false maxims adopted in government: and your errors have been no less serviceable to you than your misfortunes. For, who is the man that can pretend to rule a people wisely, who has never suffered, nor ever profited by the sufferings which his errors have occasioned?

For, who is the man that can pretend to rule a people wisely, who has never suffered, nor ever profited by the sufferings which his errors have occasioned?

"Like your father, you have filled both sea and land with your sad adventures. Go, you are now worthy of having him for your model; the passage is short and easy from here to Ithaca, where he has just now arrived. Assist him against his enemies, and be as submissive and obedient to him, as if you were the meanest of his subjects, setting thereby an example to others. He will give you Antiope, in whom you will be happy, as having been captivated less by her beauty, than her wisdom and virtue.

"When you ascend the throne, let the great object of your ambition be to renew the golden age. Let your ears be open to everyone, but let your confidence be confined to a few. Beware of trusting too much to your own judgment, and thereby deceiving yourself: but when you have committed a mistake, do not be afraid that it should be known.

"Love your people, and neglect nothing that may tend to conciliate their affection. Fear, indeed, is necessary, where love is wanting; but, like violent dangerous remedies, it ought never to be employed but where necessity compels.

"Always weigh beforehand the consequences of everything you undertake. Endeavor to foresee the greatest misfortunes that may happen; and know that true courage consists in viewing danger at distance, and despising it, when it cannot be avoided: for he that avoids thinking of it before, it is to be feared will not have courage to support the sight of it when present; whereas he who foresees all that can happen, who prevents all that can be prevented, and calmly encounters what cannot be avoided, alone deserves the character of wise and magnanimous.

"Guard against effeminacy, ostentation, and profusion; and account it your glory to maintain a simplicity of manners. Let your virtues and your good actions be the ornaments of your person and palace, and your guards. Let all the world learn from you wherin true honor consists; and remember always that kings are not promoted to the throne to gratify their own ambition, but for the good of their people; that the good they do extends to very remote ages, and that the ill goes on continually increasing to latest posterity. A weak or vicious reign often entails misery on several generations.

"Above all, be upon your guard against your own humor and caprice, which is an enemy that will never quit you till death, but will intrude into your counsels and betray you, if you listen to its suggestions. It often occasions the loss of the most valuable opportunities; it engenders childish inclinations and aversions, to the prejudice of the most important considerations; and makes the most frivolous reasons determine the greatest affairs. It disgraces a man's talents, and his courage, and makes him appear unequal, weak, contemptible, and insupportable. Beware, therefore, O Telemachus, of such an enemy.

"Fear the gods, O Telemachus. Such fear is the greatest treasure the heart of man can be possessed of: by it you will obtain wisdom, virtue, peace, joy, genuine pleasures, true liberty, sweet plenty, and unspotted glory.

"I am now going to leave you, son of Ulysses; but my wisdom shall never leave you, provided you always retain a due sense of your inability to do anything well without it. It is now time that you should try to walk alone. The reason for my parting with you in Egypt and at Salente was to accustom you, by degrees, to be without me, as children are weaned, when it is time to take them from the breast, and give them more solid food."

No sooner had the goddess spoken these words, than she ascended into the air, enveloped in a cloud of gold and azure, and disappeared. Telemachus, overwhelmed with grief, wonder, and astonishment, lifted up his hands to heaven, and threw himself prostrate on the ground: then he went and waked the ship's crew, commanded them to put to sea immediately, arrived at Ithaca, and found his father at the house of the faithful Eumeus.

From François de Fénelon, *Telemachus*, edited and translated by Patrick Riley (Cambridge: Cambridge University Press, 1994). Reprinted with permission of Cambridge University Press.

NO WONDER LOUIS XIV WAS ANNOYED

"It is with sadness that I feel myself constrained to tell you hard things; but shall I betray you by concealing the truth from you? Put yourself in my place. If you have been deceived up till now, it is because you wanted to be; it is because you have feared advisors who were too sincere. Have you sought after people who were the most disinterested, and the most likely to contradict you . . . to condemn your passions and your unjust feelings? . . . No, no: let us see whether you will now have the courage to be humiliated by the truth which condemns you.

" . . . You have exhausted your riches; you have never thought of augmenting your people, nor of cultivating fertile lands. Was it not necessary to view these two things as the two essential foundations of your power—to have many good people, and well-cultivated lands to nourish them? It would require a long peace to favor the multiplication of your people. You should never think of anything but agriculture and the establishment of the wisest laws. A vain ambition has pushed you to the very edge of the precipice. By virtue of wanting to appear great, you have let yourself ruin your true greatness. Hasten to repair these faults; suspend all your great works; renounce the display which would ruin your new city; let your people breathe in peace."

—Mentor's speech to King Idomeneus of Salente,
whose misrule of Crete had caused him to be
deposed and exiled from that island,
from Fénelon's *Telemachus*

"The good historian is not from any time or any country; while he loves his fatherland he never flatters it in anything. The French historian must make himself neutral between France and England. . . . "
—François Fénelon, Lettre sur les occupations de l'Académie Française

"All these [ancient] legislators and philosophers who reasoned about laws presupposed that the fundamental principle of political society was that of preferring the public to the self—not through hope of serving one's own interests, but through the simple, pure disinterested love of the political order, which is beauty, justice, and virtue itself."
—Jean Jacques Rousseau, Economie politique, echoing Fénelon's notion of disinterested public service

QUESTIONS FOR THOUGHT AND DISCUSSION

1. In the opening paragraph, what does Telemachus say is the "most important point in government"? Why would this be so? What concerns him about this point?

2. What is Mentor's answer to Telemachus? How is his response a challenge to the way a king (or a political leader) might choose to interact with his subjects? To what areas of Telemachus's life and experience does Mentor point where this method of learning and discernment has been successful and valuable?

3. When Minerva drops her male disguise (Mentor) and addresses Telemachus as herself, she begins by recounting the history of his tutelage. What does the first paragraph of her speech say of the depth of Mentor's involvement in Telemachus's training? What does she say of his errors? What do you think of this? How would these experiences and her perspective on them prepare him for future errors he might make as king? What does she say he is now ready for?

4. How would you characterize Minerva's last words of advice to Telemachus? What areas of his life does she address?

5. Read the paragraph, "Always weigh beforehand the consequences. . ." How is this advice a continuation of his experience of being tutored? What would following—or not—this advice mean for fulfilling one's calling?

6. In the next paragraph, "Guard against . . . ," Minerva addresses some character issues. What are they? Why is it important for leaders to be of good character? She says, "A weak or vicious reign often entails misery

on several generations." What do you think? Where in history have you seen evidence to this fact?

7. What is the "enemy that will never quit you till death"? How would a leader guard against such an enemy?

8. What is your experience of being tutored/mentored/coached? And of being a tutor/mentor/coach? What difference has this relationship made for the student/apprentice? For the tutor? For the leadership or responsibility for which the young person is being prepared?

Florence Nightingale

Florence Nightingale (1820–1910) was the founder of modern nursing, a legendary pioneer in hospital reform, and a groundbreaker in the women's movement. Born in Florence, Italy to a wealthy, aristocratic English family, Nightingale received her formal training at the Institution of Deaconesses in Kaiserwerth, Germany, in 1852. During the Crimean War, she took thirty-eight nurses to Scutari, Turkey, to serve in the army hospital there. Her improvements in sanitation and discipline among the medical staff dramatically reduced the mortality rate of the wounded.

Upon her return to England in 1856, Nightingale was given a grant to establish a training school for nurses at St. Thomas's and King's College Hospital, the first of its kind. She was an active reformer, pushing for improvements in nursing, hospital sanitation, army conditions, and the public health and independence of India. A prolific writer, her Notes on Nursing, Notes on Hospitals, Suggestions for Thought, *and collections of her letters and diaries are still in print today.*

Nightingale was a woman much ahead of her time, breaking numerous social taboos to become a nurse. Presented to Queen Victoria on her social debut, Nightingale came from an elite family that associated with the likes of Lord Palmerston and Lord Shaftesbury. Although her father was a nonconformist who himself educated his daughters in the classics and enlightened them on the political reforms of the day, her mother was strictly conventional and was shocked by Florence's interests.

Perhaps known best as "the lady with the lamp," this idealized symbol does little to convey the radical path she took in life, creating an acceptable vocation for educated women of all classes, nor the dramatic improvements she made in the medical sector.

The passages below, from Barbara Montgomery Dossey's biography, Florence Nightingale, *show the strong social barriers Nightingale had to surmount in answering her call of God.*

BE WHO YOU ARE

"God has always led me of Himself. . . . The first idea I can recollect when I was a child was a desire to nurse the sick. My day dreams were all of hospitals and I visited them whenever I could. I never communicated it to any one, it would have been laughed at; but I thought God had called me to serve Him in that way."

—Florence Nightingale, Curriculum Vitae, 1851

A FIERY COMET

"My principle has always been: that we should give the best training we could to any woman of any class, of any sect, 'paid' or unpaid, who had the requisite qualifications, moral, intellectual & physical, for the vocation of a Nurse."

—Florence Nightingale, in a letter to Dr. William Farr, 1866

"Fifty years ago, the various facilities for nursing the wounded which are available today did not exist. People did not come out to render aid in large numbers as they do now. Surgery was not as efficacious then as it is today. There were in those days very few men who considered it an act of mercy and merit to succour the wounded. It was at such a time that this lady, Florence Nightingale, came upon the scene and did good work worthy of an angel descended from heaven. She was heart-stricken to learn of the sufferings of the soldiers.

"Born of a noble and rich family, she gave up her life of ease and comfort and set out to nurse the wounded and the ailing, followed by many other ladies. She left her home on October 21, 1854. She rendered strenuous service in the battle of Inkerman. At that time there were neither beds nor other amenities for the wounded. There were 10,000 wounded under the charge of this single woman. The death rate among the wounded which was 42 per cent, before she arrived, immediately came down to 31 per cent, and ultimately to 5 per cent. This was miraculous, but can be easily visualized. If bleeding could be stopped, the wounds bandaged and the requisite diet given, the lives of many thousands would doubtless be saved. The only thing necessary was kindness and nursing, which Miss Nightingale provided.

"It is said that she did an amount of work which big and strong men were unable to do. She used to work nearly twenty hours, day and night. When the women working under her went to sleep, she, lamp in hand, went out alone at midnight to the patients' bedside, comforted them, and herself gave them whatever food and other things were necessary. She was not afraid of going even to the battle-front, and did not know what fear was. She feared only God. Knowing that one has to die some day or other, she readily bore whatever hardships were necessary in order to alleviate the suffering of others."

—Mohandas Ghandi, *Indian Opinion*, 1915

"Like a fiery comet, Florence Nightingale streaked across the skies of 19th-century England and transformed the world with her passage. She was a towering genius of both intellect and spirit, and her legacy resonates today as forcefully as during her lifetime."

—Barbara Montgomery Dossey, *Florence Nightingale*

"Thanks to Nightingale and her colleagues, the image of the nurse was also completely transformed: She was now seen as an angel of mercy with a high calling. By proving that women could successfully serve as nurses in military hospitals, Nightingale had almost single-handedly awakened England to the idea that women did indeed have a capacity for purposeful work and could make major contributions to society. . . .

"From the beginning of the war, Nightingale's popularity with the British public had been enormous because of the letters that the soldiers wrote to family and friends about her and the articles in the *Times* that described her tireless work on behalf of the sick and wounded. As word of her accomplishments spread, she became a kind of national heroine-cum-saint in Britain and beyond."

—Barbara Montgomery Dossey, *Florence Nightingale*

The Lady with the Lamp

By the time she was a teenager, Florence's life had already begun to revolve around helping her poor and ill neighbors. As a girl of 15 or so, she often disappeared in the evening, only to be found by her mother at the bedside of an ailing villager, saying "she could not sit down to a grand 7 o'clock dinner while this was going on . . . " Looking back, Florence wrote that she had always been in the habit of visiting the poor at home: "I longed to live like them and with them and then I thought I could really help them. But to visit them in a carriage and give them money is so little like following Christ, who made Himself like His brethren."

Florence had been elated when she first became responsible for caring for her nephew Shore when Nurse Gale fell ill. As she began to grow in size and strength and flourish in her education, her innate gifts as a healer and her desire to be of service began to find expression in caring for her extended family and the larger world.

When Aunt Julia visited Lea Hurst, Florence went with her to visit the poor people in the nearby villages. Florence admired Aunt Julia, who not only did good, but also had an efficient system for doing so. Julia kept track of who was sick and needed return visits; which families needed clothing, shoes, blankets, or food; and which mothers needed help tending their flocks of children amidst the filth and poverty.

Although Florence's mother also paid visits to villagers, usually to distribute food from the Nightingale's table or to offer practical advice, "poor-peopling" was only a sidelight in her life; she was consumed with ambition for social success—not social service—for herself and her daughters.

[*In 1837, when she was just 16, Florence sensed dramatically that God was calling her. To what exact path, she was not certain, but she increased dramatically her nursing work among the poor.*]

"I longed to live like them and with them and then I thought I could really help them. But to visit them in a carriage and give them money is so little like following Christ, who made Himself like His brethren."
—FLORENCE NIGHTINGALE

. . . While Florence inwardly longed to find meaningful work, her duty to family continued to dictate her life. As a young lady in society, she was expected to be at the disposal of her parents, available at all times to show guests around the estates and make pleasant conversation. The family received many distinguished visitors, leaving Florence no time for the serious studies she wished to undertake. Although she accompanied the family on the regular round of seasonal visits and parties at Embley, Lea Hurst, and London, her thoughts were far away—with the plight of women and poor people who were the subject of the debate over Lord Ashley's Ten Hours Bill.

Mrs. Nightingale had no idea of the serious thoughts and desire for a meaningful life that occupied her younger daughter's mind. Fanny's plans for her daughters and her social ambitions were moving forward nicely. . . .

In the summer of 1844, family friends introduced the Nightingales to the famed American educator and philanthropist Dr. Samuel Gridley Howe, and his wife, Julia Ward Howe. Mrs. Howe would later become a well known suffragette and reformer as well as the composer of the "Battle Hymn of the Republic." The Howes knew England well; as philanthropists, they had previously visited numerous public institutions, including schools, workhouses, prisons, and insane asylums. On a visit to a prison with novelist Charles Dickens, the group watched the prisoners' daily routine of "ungrateful work," and Dickens commented, "My God! if a woman thinks her son may come to this, I don't blame her if she strangles him in infancy."

One morning, Florence asked to meet with Dr. Howe. She came straight to the point: "Dr. Howe, do you think it would be unsuitable and unbecoming for a young Englishwoman to devote herself to works of charity in hospitals and elsewhere as Catholic sisters do? Do you think it would be a dreadful thing?" From his conversations with family friends, Dr. Howe was well aware of Florence's struggles with her parents over her desire for a meaningful vocation, but his answer reflected his own conscience and his American understanding of the strictures of English society:

"You will find that there is never anything unbecoming or unladylike in doing your duty for the good of others."
—Dr. Samuel Gridley Howe

My dear Miss Florence, it would be unusual, and in England whatever is unusual is apt to be thought unsuitable; but I say to you, go forward if you have a vocation for that way of life; act up to your inspiration, and you will find that there is never anything unbecoming or unladylike in doing your duty for the good of others. Choose, go on with it wherever it may lead you, and God be with you.

At this time in England, "nurses" were generally drawn from the ranks of the poor and unskilled, and usually remained in that state, with the exception of those women with natural healing instincts and intelligence. They also had a reputation for drunkenness and immoral conduct. This sad state of affairs had evolved for three centuries as nursing passed into its "dark ages" in England. Since the Reformation and the suppression of monasteries, the quality of nursing and hospitals had suffered in all the Protestant European countries but most severely in England.

When Henry VIII established the Church of England in 1534, he seized over 600 charitable institutions and suppressed all religious orders. This seizure of church properties had a direct negative effect on women and nursing—women lost political and administrative control of nursing operations. Inexperienced civil administrators took over from religious professionals who were steeped in a culture of care that had evolved since the beginning of the Christian church. Women lost their voice in both hospital administration and nursing management. The whole medical system began a downward spiral of mismanagement, crowding, filth, and contagion. It was these conditions that prompted Howe to tell Florence that her avocation might be thought "unusual." . . .

This seizure of church properties had a direct negative effect on women and nursing—women lost political and administrative control of nursing operations.

By late 1845, Florence had come to realize the need for training to learn the rudiments of nursing. . . . With the agreement of family friend Dr. Richard Fowler, for many years a doctor at Salisbury Hospital, Florence proposed to her family that she go to study under his direction for 3 months. . . .

The plans of the two forward thinkers ran into a wall of absolute conventionality. Mrs. Nightingale was horrified and called Florence "odd"; such a venture was totally beneath their class and unequivocally forbidden. It was unbelievable that Florence would even consider such unladylike behavior. What if men who weren't "gentlemen" made advances to her? Didn't she care what others thought of her? Even Dr. Fowler's wife, upon whose sympathy Florence had depended, felt that conditions at Salisbury Hospital were far too coarse for a lady of Florence's upbringing. At this time in England, as Florence would later write, caregivers were "merely women who would be servants if they were not nurses . . . it was as if I had wanted to be a kitchen-maid."

At this time in England, as Florence would later write, caregivers were "merely women who would be servants if they were not nurses . . . it was as if I had wanted to be a kitchen-maid."

It wasn't just the field of nursing to which the Nightingales so vehemently objected; doctors and hospitals were also included in their concerns. A unified medical profession, in the sense now known, didn't exist. The rapid modernization and industrialization that was creating many new professions in England and changing others for the better hadn't begun to reach the medical sector. Doctors were regarded as little better than tradesmen, and hospitals and nursing were little changed from the previous 3 centuries. The filth and stench of hospitals were such that only the poor and the destitute went there; those who could afford it were nursed at home.

Crushed, Florence poured out her feelings to cousin Hilary [Bonham Carter]. In a torrent of emotion, she revealed that she was thinking not only of nursing for herself, but also in terms of plans for an organization:

> I have always found that there was so much truth in the suggestion that you must dig for hidden treasures in silence or you will not find it; and so I dug after my poor little plan in silence, even for you. It was to go to be a nurse at Salisbury Hospital for these few months to learn the 'prax'; and then to come home and make such wondrous intimacies at West Wellow under the shelter of a rhubarb powder and a dressed leg; let alone that no one could ever say to me again, your health will not stand this or that. I saw a poor woman die before my eyes this summer because there was no one but fools to sit up with her, who poisoned her as much as if they had given her arsenic. And then I had such a fine plan for those dreaded latter days (which I have never dreaded), if I should outlive my immediate ties, of taking a small house in West Wellow. Well, I do not like much talking about it, but I thought something like a Protestant Sisterhood, without vows, for women of educated feelings, might be established.
>
> But there have been difficulties about my very first step, which terrified Mama. I do not mean the physically revolting parts of a hospital, but things about the surgeons and nurses which you may guess. Even Mrs. Fowler threw cold water upon it; and nothing will be done this year at all events, and I do not believe—ever; and no advantage that I see comes of my living on, excepting that one becomes less and less of a young lady every year, which is only a negative one. You will laugh, dear, at the whole plan, I daresay; but no one but the mother of it knows how precious an infant idea becomes; nor how the soul dies between the destruction of one and the taking up of another. I shall never do anything, and am worse than dust and nothing. I wonder if our Savior were to walk to the earth again, and I were to go to Him and ask, whether He would send me back to live this life again, which crushes me into vanity and deceit. Oh for some strong thing to sweep this loathsome life into the past. . . .

"No one but the mother of it knows how precious an infant idea becomes; nor how the soul dies between the destruction of one and the taking up of another."
—FLORENCE NIGHTINGALE

[*1849 and 1850 proved to be life-changing years for Florence. Seeing marriage as a definite barrier to becoming a nurse, she turned down a second proposal, much to her family's disapproval. Family friends, the Bracebridges, took Florence on a trip to Egypt, Greece and Europe to relieve the tension in the Nightingale household. During this tour, particularly while in Egypt, Florence sensed another call from God.*]

[March] 7. Thursday. Gale all night & all day . . . God called me in the morning & asked me "Would I do good for Him, for Him alone without the reputation [self-interest]."

8. Friday. Thought much upon this question. My Madre [a nun she had met the previous year in Rome who advised her on hearing God] said to me, Can you hesitate between the God of the whole Earth & your little reputation?

9. Saturday. During half an hour I had by myself in the cabin . . . settled the question with God.

11. Monday. Thought how our leaving Thebes was quite useless owing to this contrary wind . . . but without it I might not have had this call from God.

12. Tuesday. Very sleepy. Stood at the door of the boat looking out upon the stars & the tall mast in the still night against the sky . . . & tried to think only of God's will—& that every thing is desirable only as He is in it or not in it—only as it brings us nearer or farther from Him. He is speaking to us often just when something we think untoward happens.

15. Friday. Such a day at Memphis & in the desert of Sakkara . . . God has delivered me from the great offense—& the constant murderer of my thoughts.

16. Saturday—17. Sunday. Tried to bring my will one with God's . . . Can I not serve God as well in Malta as in Smyrna, in England as at Athens? Perhaps better—perhaps it is between Athens & Kaiserwerth [a training school for nurses in Germany]—perhaps this is the opportunity my

God called me in the morning & asked me "Would I do good for Him, for Him alone without the reputation [self-interest]."
—FLORENCE NIGHTINGALE

30th year was to bring me. Then as I sat in a large dull room waiting for the letters, God told me what a privilege he had reserved for me, what a preparation for Kaiserwerth in choosing me to be with Mr. B. during his time of ill health & how I had neglected it—& had been blind to it. If I were never thinking of the reputation, how I should be better able to see what God intends for me . . .

In her diary at Cairo she wrote: "Oh God, thou puttest into my heart this great desire to devote myself to the sick and sorrowful. I offer it to thee, Do with it what is for thy service."

[Marking her 30th birthday, May 12, 1850, Florence responded to God's call with a deliberate vow, which she recorded in her diary.]

"Today I am 30—the age Christ began his Mission. Now no more childish things, no more vain things, no more love, no more marriage. Now, Lord let me only think of Thy will, what Thou willest me to do. O, Lord, Thy will, Thy will."

[The Bracebridges took Florence to Kaiserwerth, Germany, to see the nursing school. She became even more determined to become a trained nurse. However, her return to England proved nothing had changed at home. Her family did everything possible to distract her and thwart her plans. She recorded her frustration and near despair in her diary.]

What am I that I am not in harmony with all this, that their life is not good enough for me? Oh God, what am I? The thoughts & feelings that I have now I can remember since I was 6 years old. It was not I that made them. Oh God, how did they come? Are they the natural cross of my father and mother? What are they? A profession, a trade, a necessary occupation, something to fill & employ all my faculties, I have always felt essential to me, I have always longed for, consciously or not . . . The first thought I can remember & the last was nursing work & in the absence of this, education work, but more education of the bad than of the young. . . .

But why, oh my God, cannot I be satisfied with the life which satisfies so many people? I am told that the conversations of all these good clever men ought to be enough for me—why am I starving, desperate, diseased upon it? . . . My God, what am I to do? teach me, tell me, I cannot go on any longer waiting till my situation sh'd change. . . .

[The next year, in 1851, Florence met and spent considerable time with Dr. Elizabeth Blackwell, the first woman doctor in America, discussing women and medicine. Dr. Blackwell encouraged her in her pursuit of formal nursing, and this friendship gave her the strength to go against her family's expectations. Her notes in her diary sounded more optimistic and determined.]

I must place my intercourse with those three [her parents and sister] on a true footing . . . I must expect no sympathy or help from them. I have so long craved for their sympathy that I can hardly reconcile myself to this. I have so long struggled to make myself understood . . . insupportably fretted by not being understood (at this moment I feel it when I retrace these conversations in thought) that I must not even try to be understood . . . Parthe [her sister] says that I blow a trumpet—that it gives her indigestion—that also is true. Struggle must make a noise—and everything that I have to do that concerns my real being must be done with a struggle.

[Her parents finally relented, and in October of 1851, Florence enrolled at Kaiserwerth, at long last launching her revolutionary career as nurse and medical reformer. About three years later, fully into nursing at this point, Florence writes her Aunt Hannah, revealing her deep conviction and satisfaction in pursuing her calling.]

Our vocation is a difficult one, as you, I am sure, know—& though there are many consolations & very high ones, the disappointments are so numerous that we require all our faith & trust. But that is enough. I have never repented nor looked back, not for one moment. And I begin the New Year with more true feeling of a happy New Year than ever I had in my life.

"Struggle must make a noise—and everything that I have to do that concerns my real being must be done with a struggle."
—FLORENCE NIGHTINGALE

From Barbara Montgomery Dossey, *Florence Nightingale: Mystic, Visionary, Healer* (Springhouse, PA: Springhouse Corp., 2000). Reprinted with permission.

HOW WARM MY ADMIRATION

"You are, I know, well aware of the high sense I entertain of the Christian devotion which you have displayed during this great and bloody war, and I need hardly repeat to you how warm my admiration is for your services, which are fully equal to those of my dear and brave soldiers, whose sufferings you have had the privilege of alleviating in so merciful a manner. I am, however, anxious for marking my feelings in a manner which I trust will be agreeable to you, and therefore send you with this letter a brooch, the form and emblems of which commemorate your great and blessed work, and which, I hope, you will wear as a mark of the high approbation of your Sovereign!

"It will be a very great satisfaction to me, when you return at last to these shores, to make the acquaintance of one who has set so bright an example to our sex. And with every prayer for the preservation of your valuable health, believe me, always, yours sincerely, Victoria R."

—Queen Victoria of Great Britain, 1855,
in a letter thanking Nightingale for her service in the Crimean War

"The wounded from the battle-plain,
In dreary hospitals of pain,
The cheerless corridors,
The cold and stony floors.
Lo! in that house of misery
A lady with a lamp I see
Pass through the glimmering gloom,
And flit from room to room.
And slow, as in a dream of bliss,
The speechless sufferer turns to kiss
Her shadow, as it falls
Upon the darkening walls . . . "

—Henry Wadsworth Longfellow, "*Santa Filomena,*" 1857

"At a Court of Common Council, 13 February, 1908, it was resolved unanimously: That the Honorary Freedom of this City, in a Gold Box of the value of one hundred Guineas, be presented to Miss Florence Nightingale, in testimony of this Court's appreciation of her philanthropic and successful efforts for the improvement of hospital nursing and management, whereby invaluable results have been attained for the alleviation of human suffering."

—the resolution awarding Nightingale the Freedom of the City of London, 1908

QUESTIONS FOR THOUGHT AND DISCUSSION

1. What is unusual about Nightingale's early involvement in helping the sick? How would you compare her service to that of her mother? What in particular did Nightingale learn from her aunt?

2. In the next section, Nightingale's "inward longing" is contrasted with the social constraints of her day. What do you suppose she felt during this time? Why do you think Mrs. Nightingale "had no idea" of her daughter's desire for more than high society?

3. What is revealed in Nightingale's questions to Dr. Howe? Why do you think she asked him? How does he answer her? What were the circumstances that would make nursing an "unusual" career? Why does he say it would not be "unladylike"?

4. What are the components of the "wall of absolute conventionality" that Nightingale encountered in her proposal to work for Dr. Fowler? Why was this so? In her letter to her cousin Hilary, how did she describe the event? Considering the circumstances, do you think her mother was being unreasonable?

5. Where did Nightingale think her dream stood at this point? How was she feeling? Do you think she was being melodramatic? She said her life "crushes me into vanity and deceit." What did she mean?

6. Nightingale told Hilary, "you must dig for hidden treasures in silence or you will not find it." What did she mean? Do you think this would always be so? Why or why not?

7. How did her letter to Hilary reveal that her dream of nursing had grown? In what ways?

8. In her diary excerpts from her trip to Egypt, what main issue was Nightingale wrestling with? Why is this issue so powerful? How did she overcome it? How would you describe her vows to God? What is the significance of her age? How long had it been since her first sense of calling?

9. In her diary entry, "What am I that I am not in harmony . . . ," what was Nightingale's main frustration? What is the significance of all the questions she poses to God?

10. In the next entry she said, "Parthe says that I blow a trumpet." How so? Do you agree that "struggle must make a noise"? What is the connection between Nightingale's "real being" and her sense of God's call on her life?

11. In the final paragraph, what strikes you about Nightingale's tone and message to her aunt? How would you describe her outlook on her chosen vocation, now that she has been at it for a couple of years? What is the significance of her saying, "I have never repented nor looked back, not for one moment"?

12. What do you take away from Florence Nightingale's story? Have you encountered similar barriers or social restraints in the pursuit of your own calling? What did they cost you?

George Sayer

George Sayer's Jack *is arguably the best biography of C. S. Lewis, who was the leading light of the Oxford literary group, the Inklings. Clive Staples Lewis (1898–1963) was a scholar, a writer, and a celebrated and much-loved Christian apologist. Born in Belfast, Northern Ireland, he was educated at University College, Oxford. After a brief service in World War I, he resumed his studies at Oxford where he became a fellow in English Language and Literature at Magdalen College. For the last seven years of his life he was a professor at Cambridge University, but insisted on still living at Oxford.*

Lewis was an excellent scholar in his field, but his enormous reputation rests on his writings. Three dozen of his titles are still available with over forty million in print—making Lewis the best-selling Christian author of all time. His scholarly study The Allegory of Love *was awarded the Hawthornden Prize in 1936, but he became known popularly through such books as* The Screwtape Letters *and* Mere Christianity, *and later through his children's stories* The Chronicles of Narnia *and his science fiction trilogy.*

Lewis, known to friends as Jack, was by any standards a courageous and independent thinker. But he derived enormous stimulation and encouragement from the Inklings, a discussion group that met in his college rooms and in an Oxford pub— the Eagle and Child. The group included such other writers as J. R. R. Tolkien, Charles Williams, and Dorothy L. Sayers. Although they did not pursue any outside agenda—as did the conscious reformers of the Clapham Circle—the influence of the Inklings through their writings has been incalculable.

The following reading is from Jack, *by George Sayer, who headed the English department at Malvern College in Worcestershire until his retirement in 1974. Sayer is a former student of C. S. Lewis who later became a personal friend. He went with Lewis on several of his celebrated walking tours and occasionally attended meetings of the Inklings.*

IRON SHARPENS IRON

"As iron sharpens iron,
so one man sharpens another."

—Proverbs 27:17

"The greatest misfortune a man can have is to outlive all his friends."
—Giovanni Giacomo Casanova

"When friends plan and do together, their minds become one mind and the last secret disappears."
—W. B. Yeats, *Autobiographies*

The Inklings

For years no regular event delighted Jack more than the Thursday evening meetings of the little group of friends called the Inklings. His was the second group to use this name. Its predecessor was founded in about 1930 by a University College undergraduate named Tangye Lean. Members met in each other's rooms to read aloud their poems and other work. There would be discussion, criticism, encouragement, and frivolity, all washed down with wine or beer. Lean's group consisted mainly of students, but a few sympathetic dons were invited to join, including Tolkien and Jack, who may have been Lean's tutor. Lean graduated in June 1933, and that autumn Jack first used the name *the Inklings* to describe the group that had already begun to meet in his rooms.

It was always utterly informal. There were no rules, no officers, and certainly no agenda.

It was always utterly informal. There were no rules, no officers, and certainly no agenda. To become a member, one had to be invited, usually by Jack. Nearly all members were his friends.

The first was J. R. R. Tolkien, elected Bosworth Professor of Anglo-Saxon in 1935. He was forty-two and full of energy. Coming from Leeds, he found the Oxford English School disappointing because it seemed to him that too much time was given to Victorian and modern literature and far too little to Anglo-Saxon and Middle English language and literature. He set out to remedy this with a remarkable energy and practicality. He also encouraged the study of Icelandic literature by forming another group of dons, called the Coalbiters, to read and translate the Sagas and Eddas. Most members of this group had a good knowledge of the language, but a few beginners, including Jack and Nevill Coghill, were invited to join. Tolkien presided and corrected everyone's mistakes.

Jack's first impressions of Tolkien were not entirely favorable, but he found the meetings of the Coalbiters exciting. He loved both the language and the literature, and the study revived his taste for "northernness" and brought back "the old authentic thrill" he had experienced as a child. Tolkien was a rather diffident and private person. He was a domestic man, deeply concerned with his home life and growing family. He was also a most gifted philologist and an inspired storyteller, combining these talents in the languages and people he invented for such books as *The Silmarillion*. A conservative Roman Catholic, he was rather quick to draw his sword if he thought his faith was under attack. He kept the best of himself for his own secret creative world as a storyteller, of which few indeed had any idea in the 1930s.

Although Jack studied Icelandic literature under Tolkien every few weeks, he did not realize until December 3, 1929, that they shared a taste for "northernness" and a delight in Norse mythology. Jack invited Tolkien to come back to his rooms after a Coalbiters meeting for a chat and some whiskey. He stayed for three hours, "discoursing of the gods and giants of Asgard." The visit was longer than Jack had intended, but "who could turn him out, for the fire was bright and the talk good."

This discussion was the germ of the Inklings and the beginning of one of the most important literary friendships of the twentieth century. A few days later, Tolkien asked Jack to give his opinion on two poems, lyrical versions of some of the stories later published as *The Silmarillion*. Jack wrote encouragingly and suggested improvements. Although Tolkien did not care for many of these, he was delighted by Jack's genuine interest and suggested that they might meet once a week so that he could read the rest of *The Silmarillion* to Jack.

The duo became a trio in 1933 by the addition of Warren, who had been collecting books on the age of Louis XIV since World War I and was probably considering how to approach the study he hoped to write for publication. Although he did not begin his "doggerel history of the reign" until June 1934, meetings of the Inklings were for him among the high points of the week. He brought to the sessions a keen mind, an experience of army life at home and overseas, and a knowledge of a large number of unusual subjects.

In 1934 Hugo Dyson and Dr. Robert E. Havard made it a group. Dyson, a lecturer at Reading University, was volatile, exuberant, and eccentric, a quick-witted comedian; Jack enjoyed his sort of humor. Dyson's encounter with Councillor Brewer, a man of vast bulk, in an Oxford pub is typical. Hugo addressed him with an almost servile deference, "You will pardon the liberty, sir. I trust you don't think I presume, but I shall call you Fred." Then, gazing intently at his full pale face, broke in again, "You'll excuse me, sir, but am I looking at your full face or your profile?" The Councillor, still smiling determinedly, turned to his friend and began to reminisce about their having rowed together in the

Teddy Hall boat the year Teddy Hall was bottom of the river. But we had never heard the story. "Bottom? Bottoms?" said Hugo. "Admirable things if ample enough, but you, sir, of course, could have no difficulty about that!" He much preferred talking to listening, and he disliked *The Hobbit* and *The Lord of the Rings*. For these reasons, people sometimes found him irritating.

Dr. Havard (always called Humphrey, a name given to him by Dyson) was Jack's and Warren's doctor from 1934 on. Although he was too busy to write much, he was well-read and keenly interested in the processes of literature and in theology. Havard did much to encourage Jack in the writing of the Narnia stories, the first of which was dedicated to his daughter. He was an entirely delightful man and much respected for his concern with the whole person, rather than just the physical body. I remember a reminiscence of Tolkien's that illustrates this point. "I told him that I was feeling depressed, so depressed that I hadn't been to Mass for a couple of weeks. I wasn't sleeping well either. He said I didn't need drugs, what I needed was to go to Confession. He was at my house at 7:30 the following morning to take me to Confession and Mass. Of course I was completely cured. Now that's the sort of doctor to have!"

Nevill Coghill, who read light verse, and Charles Wrenn, who tutored Jack's third-year pupils in Old English, sometimes came to the group, as did Owen Barfield and other friends of Jack's who happened to be in Oxford on Thursday evenings.

After the arrival of Charles Williams from London at the start of the war, still others joined the Inklings. Membership required the group's general agreement. As Warren put it, "We all knew the sort of man we wanted—and did not want." The latter included dogmatic men who relied, not on evidence, but on cliché—"The sort of fellow," Jack would say, "who uses language not to communicate thought but instead of thought."

The ritual never varied. When most of the expected members had arrived (and maybe only three or four would come), Warren would brew a pot of strong tea, the smokers would light their pipes, and Jack would say, "Well, has nobody got anything to read us?" If no one else produced a manuscript, Jack might read something of his own. This was not a mutual admiration society. "Praise for good work was unstinted but censure for bad, or even not so good, was often brutally frank." To read could be a formidable ordeal.

Warren has left an account of the meetings in 1946, which he describes as a vintage year:

As Warren put it, "We all knew the sort of man we wanted—and did not want." The latter included dogmatic men who relied, not on evidence, but on cliché—"The sort of fellow," Jack would say, "who uses language not to communicate thought but instead of thought."

"Praise for good work was unstinted but censure for bad, or even not so good, was often brutally frank."
—C. S. LEWIS

... [W]e had at most meetings a chapter of what I call "the new Hobbit" from Tolkien; this being the book or books ultimately published as "The Lord of the Rings." [O]n 30th October ... there was a long argument on the ethics of cannibalism, and on 28th November Roy Campbell read his translation of a couple of Spanish poems and John Wain won an outstanding bet by reading a chapter of "Irene Iddesleigh" without a smile. At our next meeting David Cecil read a chapter of his forthcoming book on Gray.

Sometimes, but not often, it would happen that no one had anything to read to us, and on these occasions the fun would grow riotous, with Jack at the top of his form and enjoying every minute—"No sound delights me more," he once said, "than male laughter." At the Inklings his talk was an outpouring of wit, nonsense, whimsy, dialectical swordplay, and pungent judgements. . . .

The same company used to meet on Tuesdays (later Mondays) for an hour or two before lunch at the Eagle and Child (a pub that was always referred to in University circles as "The Bird and Baby"). This particular inn was chosen partly because of its small back room, but mainly because of the character of its landlord, Charles Blagrove, who had "endless stories of an Oxford which is as dead as Dr. Johnson's an Oxford in which it was not uncommon for undergrads to *fight* a landlord for a pint of beer: both would strip to the waist, have a mill in the backyard, and then the battered undergrad would throw down a sovereign and depart." Blagrove had begun life as a cab driver. He remembered undergraduates who were so fastidious that they would give him their new suits if they did not fit perfectly. He could talk about the lavish tips he had received for driving "what he used to call 'fancy goods' to secluded spots; of the people who used to hire his cab to be taken 'somewhere where they could find a fight'; of rags, dinners, that general reckless extravagance and panache which prevailed when the security of the upper classes was still absolute, and England ruled the world. . . . "

Jack held meetings of the Inklings in his rooms for fifteen years, until one horrible Thursday in October 1949 when nobody turned up. What were his motives? In his brilliant book, *The Inklings,* Humphrey Carpenter suggests that he sought to protect himself through the formation of a circle of friends against the powerful inner circle that seemed to him to dominate Magdalen and university politics. This seems to me to be true. He felt isolated during his early years at Magdalen and under dialectical attack during the later ones. For reassurance, he needed fairly frequent meetings with his friends, men who held similar views. Though few who met him casually would have guessed it, he was beneath the surface plagued by Celtic melancholy and a streak of pessimism, qualities the Inklings held at bay. He loved his friends and liked to think that he was of service to them in their literary careers. Meetings of the Inklings made him utterly happy.

From George Sayer, *Jack: A Life of C. S. Lewis* (Wheaton: Crossway Books, 1994), pp. 248–254. Reprinted by permission of Crossway Books and Hodder and Stoughton Publishers.

A DISSENTING VIEW

"May I venture to indicate one last trait of my nature which creates for me no little difficulty in my relations with others? I possess a perfectly uncanny sensitivity of the instinct for cleanliness, so that I perceive physiologically—*smell*—the proximity or—what am I saying?—the innermost parts, the 'entrails', of every soul . . . I have in this sensitivity psychological antennae I touch and take hold of every secret: all the *concealed* dirt at the bottom of many a nature, perhaps conditioned by bad blood but whitewashed by education, is known to me almost on first contact. . . . This makes traffic with people no small test of my patience; my humanity consists, *not* in feeling for and with man, but in *enduring* that I do feel for and with him . . . My humanity is a continual self-overcoming.—But I have need of *solitude*, that is to say recovery, return to myself, the breath of a free light playful air . . . My entire Zarathustra is a dithyramb on solitude or, if I have been understood, on *cleanliness*."

—Friedrich Nietzsche, *Ecce Homo*

I am convinced that "to know how to remain alone for a year in a poor room teaches a man more than a hundred literary salons and forty years of experience of 'Parisian life.'"

—Albert Camus, *Notebooks*

"I withdrew from the world not because I had enemies there, but because I had friends. Not because they did me an injustice as usually happens, but because they believed me better than I am. It's a lie I can't accept."

—Albert Camus, *Notebooks*

QUESTIONS FOR THOUGHT AND DISCUSSION

1. The Inklings were clearly an unusual group. How would you describe their character and genius? How were they similar to and different from Wilberforce's Clapham Sect?

2. What brought this group of people together? Was this purely for professional development? How is this type of friendship different from other kinds of relationships and social gatherings?

3. What do you think of Dr. Havard's advice to Tolkien to go to confession? What does this say of how well they knew each other?

4. How did people join this group? What were the requirements for membership? How do you find this exclusivity? What would it have meant for the group if they had let anyone in who had wanted to join?

5. What was an average evening like? Sayer says, "This was not a mutual admiration society. . . . To read could be a formidable ordeal." Do you think they were harsh with each other? What does brutal frankness say of their relationships? Of their callings?

6. Sayer quotes Warren describing C. S. Lewis in the meetings: "At the Inklings his talk was an outpouring of wit, nonsense, whimsy, dialectical swordplay, and pungent judgements." Do you think this is sheer horseplay or creative inspiration on Lewis's part? What is the potential impact of this interaction?

7. What motives does Sayer suggest C. S. Lewis had in pulling this group together weekly? What does this say of the importance of having a group of like-minded friends in keeping us focused on our calling?

8. What other small groups do you know that have influenced the course of history? Why are such groups so powerful? What is the place of such a group in your experience?

Ludwig Van Beethoven

Ludwig van Beethoven (1770–1827) was a pianist, organist, composer, and musical genius of the highest order—usually ranked only with Johann Sebastian Bach and Wolfgang Amadeus Mozart. Born in Bonn, Germany, the son of a tenor, he was groomed to be a musician from an early age. Leaving school at eleven, he began as assistant organist in the court of Bonn and was taught by both Mozart and Haydn before moving permanently to Vienna, where he wrote and published his most famous works.

In 1802 Beethoven began to suffer seriously from depression brought about by realization that his growing deafness, first noticed in 1796, would be incurable. Deafness did not affect his ability to compose, but it curtailed his ability to perform, conduct, and teach. More and more tormented by this deafness, he became increasingly irascible. In 1812 Goethe described him as "an utterly untamed personality." But friends wrote more sympathetically that "despite all these absurdities, there was something so touching and ennobling about him that one could not help admiring him and feeling drawn to him."

In his despair, Beethoven wrote a will-like document to his two brothers that has become known as the Heiligenstadt Testament. He confesses his misery and feels close to death. He recovered, however, and his creative middle period is often called his "heroic period" because of his determination to strive creatively in the face of despair—in his own words, "seizing fate by the throat."

His creative middle period is often called his "heroic period" because of his determination to strive creatively in the face of despair—in his own words, "seizing fate by the throat."

The following reading is taken from a manuscript in Beethoven's own writing that was discovered after his death and later owned by such people as Franz Liszt and Jenny Lind. The manuscript is currently in the Library of Hamburg. It illustrates how many great leaders and creators have achieved their noblest work in the face of great handicaps—among others, John Milton overcoming blindness, Leo Tolstoy suicidal meaninglessness, Fyodor Dostoyevsky epilepsy, Blaise Pascal and Simone Weil excruciating pain, and Winston Churchill the "black dog" of depression.

LIMPING BUT ALIVE

"That night Jacob got up and took his two wives, his two maidservants and his eleven sons and crossed the ford of the Jabbok. After he had sent them across the stream, he sent over all his possessions.

"So Jacob was left alone, and a man wrestled with him till daybreak. When the man saw that he could not overpower him, he touched the socket of Jacob's hip so that his hip was wrenched as he wrestled with the man. Then the man said, 'Let me go, for it is daybreak.'

"But Jacob replied, 'I will not let you go unless you bless me.'

"The man asked him, 'What is your name?'

"'Jacob,' he answered.

"Then the man said, 'Your name will no longer be Jacob, but Israel, because you have struggled with God and with men and have overcome.'

"Jacob said, 'Please tell me your name.' But he replied, 'Why do you ask my name?' Then he blessed him there.

"So Jacob called the place Peniel, saying, 'It is because I saw God face to face, and yet my life was spared.'

"The sun rose above him as he passed Peniel, and he was limping because of his hip. Therefore to this day the Israelites do not eat the tendon attached to the socket of the hip, because the socket of Jacob's hip was touched near the tendon."

—Genesis 32:22–32

"To keep me from becoming conceited because of these surpassingly great revelations, there was given me a thorn in my flesh, a messenger of Satan, to torment me. Three times I pleaded with the Lord to take it away from me. But he said to me, 'My grace is sufficient for you, for my power is made perfect in weakness.' Therefore I will boast all the more gladly about my weaknesses, so that Christ's power may rest on me. That is why, for Christ's sake, I delight in weaknesses, in insults, in hardships, in persecutions, in difficulties. For when I am weak, then I am strong."

—Paul, in 2 Corinthians 12:7–10

The Heiligenstadt Testament ❧

Heiligenstadt, October 6, 1802

For my brothers Carl and —————— Beethoven

O my fellow men, who consider me, or describe me as, unfriendly, peevish, or even misanthropic, how greatly do you wrong me. For you do not know the secret reason why I appear to you to be so. Ever since my childhood my heart and soul have been imbued with the tender feeling of goodwill; and I have always been ready to perform even great actions. But just think, for the last six years I have been afflicted with an incurable complaint which has been made worse by incompetent doctors. From year to year my hopes of being cured have gradually been shattered and finally I have been forced to accept the prospect of a *permanent infirmity* (the curing of which may perhaps take years or may even prove to be impossible).

Though endowed with a passionate and lively temperament and even fond of the distractions offered by society I was soon obliged to seclude myself and live in solitude. If at times I decided just to ignore my infirmity, alas! how cruelly was I then driven back by the intensified sad experience of my poor hearing. Yet I could not bring myself to say to people: "Speak up, shout, for I am deaf." Alas! how could I possibly refer to the impairing *of a sense* which in me should be more perfectly developed than in other people, a sense which at one time I possessed in the greatest perfection, even to a degree of perfection such as assuredly few in my profession possess or have ever possessed—Oh, I cannot do it; so forgive me, if you ever see me withdrawing from your company which I used to enjoy.

Moreover my misfortune pains me doubly, inasmuch as it leads to my being misjudged. For me there can be no relaxation in human society, no refined conversations, no mutual confidence. I must live quite alone and may creep into society only as often as sheer necessity demands; I must live like an outcast. If I appear in company I am overcome by a burning anxiety, a fear that I am running the risk of letting people notice my condition—And that has been my experience during the last six months which I have spent in the country. My sensible doctor by suggesting that I should spare my hearing as much as possible has more or less encouraged my present natural inclination, though indeed when carried away now and then by my instinctive desire for human society, I have let myself be tempted to seek it. But how humiliated I have felt if somebody standing beside me heard the sound of a flute in the distance and *I heard nothing*, or if somebody heard *a shepherd sing* and again I heard nothing—

Such experiences almost made me despair, and I was on the point of putting an end to my life—The only thing that held me back was *my art*. For indeed it seemed to me impossible to leave this world before I had produced all the works that I felt the urge to compose; and thus I have dragged on this miserable existence—a truly miserable existence, seeing that I have such a sensitive body that any fairly sudden change can plunge me from the best spirits into the worst of humours—*Patience*—that is the virtue, I am told, which I must now choose for my guide; and I now possess it—I hope that I shall persist in my resolve to endure to the end, until it pleases the inexorable Parcae to cut the thread; perhaps my condition will improve, perhaps not; at any rate I am now

Alas! how could I possibly refer to the impairing of a sense which in me should be more perfectly developed than in other people, a sense which at one time I possessed in the greatest perfection, even to a degree of perfection such as assuredly few in my profession possess or have ever possessed.

If I appear in company I am overcome by a burning anxiety, a fear that I am running the risk of letting people notice my condition.

For indeed it seemed to me impossible to leave this world before I had produced all the works that I felt the urge to compose; and thus I have dragged on this miserable existence—a truly miserable existence, seeing that I have such a sensitive body that any fairly sudden change can plunge me from the best spirits into the worst of humours.

resigned—At the early age of 28 I was obliged to become a philosopher, though this was not easy; for indeed this is more difficult for an artist than for anyone else—Almighty God, who look down into my innermost soul, you see into my heart and you know that it is filled with love for humanity and a desire to do good. Oh my fellow men, when someday you read this statement, remember that you have done me wrong; and let some unfortunate man derive comfort from the thought that he has found another equally unfortunate who, notwithstanding all the obstacles imposed by nature, yet did everything in his power to be raised to the rank of noble artists and human beings.—

And you, my brothers Carl and [Johann], when I am dead, request on my behalf Professor Schmidt, if he is still living, to describe my disease, and attach this written document to his record, so that after my death at any rate the world and I may be reconciled as far as possible—At the same time I herewith nominate you both heirs to my small property (if I may so describe it)—Divide it honestly, live in harmony, and help one another. You know that you have long ago been forgiven for the harm you did me. I again thank you, my brother Carl, in particular, for the affection you have shown me of late years. My wish is that you should have a better and more carefree existence than I have had. Urge your children to be *virtuous*, for virtue alone can make a man happy. Money cannot do this. I speak from experience. It was virtue that sustained me in my misery. It was thanks to virtue and also to my art that I did not put an end to my life by suicide—Farewell and love one another—I thank all my friends, and especially *Prince Lichnowsky* and *Professor Schmidt*. I would like Prince L[ichnowsky]'s instruments to be preserved by one of you, provided this does not lead to a quarrel between you. But as soon as they can serve a more useful purpose, just sell them; and how glad I shall be if in my grave I can still be of some use to you both—

It was thanks to virtue and also to my art that I did not put an end to my life by suicide.

Well, that is all—Joyfully I go to meet Death—should it come before I have had an opportunity of developing all my artistic gifts, then in spite of my hard fate it would still come too soon, and no doubt I should like it to postpone its coming—Yet even so I should be content, for would it not free me from a condition of continual suffering? Come then, Death, *whenever* you like, and with courage I will go to meet you—Farewell; and when I am dead, do not wholly forget me. I deserve to be remembered by you, since during my lifetime I have often thought of you and tried to make you happy—Be happy—

Ludwig van Beethoven

For my brothers Carl and ————————

To be read and executed after my death—

HEILIGENSTADT, October 10, 1802—Thus I take leave of you—and, what is more, rather sadly—yes, the hope I cherished—the hope I brought with me here of being cured to a certain extent at any rate—that hope I must now abandon completely. As the autumn leaves fall and wither, likewise—that hope has faded for me. I am leaving here—almost in the same condition as I arrived—Even that high courage—which has often inspired me on fine summer days—has vanished—Oh Providence—do but grant me one day *of pure joy*—For so long now the inner echo of real joy has been unknown to me— Oh when—oh when, Almighty God—shall I be able to hear and feel this echo again in the temple of Nature and in contact with humanity—Never?— No!—Oh, that would be too hard.

From George R. Marek, *Beethoven: Biography of a Genius*, trans. Emily Anderson (New York: Funk & Wagnalls).

PAYING THE PRICE?

"Such are the happy effects of adversity; it teaches princes moderation, and makes them feel the pains of others. When they have never drunk but from the sweet poisoned cup of prosperity, they look upon themselves as gods; they would have the mountains humble themselves into plains to please them; they count men as nothing; they expect that all nature should be subservient to their will. When mention is made of suffering, they know not what it mean: they have no idea of it, having never known the difference between happiness and misery. It is misfortune alone that can teach them humanity, and soften their obdurate hearts: then they find they are only men, and that they ought to study the ease and happiness of other men, who are like them."

—Mentor to young Telemachus, son of Ulysses
in François Fénelon's *Telemachus*

"The curse of God is upon me."

—the reformer Lord Shaftesbury,
at the low point of a black depression, 1827

"In any large undertaking, there are rough times to go through, & of course success may not come till after one is dead—but those things don't matter if one is in earnest."

—Bertrand Russell, letter to a friend, 1916

"I always feel as if I stood naked for the fire of Almighty God to go through me—and it's rather an awful feeling. One has to be terribly religious, to be an artist."

—D. H. Lawrence

"Of recorded dramas of the soul, that of Tolstoy's relations to God is among the most absorbing and majestic. In contemplating it one is haunted by the notion that the forces engaged on either side were not infinitely disparate in magnitude. This is a notion which a number of great artists bring to mind. I have heard students of music infer a similar confrontation from the late compositions of Beethoven, and there are pieces of statuary by Michelangelo which hint at awesome encounters between God and the more god-like of His creatures. To have carved the figures in the Medici Chapel, to have imagined Hamlet and Falstaff, to have heard the Missa Solemnis out of deafness is to have said, in some mortal but irreducible manner, 'Let there be light.' It is to have wrestled with the angel. Something of the artist is consumed or mutilated in the combat. Art itself has its emblem in the image of Jacob limping away from the Jabbok, blest, wounded, and transformed by his dread match. This, perhaps, is why one fancies that there was in Milton's blindness, in Beethoven's deafness, or in Tolstoy's final, hunted pilgrimage towards death some terrible but appropriate justice. How much mastery over creation can a man achieve and yet remain unscathed?"

—George Steiner, *Tolstoy or Dostoevsky*

"What made the success of my books is what makes them lies to me. In fact I am an average man + demands."

—Albert Camus, *Notebooks*

"It wd. be better that the door of my prison had never been opened than if it now bangs in my face! How hard to submit to God's will."

—C. S. Lewis,
after giving up a much-needed vacation in Ireland
with a childhood friend because of his brother's alcoholism

QUESTIONS FOR THOUGHT AND DISCUSSION

1. How would you gauge Beethoven's overall response to this terrible affliction? What is the tone of his letter to his brothers? At this point, how long has he been suffering from the loss of his hearing?

2. What must it have been like for a musical genius to lose the one sense that mattered to him?

3. Several times he addresses "O my fellow men" as well as "Almighty God." How do you understand this appeal? Is he merely talking to his brothers? What do you think his purpose was in writing the letter?

4. What is Beethoven's explanation for withdrawing from society? How do you think the withdrawal affected him? How does he describe his life? Do you think the isolation bothered him as much as "being misjudged"? He says, "If I appear in company I am overcome by a burning anxiety" that people will find out he is deaf. Why did he not tell people of his malady?

5. What keeps him from "putting an end to [his] life"? What is left to accomplish? How is he able to keep on going?

6. With statements such as "remember that you have done me wrong" and "that . . . the world and I may be reconciled as far as possible," what is he saying? What do you think he wants?

7. In the second, short letter to his brothers, Beethoven pleads with God: "Oh Providence—do but grant me one day *of pure joy* . . . Oh when . . . shall I be able to hear and feel this echo again. . . ?" How do you understand this passage? What does it say of Beethoven's love for his art?

8. Read George Steiner's words in the box, "Paying the Price?" What do you think of his explanation of Beethoven's deafness? How would a biblical explanation differ?

William Manchester

William Manchester (born 1922) is a writer, historian, and professor emeritus at Wesleyan University in Middletown, Connecticut. Born in Attleboro, Massachusetts, his eighteen books include Death of a President, American Caesar, The Last Lion (a much-praised biography of Winston Churchill), and A World Lit Only by Fire.

"One Man Alone," a stirring essay on Ferdinand Magellan, is from the latter. Agonizingly and almost inexplicably, a feat of unprecedented courage and heroism degenerates into an act of reckless folly. As so often, success breeds hubris, the pride that swells with the illusion of its own invulnerability.

As so often, success breeds hubris, the pride that swells with the illusion of its own invulnerability.

DREAMERS OF THE DAY

"O Lord God, when thou givest to thy servants to endeavour any great matter, grant us also to know that it is not the beginning, but the continuing of the same to the end, until it be thoroughly finished, which yieldeth the true glory; through him who for the finishing of thy work laid down his life, our Redeemer, Jesus Christ."

—Anglican prayer adapted from the writings of the Elizabethan
sailor and adventurer Sir Francis Drake

"Dare you see a Soul *at the White Heat?*"

—Emily Dickinson

"Have we not all of us more or less taken our desires for realities? Indeed, I would not accept as a friend any young man who in his daydreams had not crowned himself with a laurel wreath, erected some pedestal or imagined himself embracing compliant mistresses. I myself have often been a general or an emperor. I have been a Byron, and then nothing at all. After disporting myself on the summit of human achievement, I perceived that all my mountains were still to be climbed and all obstacles still to be overcome."

—Honoré de Balzac, *The Wild Ass's Skin*

"In teaching able men it seems to me one's relation to them should be like that of Columbus to his crew—tempting them by courage & passion to accompany one in an adventure of which one does not know the outcome."

—Bertrand Russell

"All men dream, but not equally. Those who dream by night in the dusty recesses of their minds wake in the day to find it was vanity: but the dreamers of the day are dangerous men, for they may act their dreams with open eyes, to make it possible."

—T. E. Lawrence, *Seven Pillars of Wisdom*

"Every man is made to reach out beyond his grasp."

—Oswald Chambers

"I know why logs spit. I know what it is to be consumed."

—Winston Churchill,
on sitting by a fireplace and staring into the flames

One Man Alone: Ferdinand Magellan ✍

In the teeming Spanish seaport of Sanlúcar de Barrameda it is Monday, September 19, 1519.

Capitán-General Ferdinand Magellan, newly created a Knight Commander of the Order of Santiago, is supervising the final victualing of the five little vessels he means to lead around the globe: *San Antonio, Trinidad, Concepción, Victoria,* and *Santiago.* Here and in Seville, whence they sailed down the river Guadalquivir, Andalusians refer to them as *el flota,* or *el escuadra:* the fleet. However, their commander is a military man; to him they are an armada—officially, the Armada de Molucca. They are a battered, shabby lot, far less imposing than the flota Christopher Columbus led from this port twenty-one years ago, leaving Spain for his third crossing of the Atlantic.

. . . Proud of his lineage, meticulous, fiercely ambitious, stubborn, driven, secretive, and iron-willed, the capitán-general, or admiral, is possessed by an inner vision which he shares with no one. There is a hidden side to this seasoned skipper which would astonish his men. He is imaginative, a dreamer; in a time of blackguards and brutes he believes in heroism. Romance of that stripe is unfashionable in the sixteenth century, though it is not altogether dead. Young Magellan certainly knew of El Cid, the eleventh-century hero Don Rodrigo, whose story was told in many medieval ballads, and he may have been captivated by tales of King Arthur. Even if he had missed versions of Malory's *Morte d'Arthur*, he would have been aware of Camelot; the myths of medieval chivalry had persisted for centuries, passed along from generation to generation. . . .

[His first great test came from his realization that the Río de la Plata was only a bay, not the passage through to the Pacific.]

Each day the weather grew more depressing. No European had ever been this close to the South Pole. The days grew shorter, the nights longer, the winds fiercer, the seas grayer; the waves towered higher, and the southern winter lay ahead. To grasp the full horror of the deteriorating climate, it is necessary only to translate degrees of southern latitude into northern latitude. Rio de Janeiro, where they had first landed, is as far below the equator as Key West is above it. By the same reckoning the Río de la Plata is comparable to northern Florida, the Golfo San Matías to Boston, and Puerto San Julián, which they reached after thirty-seven days of struggling through shocking weather, to Nova Scotia. The sails of their five little ships were whitened by sleet and hail. Cyclones battered them twice a week or more. Both forecastles and aftercastles had been repeatedly blown away on every vessel and replaced by ship's carpenters. Crews shrank as the corpses of men pried loose from frozen rigging slid to briny graves. Yet the paso remained as elusive as ever. . . .

[His second great test was in overcoming a serious mutiny.]

His desolation was ironic, for during those eight fearful, brooding weeks, from August 26 to October 18, he was only 150 miles—two sailing days—from immortality.

On Sunday, October 21, 1520, a day of high, harsh, howling winds, lookouts clinging to the fleet's topmasts sighted a steep eminence which, as they approached, was perceived as a wall of naked white cliffs. Closing, they saw that these formed a cape, beyond which lay an immense bay of black water. The day was St. Ursula's. In remembrance of her, Magellan christened the peninsula Cabo de los Vírgenes. But his officers, still dreaming of the south seas, were unimpressed. The sound, all four pilots agreed, was a fjord similar to those which had been observed in Norway. "We all believed," Don Antonio Pigafetta wrote afterward, "that it was a blind alley." Only their commander was curious. However, because he had wasted over three weeks investigating the Río de la Plata nine months earlier, he could spare little for this exploration. He told *San*

Antonio and *Concepción* that he wanted them to see how far westward they could sail into the bay, but he wanted them back in five days at most. . . .

After a month in the seaway no one doubted that they had found the legendary paso. Three hundred miles of it lay behind them, and now unfamiliar birds flew overhead, a sure sign of another ocean ahead. Another fork confronted them. After ordering *San Antonio* and *Concepción* to spend a maximum of five days investigating the southeastern route—*Trinidad* and *Victoria* would wait here—Magellan called a meeting of his officers. He faced a decision—whether to sail home with news of their discovery or continue on to the Spice Islands—and he wanted their reports on the amount of provisions left. All told the same story: soon they would be running short. The holds contained three months of supplies, no more. Estevão Gomes, pilot of the *San Antonio*, argued vehemently that they should turn back. Stores were not the only consideration, he said; the ships were badly in need of refitting. Furthermore, no one knew the distance between them and the islands. If it was far, the entire fleet might perish on the merciless ocean, victims of thirst and starvation, their fate forever unknown.

It was good advice. Magellan chose to ignore it. They would push on, he said; no doubt there would be hardships, but even if they had to eat the leather on the ships' yards, he would keep his promise to King Carlos, trusting to God to help them and provide them with good fortune (*"de pasar adelante y descubrir lo que había prometido"*). The captains were enjoined, on pain of death, from telling their men of the supply shortage. Gomes was unconvinced, however; the prospect of sailing onward frightened him even more than Magellan's threat of death and mutilation for mutineers. He decided to quit the armada with his ship. During the scouting of the southeastern channel, *San Antonio*, with Mesquita in command, showed Serrano's *Concepción* its heels. Serrano did not know precisely what had happened, but since desertion by the capitán-general's cousin was impossible, he inferred that the pilot had led a successful revolt against the captain. Magellan had to face the hard fact that his biggest ship, with the bulk of his stores, was headed homeward. He was now down to three bottoms, and the supply situation, bad as it had been, was now worse. Yet he never considered altering his course. In an order issued "in the Channel of Todos los Santos, off the mouth of the Río del Isleo, on November 21, fifty-three degrees south of the equator," he declared that as "capitán-general of this armada" he had taken the "grave decision to continue the voyage."

His resolution was strengthened when another pinnace, sent ahead, reappeared on the third day with the electrifying news that Balboa's Mar del Sur had been found. Hurrying there, the admiral looked out on the prize

He would keep his promise to King Carlos, trusting to God to help them and provide them with good fortune.

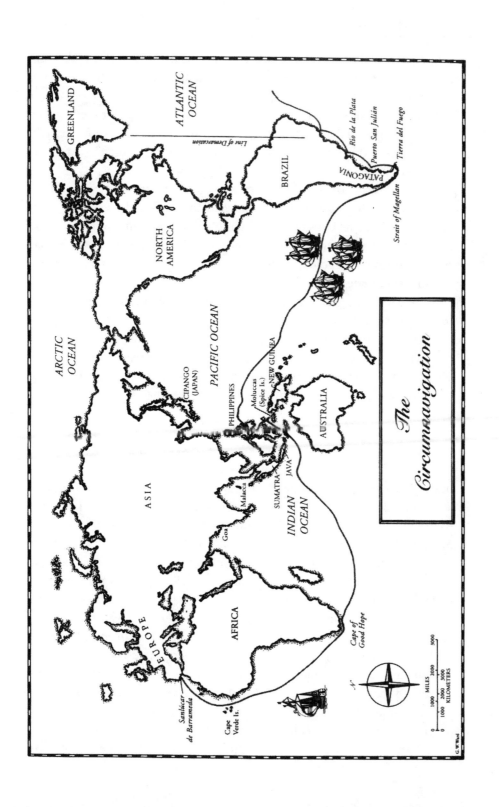

ARCTIC
OCEAN

GREENLAND

ATLANTIC
OCEAN

Line of Demarcation

NORTH
AMERICA

BRAZIL

Rio de la Plata

Puerto San Julián

PATAGONIA

Tierra del Fuego

Strait of Magellan

PACIFIC OCEAN

CIPANGO
(JAPAN)

PHILIPPINES

ASIA

Moluccas
(Spice Is.)

NEW GUINEA

AUSTRALIA

JAVA

SUMATRA

Malacca

Goa

INDIAN
OCEAN

EUROPE

AFRICA

Cape of
Good Hope

Sanlúcar
de Barrameda

Cape
Verde Is.

The
Circumnavigation

N

MILES
1000   2000   3000
1000   2000   3000
KILOMETERS

G. W Ward

Columbus, Cabot, Vespucci, and Pinzón had sought in vain: the mightiest of oceans, stretching to all horizons, deep and blue and vast with promise. Its peaceful, *pacífico* appearance inspired his name for it, though that came later. In that first rapturous moment he could not speak. Perhaps for the first time in his adult life, he was overcome by emotion, and his reserve broke. Don Antonio writes that *"il capitano-generale lacrimó per allegrezza"*—Magellan had burst into tears.

The little armada's 12,600-mile crossing of the Pacific, the greatest physical unit on earth, is one of history's imperishable tales of the sea, and like so many of the others it is a story of extraordinary human suffering, of agony so excruciating that only those who have been pushed to the extremes of human endurance can even comprehend it. Lacking maps, adequate navigational instruments, or the remotest idea of where they were, they sailed onward for over three months, from November to March, moving northwestward under frayed rigging, rotting sails, and a pitiless sun.

Even for the age of discovery, Magellan's situation was unique. Previous explorers had known that if all else failed, they could always return to Europe. That option was closed to him. Ignorant of South America—having started from the mouth of a strait known only to him—he had no base to fall back upon. Once he had left the eastern horizon behind, he had to sail on—and on, and on. . . .

The expedition had left Sanlúcar with 420 casks of wine. All were drained. One by one the other staples vanished—cheese, dried fish, salt pork, beans, peas, anchovies, cereals, onions, raisins, and lentils—until they were left with kegs of brackish, foul-smelling water and biscuits which, having first crumbled into a gray powder, were now slimy with rat droppings and alive with maggots. These, mixed with sawdust, formed a vile muck men could get down only by holding their noses. Rats, which could be roasted, were so prized that they sold for half a ducat each. The capitán-general had warned them that they might have to eat leather, and it came to that. Desperate to appease their stomach pangs, "the famine-stricken fellows," wrote Antonio Pigafetta, who was one of them, "were forced to gnaw the hides with which the mainyard was covered to prevent chafing." Because these leather strips had been hardened by "the sun and rain and wind," he explained, "we were obliged to soften them by putting them overboard four or five days, after which we cooked them on embers and ate them thus."

The serenity of the Pacific maddened the crews. Yet, as Don Antonio realized, it also saved them: "But for the grace of God and the Blessed Virgin in

The little armada's 12,600-mile crossing of the Pacific, the greatest physical unit on earth, is one of history's imperishable tales of the sea, and like so many of the others it is a story of extraordinary human suffering, of agony so excruciating that only those who have been pushed to the extremes of human endurance can even comprehend it.

sending us such magnificent weather, we should all have perished in this gigantic ocean." Some died anyhow; nineteen succumbed to starvation and were heaved overboard. Those left were emaciated, hollow-cheeked wraiths, their flesh covered with ulcers and bellies distended by edema. Scurvy swelled their gums, teeth fell out, sores formed inside their mouths; swallowing became almost impossible, and then, for the doomed, completely impossible. Too weak to rise, some men sprawled on decks, cowering in patches of shade; those able to stand hobbled about on sticks, babbling to themselves, senile men in their early twenties.

No other vessels crossed their path; indeed, in the six months that passed after they left San Julián they did not encounter another soul. False hopes were raised twice, about halfway through their ordeal, when islands were sighted which proved to be uninhabited and with no bottom for anchoring. Finally, on March 6, 1521, when the life expectancy of the hardiest of them could have been measured in days, they made a genuine landfall. It was Guam in the Marianas, then a nameless isle . . .

[Euphoric over his success, Magellan decides on a showcase invasion to display the Europeans' invincibility.]

Now in late April of 1521, on the eve of this wholly unnecessary battle, Magellan was everything he had never been. He had never before been reckless, imprudent, careless, or forgetful of the tactical lessons he had learned during Portuguese operations in East Africa, India, Morocco, and Malaya. But he had not been a soldier of Christ then. Here, shielded by divine intervention, he scorned the precautions observed by mortal men preparing for action. Professional fighting men value deception, secrecy, surprise. He announced to Spaniards and Filipinos alike that he would invade Mactan on Saturday, April 27—he believed it was his lucky day—and he invited the people of Cebu to come watch. Before going into action professional fighters study the terrain, and, if the operation is to be amphibious, the tides. Because he disdained all he had learned, he was unaware of Mactan's encircling reef, which at low tide—at the hour he had chosen for his attack—would prevent his ships from providing covering fire. Professionals court allies. He loftily declined the rajah-king's offer of a thousand veteran warriors, rejected Crown Prince Lumai's suggestion that he take the enemy from the rear with a diversionary landing, and rebuffed the Cacique Zula, a Mactan rival of Lapulapu, who proposed that he attack the flank of the rebel chief as the Spaniards waded ashore. Magellan urged each of them to join the spectators, including all the converted chieftains, who would watch from a score of balangays—native canoes—offshore. He needed no help, he said; he and his men could, and would, do the job alone.

. . . He might have pulled it off, had he picked the right men, and enough of them, and then handled them properly. Estimates of the force which would oppose him range from 1,500 to 2,000 natives, but they were an undisciplined mob, a prey to panic, armed with only the most primitive weapons. The whole lot could have been easily routed by 150 properly equipped Spaniards trained in the use of crossbows and harquebuses and led by Gómez de Espinosa, the armada's alguacil, and his disciplined marines. Cortés and Francisco Pizarro, similarly outnumbered, vanquished the Mexicans and Peruvians. But Magellan spurned conventional approaches. He limited his landing party to 60 seamen because, he said, he intended to show the Filipinos a victory won by Christian soldiers against the greatest odds imaginable. And he wanted to lead only volunteers, 20 from each vessel. This meant that the party would include none of the tough marines, who, deeply offended, stayed on their ships. In the end, according to Don Antonio, Magellan wound up with a motley contingent of unseasoned, unblooded cooks, stewards, and cabin boys—crew temperamentally unsuited for the job ahead, unfamiliar with their weapons, and, as it turned out, inadequately protected by armor, which should have been one of their chief advantages in the fight; corselets and helmets were issued to them, but not—and this was to prove decisive—greaves or leg armor. Lastly, their capitán-general was to be their only officer. That, too, was his doing. Because the members of the council had disapproved of his plan, he had excluded them.

. . . When the Saturday sun rose on an ebb tide, they found themselves stranded on the reef, still far from the beach. Realizing that the boats could not negotiate the intervening coral, Magellan detailed eleven men to remain aboard and cover the landing with the bateaux bombards. Then he stepped out into thigh-deep water and ordered the remaining seamen to follow him and storm the shore. Several of the crew repeatedly implored him not to lead, writes Pigafetta, "but he, like a good shepherd, refused to abandon his flock."

As they stumbled forward, encumbered by their armor and waist deep in water, it dawned upon the more experienced of them that there would be no covering fire. The reef was too far out; the boats' small cannons could not reach the enemy. Broadsides from the more powerful guns of the fleet might have been feasible, but Barbosa and Serrano, having been excluded from the mission, were sulking in their bunks below decks, and there was no way their commander could reach them.

The attackers, wading in with all their equipment, were exhausted even before they reached the surf line. There they became confused. Facing them were three forces of naked warriors drawn up, not at the water's edge, as they had expected, but well inland. According to Pigafetta, Lapulapu, displaying an intuitive grasp of tactics, had deployed his troops behind a triple line of trenches, forming a crescent to envelop the advancing invaders. He had also stationed himself and his bodyguard behind the deepest part of the crescent, out of the Spaniards' range. If they wanted him, they would have to come after him. Magellan's experience dictated a prudent withdrawal, but after all his grandiloquence that would mean a shaming loss of face. Instead he issued the command to open fire. Those seamen trained in the use of harquebuses and crossbows responded as best they could, but their ragged volley accomplished nothing. None of the balls, bolts, and arrows reached the mini-rajah, and the rest of them rattled ineffectively off the wooden shields of his men. According to Pigafetta, who was to remain with his capitán-general until the end, the noise of the muskets at first frightened the defenders into backing away, but the respite was brief. Magellan, "wishing to reserve the ammunition for a later stage of the encounter," in Don Antonio's words, called out, "¡Alto el fuego!"— "Cease fire!" — "but," Pigafetta continues, "his order was disregarded in the confusion. When the islanders realized that our fire was doing them little or no harm, they ceased to retire. Shouting more and more loudly, and jumping from side to side to disconcert our aim, they advanced simultaneously, under cover of their shields, assailing us with arrows, javelins . . . stones, and even filth, so that we were scarcely able to defend ourselves. Some of them began to throw lances with brazen points against our captain."

. . . Alarmed at last, the capitán-general ordered a withdrawal to the boats. He handled it skillfully, dividing his vastly outnumbered party in half, one half to hold the spearmen at bay while the others recrossed the ditches. All went well until, negotiating the last trench, they struck a snag and were held up. Lapulapu scented triumph. Splitting his own force, he sent men racing around both Spanish flanks in a bold attempt to cut them off before they could reach the bateaux.

It was at that point that Magellan paid the ultimate price for having left his marines behind. Discipline in the landing force disintegrated; nearly forty of his men broke for the sea. They lurched across the coral, reached the boats, and cowered there, leaving their embattled leader to fight his last, terrible fight with a loyal remnant: Don Antonio and a handful of others. The uneven struggle lasted over an hour and was fought out in full view of a

Magellan's experience dictated a prudent withdrawal, but after all his grandiloquence that would mean a shaming loss of face.

floating, mesmerized, horrified, but largely immobile audience: the rajah-king of Cebu, Prince Lumai, the Cacique Zula, the other baptized chieftains in the balangays, and the timorous men in the bateaux. The newly converted Filipinos awaited divine intervention by the Madonna, the saints, Our Lady of Victory, or Jesus Christ himself. It never came. Ferdinand Magellan, Knight Commander of the Order of Santiago and emissary of His Christian Majesty of Spain, had no miracles left. Toward the end a small band of his new Christians, Cebu warriors unable to endure the awful spectacle, landed on Mactan to rescue their godfather, but the moment they were ashore a Spanish gunner out in the armada, where no one had stirred till now, fired a medieval culverin at the beach. Castilian luck being what it was that Saturday, the wild shot scored a direct hit on the rescuers, killing four instantly and dispersing the others.

But it took a lot to kill the capitán-general. A poisoned arrow struck his unarmored right foot; reaching down, he ripped it out and fought on. He and his embattled band were knee deep in surf now, showered by stones, sod, and spears—Pigafetta writes that the natives would retrieve the spears and hurl the same one five or six times. Twice Magellan's helmet was knocked off; twice his men recovered and replaced it. Then he was speared in the face. Half blinded by his own blood, he slew his attacker with his lance, but the weight of the falling spearman wrenched the lance from his grip. Empty-handed, he started to draw his sword and found he couldn't; an earlier wound had severed the muscles in his sword arm. Seeing him helpless, Lapulapu's warriors closed in. All but four of Magellan's men were dead. The survivors tried to cover him with their bucklers, but a native wielding a long *terzado*—a scimitar—slashed beneath the shields, laying Magellan's game leg open. As he fell face downward in the water, Pigafetta, bleeding himself from an arrow, saw a dozen warriors "rush upon him with iron and bamboo spears and with their cutlasses, until they killed our mirror, our light and comfort, and our true guide." Somehow Don Antonio, Enrique, and the two others fought free. "Beholding him dead," Don Antonio writes, "we, being wounded, retreated as best we could to the boats, which were already pulling off."

Nothing of Magellan's person survived. That afternoon the grieving rajah-king, hoping to recover his remains, offered Mactan's victorious chief a handsome ransom of copper and iron for them. Lapulapu was elated; he had not possessed so much wealth in his lifetime. However, he was unable to produce the body. He could not find it. He searched; accompanied by a delegation from Cebu, he and his warriors carefully examined the shallow surf where

Magellan had thrashed his last. The corpses of the other victims lay where they had fallen among the battlefield debris—arrows, discarded spears, fragments of armor—but that was all. None of the capitán-general's parts turned up; no shred of flesh or tissue, no shard of bone. The only explanation, as inescapable as it is gruesome, is that Mactan's defenders, in their murderous fever, literally tore him apart, and the sea, which had brought him so far, bore his blood away. Since his wife and child died in Seville before any member of the expedition could return to Spain, it seemed that every evidence of Ferdinand Magellan's existence had vanished from the earth.

From William Manchester, *A World Lit Only by Fire: The Medieval Mind and the Renaissance; Portrait of an Age* (New York: Little, Brown and Company, 1992). © 1992 William Manchester. Reprinted with permission of Little, Brown and Company and Don Congdon Associates Inc.

THE PRICE OF SUCCESS

"Do you know what is the greatest enemy of the artist? Talent, the gift he's born with; facility, dexterity. In a word, *chic* is what spoils us and ruins us. We think we've arrived at the summit of our art no sooner than we've produced something, and we look no further. And not only that; we then underrate those who don't have the same facility."

—Auguste Rodin

"14 June 1947. Gandhi was 'reduced to despair.' For him, partition was a 'spiritual tragedy.' On the day he had been waiting for all his life, the day of the proclamation of independence—15 August 1947— he refused to take part in the ceremonies. The Indians had betrayed those principles of non-violence which, in his eyes, counted for more than independence itself. 'If God loves me, He will not leave me on earth for more than a moment longer,' he said. . . . The longed-for independence brought him nothing but despair. . . . He put principle before reality, the means before the end: and the result was a contradiction of his whole lifetime's purpose. There are not many fates more tragic for a man than that of seeing his course of action fundamentally perverted in the very moment of accomplishment."

—Simone de Beauvoir, *The Coming of Age*

"First I am not. I do not deign to be second. I am Mouton."

—motto of winemaker Baron Philippe de Rothschild
of the Château Mouton-Rothschild, embossed on all his bottles

"With success, there always comes a day of reckoning.

"I started out with a vision. I put together a partnership, bought land, and then built a home where my vision could take root and flower. Together with my family and extended family, we created a quality product line, established our image and brand name, educated retailers and consumers, and built a national market for our products. And all along the way we worked hard to raise public consciousness and earn respect and support for our guiding vision.

"Then came the hard part: success."

—Robert Mondavi, *Harvests of Joy*

QUESTIONS FOR THOUGHT AND DISCUSSION

1. Starting with "Proud of his lineage," what are some of the characteristics of Magellan cited? Which lend themselves to success? Which to folly?

2. In the paragraph, "It was good advice . . . ," what is Magellan's motivation for continuing the journey? Do you see it as heroism or hubris?

3. What do you think he must have felt as "he was overcome with emotion" when they first gazed out on the Pacific Ocean?

4. What were some of the difficulties they faced as they continued westward? What were their conditions when they arrived in Guam? What were the reactions of some of Magellan's men when he was planning the battle just six weeks later?

5. Manchester says, "Here, shielded by divine intervention, he scorned the precautions observed by mortal men preparing for action." How is this stance different from the "trusting in God" Magellan experienced in South America?

6. What are some of the specific steps Megallan took—to prove how strong they were—that were their undoing? Where did he ignore the voice of his own experience?

7. Magellan's feat and Magellan's folly were almost unfathomable. How were they linked? How would you compare his attitude in each situation?

8. Can you think of similar examples of hubris, where a great leader, or someone in your own experience, was undermined by his or her pride and the illusion of invulnerability?

FOUR
A TIME TO APPRAISE

AT SOME POINT IN ALL OUR LIVES THERE COMES A TIME TO TAKE STOCK. SOME PEOPLE *have succeeded in pursuing their quests but need to assess how far they have come, how much further they will endeavor to go, and who they have become in the process. Others have succeeded too, but in pressing down the wrong roads only to find themselves bogged down by futility. They have mounted ladders set against the wrong walls, as it is often put today. Still others have betrayed their quest or the promise of their youth and wonder whether there is time to regroup and set out again—or whether they are condemned to spend their final days only as spectators on the sidelines.*

Where am I now? What have I accomplished? Did I do it well or poorly? What value am I to society, to my family and friends, to myself? The greater the gap between dreams and fulfillment, the greater the doubts. But success has its own kinds of "emptiness" and "trappedness" too. In his autobiography, nineteenth-century writer Van Wyck Brooks surveyed his life and concluded that his efforts had been sown in an environment where they could not grow and not even the furrow could remain. He had "ploughed the sea." The great Irish poet W. B. Yeats wrote similarly in his autobiography: "All life weighed in the scale of my own life seems a preparation for something that never happens."

The idea of a time for appraisal has long been present in the literature of chivalry and in the experience of "transitions" and "midlife crises." Recently it has gained fresh currency in such books as Bob Buford's Half Time. "Time out," or what traditional writers would have termed the spiritual discipline of "solitude," is a regular requirement that is not for mid-life only. But it is a special part of the transitions of the middle years. As novelist James Baldwin wrote, "When more stretches behind than stretches before one, some assessments, however reluctantly and incompletely, begin to be made."

Geniuses make their mark earlier and exceptions continue to exert their influence longer. But for most people, middle adulthood is where they make their greatest contributions. This is what makes the forty- to sixty-year-olds "the Dominant Generation." But it is also what sets them up for a time of transition heavy with doubts and decline.

Part 4 addresses these transitions and these doubts. Beginning with Leo Tolstoy's delightful story "Two Old Men," the readings are an invitation to a time for appraisal, a personal challenge to an opportunity for renewal.

Leo Tolstoy

Leo Tolstoy (1828–1910) was a Russian novelist and social reformer, famous for his novels War and Peace *and* Anna Karenina, *considered by many the greatest novels ever written. Born to a noble, landed family, his early years were marked by a dissolute life and a violent reaction to the horrors of the Crimean War. In 1862 he married and settled down, producing thirteen children and a burst of literary successes. After writing* Anna Karenina *he experienced a profound spiritual crisis and renounced his literary ambitions, believing them to be incompatible with his deepest convictions. His numerous later works were on religious and moral subjects. The following reading, written in 1885, is a classic human story that challenges us to examine our assumptions about personalities, perspectives, and priorities in life—including success and failure in business life.*

WHAT THEN?

"There is a time for everything, and a season for every activity under heaven: a time to be born and a time to die, a time to plant and a time to uproot, a time to kill and a time to heal, a time to tear down and a time to build, a time to weep and a time to laugh, a time to mourn and a time to dance, a time to scatter stones and a time to gather them, a time to embrace and a time to refrain, a time to search and a time to give up, a time to keep and a time to throw away, a time to tear and a time to mend, a time to be silent and a time to speak, a time to love and a time to hate, a time for war and a time for peace.

"What does the worker gain from his toil? I have seen the burden God has laid on men. He has made everything beautiful in its time. He has also set eternity in the hearts of men; yet they cannot fathom what God has done from beginning to end. I know that there is nothing better for men than to be happy and do good while they live. That everyone may eat and drink, and find satisfaction in all his toil—this is the gift of God."

—Ecclesiastes 3:1–13

"What good is it for a man to gain the whole world, yet forfeit his soul?"

—Jesus, in Mark 8:36

CINEAS: "The Romans are reported to be great warriors and conquerors of many nations. If God permits us to overcome them, how shall we use our victory?"

PYRRHUS: "That is an easy question. Once we conquer the Romans, there will not be any city in all of Italy that will resist us."

CINEAS: "Once we have Italy, what next?"

PYRRHUS: "Sicily, and then Carthage and Africa would then be within reach, and once we have them, who in the world would dare to oppose us?"

CINEAS: "No one, certainly. And then what shall we do?"

PYRRHUS: "Then, my dear Cineas, we will relax, and drink all day, and amuse ourselves with pleasant conversation."

CINEAS: "What prevents us from doing that now? We already have enough to make that possible without any more hard work, suffering, and danger."

—conversation between King Pyrrhus of the Greek city-state of Epirus
and his chief ambassador, as the king prepared to sail to Italy, 280 B.C.

"I suppose the point I had in mind is this—you come to a place in your life when what you've been is going to form what you will be. If you've wasted what you have in you, it's too late to do much about it. If you've invested yourself in life, you're pretty certain to get a return. If you are inwardly a serious person, in the middle years it will pay off."

—Lillian Hellman, on her play *The Autumn Garden*

"When he announced the signature of the armistice [George] Clemenceau was cheered by both chambers. A crowd gathered outside the ministry of war and insisted upon his coming out on to the balcony of his office: the ovation moved him to tears. Yet by that evening his joy had already vanished. His children took him to the Grand Hôtel so that he could see the happiness of the crowds in the Place de l'Opéra. He watched them in silence. 'Tell me you are happy,' said his daughter. 'I cannot tell you that because I am not happy. All this will turn out to have been useless.'"

—Simone de Beauvoir's *The Coming of Age*

"I have failed in an undertaking that was far too big for me."

—H. G. Wells,
1940, on realizing that his efforts to make peace were utopian
and that World War II had destroyed his hopes

"'The work is finished,' he reflected, grown old
'Just as I conceived it when I was a child;
Let fools cry out, but I have failed in nothing.
I have brought something to perfection.'
But louder still this spirit sang, 'What then?'"

—W. B. Yeats,
an imagined dialogue between an old writer and a mocking spirit

"You can get all *A*'s and still flunk life."

—Walker Percy, *The Moviegoer*

"I have the profession I like, unconditionally, the only possible one for me, and yet it doesn't make me happy. I'm sad, Mom, very often so sad."

—François Truffaut, French film director

Two Old Men ༄

"The woman saith unto him, Sir, I perceive that thou art a prophet. Our fathers worshiped in this mountain, and ye say, that in Jerusalem is the place where men ought to worship. Jesus saith unto her, Woman, believe me, the hour cometh when neither in this mountain, nor in Jerusalem, shall ye worship the Father. . . . But the hour cometh, and now is, when the true worshippers shall worship the Father in spirit and truth: for such doth the Father seek to be his worshippers."

—JOHN IV. 19–21, 23.

There were once two old men who decided to go on a pilgrimage to worship God at Jerusalem. One of them was a well-to-do peasant named Efim Tarasich Shevelev. The other, Elisha Bodrov, was not so well off. Efim was a staid man, serious and firm. He neither drank nor smoked nor took snuff, and had never used bad language in his life. He had twice served as village Elder, and when he left office his accounts were in good order. He had a large family: two sons and a married grandson, all living with him. He was pale, long-bearded, and erect, and it was only when he was past sixty that a little grey began to show itself in his beard.

Elisha was neither rich nor poor. He had formerly gone out carpentering, but now that he was growing old he stayed at home and kept bees. One of his sons had gone away to find work, the other was living at home. Elisha was a kindly and cheerful old man. It is true he drank sometimes, and he took snuff, and was fond of singing; but he was a peaceable man and lived on good terms with his family and with his neighbors. He was short and dark, with a curly beard, and, like his patron saint Elisha, he was quite bald-headed.

The two old men had taken a vow long since and had arranged to go on a pilgrimage to Jerusalem together: but Efim could never spare the time; he always had so much business on hand: as soon as one thing was finished he started

The two old men had taken a vow long since and had arranged to go on a pilgrimage to Jerusalem together: but Efim could never spare the time; he always had so much business on hand: as soon as one thing was finished he started another.

another. First he had to arrange his grandson's marriage; then to wait for his youngest son's return from the army, and after that he began building a new hut.

One holiday the two old men met outside the hut and, sitting down on some timber, began to talk.

"Well," asked Elisha, "when are we to fulfill our vow?"

Efim made a wry face.

"We must wait," he said. "This year has turned out a hard one for me. I started building this hut thinking it would cost me something over a hundred rubles, but now it's getting on for three hundred and it's still not finished. We shall have to wait till the summer. In summer, God willing, we will go without fail."

"It seems to me we ought not to put it off, but should go at once," said Elisha. "Spring is the best time."

"The time's right enough, but what about my building? How can I leave that?"

"As if you had no one to leave in charge! Your son can look after it."

"But how? My eldest son is not trustworthy — he sometimes takes a glass too much."

"Ah, neighbor, when we die they'll get on without us. Let your son begin now to get some experience."

"That's true enough; but somehow when one begins a thing one likes to see it done."

"Eh, friend, we can never get through all we have to do. The other day the women-folk at home were washing and housecleaning for Easter. Here something needed doing, there something else, and they could not get everything done. So my eldest daughter-in-law, who's a sensible woman, says: 'We may be thankful the holiday comes without waiting for us, or however hard we worked we should never be ready for it.'"

Efim became thoughtful.

"I've spent a lot of money on this building," he said, "and one can't start on the journey with empty pockets. We shall want a hundred rubles apiece — and it's no small sum."

Elisha laughed.

"Now, come, come, old friend!" he said, "you have ten times as much as I, and yet you talk about money. Only say when we are to start, and though I have nothing now I shall have enough by then."

Efim also smiled.

"Dear me, I did not know you were so rich!" said he. "Why, where will you get it from?"

"I can scrape some together at home, and if that's not enough, I'll sell half a score of hives to my neighbor. He's long wanting to buy them."

"If they swarm well this year, you'll regret it."

"Regret it! Not I, neighbor! I never regretted anything in my life, except my sins. There's nothing more precious than the soul."

"That's so; still it's not right to neglect things at home."

"But what if our souls are neglected? That's worse. We took the vow, so let us go! Now, seriously, let us go!"

I never regretted anything in my life, except my sins. There's nothing more precious than the soul.

II

Elisha succeeded in persuading his comrade. In the morning after thinking it well over, Efim came to Elisha.

"You are right," said he, "let us go. Life and death are in God's hands. We must go now, while we are still alive and have the strength."

A week later the old men were ready to start. Efim had money enough at hand. He took a hundred rubles himself, and left two hundred with his wife.

Elisha, too, got ready. He sold ten hives to his neighbor with any new swarms that might come from them before the summer. He took seventy rubles for the lot. The rest of the hundred rubles he scraped together from the other members of his household, fairly clearing them all out. His wife gave him all she had been saving up for her funeral, and his daughter-in-law also gave him what she had.

Efim gave his eldest son definite orders about everything: when and how much grass to mow, where to cart the manure, and how to finish off and roof the cottage. He thought out everything, and gave his orders accordingly. Elisha, on the other hand, only explained to his wife that she was to keep separate the swarms from the hives he had sold and to be sure to let the neighbor have them all, without any tricks. As to household affairs, he did not even mention them.

"You will see what to do and how to do it as the needs arise," he said. "You are the masters and will know how to do what's best for yourselves."

So the old men got ready. Their people baked them cakes, and made bags for them, and cut them linen for leg-bands. They put on new leather shoes and took with them spare shoes of platted bark. Their families went with them to the end of the village and there took leave of them, and the old men started on their pilgrimage.

Elisha left home in a cheerful mood and as soon as he was out of the village forgot all his home affairs. His only care was how to please his comrade, how to avoid saying a rude word to any one, how to get to his destination and home again in peace and love. Walking along the road, Elisha would either whisper some prayer to himself or go over in his mind such of the lives of the saints as he was able to remember. When he came across any one on the road, or turned in anywhere for the night, he tried to behave as gently as possible and to say a godly word. So he journeyed on, rejoicing. One thing only he could not do: he could not give up taking snuff. Though he had left his snuff-box behind, he hankered after it. Then a man he met on the road gave him some snuff, and every now and then he would lag behind (not to lead his comrade into temptation) and would take a pinch of snuff.

Efim too walked well and firmly, doing no wrong and speaking no vain words, but his heart was not so light. Household cares weighed on his mind. He kept worrying about what was going on at home. Had he not forgotten to give his son this or that order? Would his son do things properly? If he happened to see potatoes being planted or manure carted as he went along, he wondered if his son was doing as he had been told. And he almost wanted to turn back and show him how to do things or even do them himself.

III

The old men had been walking for five weeks, they had worn out their home-made bark shoes and had to begin buying new ones when they reached Little Russia. From the time they left home they had had to pay for their food and for their night's lodging, but when they reached Little Russia the people vied with one another in asking them into their huts. They took them in and fed them, and would accept no payment; and more than that, they put bread or even cakes into their bags for them to eat on the road.

The old men traveled some five hundred miles in this manner free of expense, but after they had crossed the next province, they came to a district where the harvest had failed. The peasants still gave them free lodging at night, but no longer fed them for nothing. Sometimes even they could get no bread: they offered to pay for it, but there was none to be had. The people said the harvest had completely failed the year before. Those who had been rich were ruined and had had to sell all they possessed; those of moderate means were left destitute, and those of the poor who had not left those parts, wandered about begging, or starved at home in utter want. In the winter they had had to eat husks and goosefoot.

One night the old men stopped in a small village; they bought fifteen pounds of bread, slept there, and started before sunrise to get well on their way before the heat of the day. When they had gone some eight miles, on coming to a stream they sat down, and, filling a bowl with water, they steeped some bread in it and ate it. Then they changed their leg-bands and rested for a while. Elisha took out his snuff. Efim shook his head at him.

"How is it you don't give up that nasty habit?" said he.

Elisha waved his hand. "The evil habit is stronger than I," he said.

Presently they got up and went on. After walking for nearly another eight miles, they came to a large village and passed right through it. It had now grown hot. Elisha was tired out and wanted to rest and have a drink, but Efim did not stop. Efim was the better walker of the two and Elisha found it hard to keep up with him.

"If I could only have a drink," said he.

"Well, have a drink," said Efim. "I don't want any."

Elisha stopped.

"You go on," he said, "but I'll just run in to the little hut there. I will catch you up in a moment."

"All right," said Efim, and he went on along the high road alone while Elisha turned back to the hut.

It was a small hut plastered with clay, the bottom a dark color, the top whitewashed; but the clay had crumbled away.

Evidently it was long since it had been replastered, and the thatch was off the roof on one side. The entrance to the hut was through the yard. Elisha entered the yard, and saw, lying close to a bank of earth that ran round the hut, a gaunt beardless man with his shirt tucked into his trousers, as is the custom in Little Russia. The man must have lain down in the shade, but the sun had come round and now shone full on him. Though not asleep, he still lay there. Elisha called to him and asked for a drink, but the man gave no answer.

"He is either ill or unfriendly," thought Elisha; and going to the door he heard a child crying in the hut. He took hold of the ring that served as a door-handle and knocked with it.

"Hey, masters!" he called. No answer. He knocked again with his staff.

"Hey, Christians!" Nothing stirred.

"Hey, servants of God!" Still no reply.

Elisha waved his hand. "The evil habit is stronger than I," he said.

Elisha was about to turn away, when he thought he heard a groan on the other side of the door.

"Dear me, some misfortune must have happened to the people! I had better have a look."

And Elisha entered the hut.

IV

Elisha turned the ring, the door was not fastened. He opened it and went along up the narrow passage. The door into the dwelling-room was open. To the left was a brick stove; in front against the wall was an icon-shelf and a table before it; by the table was a bench on which sat an old woman, bareheaded and wearing only a single garment. There she sat with her head resting on the table, and near her was a thin, wax-colored boy, with a protruding stomach. He was asking for something, pulling at her sleeve and crying bitterly. Elisha entered. The air in the hut was very foul. He looked round, and saw a woman lying on the floor behind the stove: she lay flat on the ground with her eyes closed and her throat rattling, now stretching out a leg, now dragging it in, tossing from side to side; and the foul smell came from her. Evidently she could do nothing for herself and no one had been attending to her needs. The old woman lifted her head and saw the stranger.

"What do you want?" said she. "What do you want, man? We have nothing."

Elisha understood her, though she spoke in the Little Russian dialect.

"I came in for a drink of water, servant of God," he said.

"There's no one—no one—we have nothing to fetch it in. Go your way."

Then Elisha asked:

"Is there no one among you, then, well enough to attend to that woman?"

"No, we have no one. My son is dying outside, and we are dying in here."

The little boy had ceased crying when he saw the stranger, but when the old woman began to speak, he began again, and clutching hold of her sleeve cried:

"Bread, Granny, bread."

Elisha was about to question the old woman, when the man staggered into the hut. He came along the passage clinging to the wall, but as he was entering the dwelling-room he fell in the corner near the threshold, and without trying to get up again to reach the bench, he began to speak in broken words. He brought out a word at a time, stopping to draw breath, and gasping.

"Illness has seized us . . . " said he, "and famine. He is dying . . . of hunger."
And he motioned towards the boy and began to sob.

Elisha jerked up the sack behind his shoulder and, pulling the straps off his arms, put it on the floor. Then he lifted it on to the bench and untied the strings. Having opened the sack, he took out a loaf of bread and, cutting off a piece with his knife, handed it to the man. The man would not take it, but pointed to the little boy and to a little girl crouching behind the stove, as if to say: "Give it to them."

Elisha held it out to the boy. When the boy smelt bread, he stretched out his arms, and seizing the slice with both his little hands, bit into it so that his nose disappeared in the chunk. The little girl came out from behind the stove and fixed her eyes on the bread. Elisha gave her also a slice. Then he cut off another piece and gave it to the old woman, and she too began munching it.

"If only some water could be brought," she said, "their mouths are parched. I tried to fetch some water yesterday—or was it to-day—I can't remember, but I fell down and could go no further, and the pail has remained there, unless some one has taken it."

Elisha asked where the well was. The old woman told him. Elisha went out, found the pail, brought some water, and gave the people a drink. The children and the old woman ate some more bread with the water, but the man would not eat.

"I cannot eat," he said.

All this time the younger woman did not show any consciousness, but continued to toss from side to side. Presently Elisha went to the village shop and bought some millet, salt, flour, and oil. He found an axe, chopped some wood, and made a fire. The little girl came and helped him. Then he boiled some soup and gave the starving people a meal.

V

The man ate a little, the old woman had some too, and the little girl and boy licked the bowl clean and then curled up and fell fast asleep in one another's arms.

The man and the old woman then began telling Elisha how they had sunk to their present state.

"We were poor enough before," said they, "but when the crops failed, what we gathered hardly lasted us through the autumn. We had nothing left by the time winter came, and had to beg from the neighbors and from any one we could. At first they gave, then they began to refuse. Some would have been glad enough to help us but had nothing to give. And we were ashamed of asking: we were in debt all round, and owed money, and flour, and bread."

"I went to look for work," the man said, "but could find none. Everywhere people were offering to work merely for their own keep. One day you'd get a short job and then you might spend two days looking for work. Then the old woman and the girl went begging, further away. But they got very little; bread was so scarce. Still we scraped food together somehow and hoped to struggle through till next harvest, but towards spring people ceased to give anything. And then this illness seized us. Things became worse and worse. One day we might have something to eat, and then nothing for two days. We began eating grass. Whether it was the grass, or what, made my wife ill, I don't know. She could not keep on her legs, and I had no strength left, and there was nothing to help us to recovery."

"I struggled on alone for a while," said the old woman, "but at last I broke down too for want of food, and grew quite weak. The girl also grew weak and timid. I told her to go to the neighbors—she would not leave the hut, but crept into a corner and sat there. The day before yesterday a neighbor looked in, but seeing that we were ill and hungry she turned away and left us. Her husband has had to go away and she has nothing for her own little ones to eat. And so we lay, waiting for death."

Having heard their story, Elisha gave up the thought of overtaking his comrade that day and remained with them all night.

Having heard their story, Elisha gave up the thought of overtaking his comrade that day and remained with them all night. In the morning he got up and began doing the housework, just as if it were his own home. He kneaded the bread with the old woman's help and lit the fire. Then he went with the little girl to the neighbors to get the most necessary things; for there was nothing in the hut, everything had been sold for bread—cooking utensils, clothing, and all. So Elisha began replacing what was necessary, making some things himself and buying some. He remained there one day, then another, and then a third. The little boy picked up strength and whenever Elisha sat down crept along the bench and nestled up to him. The little girl brightened up and helped in all the work, running after Elisha and calling,

"Daddy, daddy."

The old woman grew stronger and managed to go out to see a neighbor. The man too improved and was able to get about, holding on to the wall. Only the wife could not get up, but even she regained consciousness on the third day and asked for food.

"Well," thought Elisha, "I never expected to waste so much time on the way. Now I must be getting on."

VI

The fourth day was the feast day after the summer fast, and Elisha thought:

"I will stay and break the fast with these people. I'll go and buy them something and keep the feast with them, and tomorrow evening I will start."

So Elisha went into the village, bought milk, wheat-flour and dripping, and helped the old woman to boil and bake for the morrow. On the feast day Elisha went to church, and then broke the fast with his friends at the hut. That day the wife got up and managed to move about a bit. The husband had shaved and put on a clean shirt which the old woman had washed for him; and he went to beg for mercy of a rich peasant in the village to whom his plough-land and meadow were mortgaged.

He went to beg the rich peasant to grant him the use of the meadow and field till after the harvest; but in the evening he came back very sad and began to weep. The rich peasant had shown no mercy, but had said: "Bring me the money."

Elisha again grew thoughtful. "How are they to live now?" thought he to himself. "Other people will go haymaking, but there will be nothing for these to mow, their grass land is mortgaged. The rye will ripen. Others will reap (and what a fine crop mother earth is giving this year), but they have nothing to look forward to. Their three acres are pledged to the rich peasant. When I am gone they'll drift back into the state I found them in."

Elisha was in two minds, but finally decided not to leave that evening, but to wait until the morrow. He went out into the yard to sleep. He said his prayers and lay down; but he could not sleep. On the one hand he felt he ought to be going, for he had spent too much time and money as it was; on the other hand he felt sorry for the people.

"There seems to be no end to it," he said. "First I only meant to bring them a little water and give them each a slice of bread, and just see where it has landed me. It's a case of redeeming the meadow and the cornfield. And when I have done that I shall have to buy a cow for them, and a horse for the man to cart his sheaves. A nice coil you've got yourself into, brother Elisha! You've slipped your cables and lost your reckoning!"

Elisha got up, lifted his coat which he had been using for a pillow, unfolded it, got out his snuff and took a pinch, thinking that it might perhaps clear his thoughts.

But no! He thought and thought, and came to no conclusion.

He ought to be going; and yet pity held him back. He did not know what to do. He refolded his coat and put it under his head again. He lay thus for a long time, till the cocks had already crowed once: then he was quite drowsy. And suddenly it seemed as if some one had roused him. He saw that he was dressed for the journey with the sack on his back and the staff in his hand, and the gate stood ajar so that he could just squeeze through. He was about to pass out when his sack caught against the fence on one side: he tried to free it, but then his leg-band caught on the other side and came undone. He pulled at the sack and saw that it had not caught on the fence, but that the little girl was holding it and crying,

"Bread, daddy, bread!"

He looked at his foot, and there was the tiny boy holding him by the leg-band, while the master of the hut and the old woman were looking at him through the window.

Elisha awoke and said to himself in an audible voice:

"To-morrow I will redeem their cornfield, and will buy them a horse, and flour to last till the harvest, and a cow for the little ones; or else while I go to seek the Lord beyond the sea I may lose Him in myself."
—ELISHA

"To-morrow I will redeem their cornfield, and will buy them a horse, and flour to last till the harvest, and a cow for the little ones; or else while I go to seek the Lord beyond the sea I may lose Him in myself."

Then Elisha fell asleep and slept till morning. He awoke early, and going to the rich peasant, redeemed both the cornfield and the meadow land. He bought a scythe (for that also had been sold) and brought it back with him. Then he sent the man to mow, and himself went into the village. He heard that there was a horse and cart for sale at the public-house, and he struck a bargain with the owner and bought them. Then he bought a sack of flour, put it in the cart, and went to see about a cow. As he was going along he overtook two women talking as they went. Though they spoke the Little Russian dialect, he understood what they were saying.

"At first, it seems, they did not know him; they thought he was just an ordinary man. He came in to ask for a drink of water, and then he remained. Just think of the things he has bought for them! Why, they say he bought a horse and cart for them at the publican's only this morning! There are not many such men in the world. It's worth while going to have a look at him."

Elisha heard and understood that he was being praised, and he did not go to buy the cow, but returned to the inn, paid for the horse, harnessed it, drove up to the hut, and got out. The people in the hut were astonished when they saw the horse. They thought it might be for them, but dared not ask. The man came out to open the gate.

"Where did you get a horse from, grandfather?" he asked.

"Why, I bought it," said Elisha. "It was going cheap. Go and cut some grass and put it in the manger for it to eat during the night. And take in the sack."

The man unharnessed the horse, and carried the sack into the barn. Then he mowed some grass and put it in the manger. Everybody lay down to sleep. Elisha went outside and lay by the roadside. That evening he took his bag out with him. When every one was asleep, he got up, packed and fastened his bag, wrapped the linen bands round his legs, put on his shoes and coat, and set off to follow Efim.

VII

When Elisha had walked rather more than three miles it began to grow light. He sat down under a tree, opened his bag, counted his money, and found he had only seventeen rubles and twenty kopeks left.

"Well," thought he, "it is no use trying to cross the sea with this. If I beg my way it may be worse than not going at all. Friend Efim will get to Jerusalem without me, and will place a candle at the shrines in my name. As for me, I'm afraid I shall never fulfill my vow in this life. I must be thankful it was made to a merciful Master and to one who pardons sinners."

Elisha rose, jerked his bag well up on his shoulders, and turned back. Not wishing to be recognized by any one, he made a circuit to avoid the village, and walked briskly homeward. Coming from home the way had seemed difficult to him and he had found it hard to keep up with Efim, but now on his return journey, God helped him to get over the ground so that he hardly felt fatigue. Walking seemed like child's play. He went along swinging his staff and did his forty to fifty miles a day.

When Elisha reached home the harvest was over. His family were delighted to see him again, and all wanted to know what had happened: Why and how he had been left behind? And why he had returned without reaching Jerusalem? But Elisha did not tell them.

"It was not God's will that I should get there," said he. "I lost my money on the way and lagged behind my companion. Forgive me, for the Lord's sake!"

Elisha gave his old wife what money he had left. Then he questioned them about home affairs. Everything was going on well; all the work had been done, nothing neglected, and all were living in peace and concord.

Efim's family heard of his return the same day, and came for news of their old man, and to them Elisha gave the same answers.

"Efim is a fast walker. We parted three days before St. Peter's Day, and I meant to catch him up again, but all sorts of things happened. I lost my money and had no means to get any further, so I turned back."

The folks were astonished that so sensible a man should have acted so fool-ishly: should have started and not got to his destination, and should have squandered all his money. They wondered at it for a while and then forgot all about it; and Elisha forgot it too. He set to work again on his homestead. With his son's help he cut wood for fuel for the winter. He and the women threshed the corn. Then he mended the thatch on the outhouses, put the bees under cover, and handed over to his neighbor the ten hives he had sold him in spring and all the swarms that had come from them. His wife tried not to tell how many swarms there had been from these hives, but Elisha knew well enough from which there had been swarms and from which not. And instead of ten, he handed over seventeen swarms to his neighbor. Having got everything ready for the winter, Elisha sent his son away to find work, while he himself took to plaiting shoes of bark and hollowing out logs for hives.

VIII

All that day while Elisha stopped behind in the hut with the sick people, Efim waited for him. He only went on a little way before he sat down. He waited and waited, had a nap, woke up again, and again sat waiting, but his comrade did not come. He gazed till his eyes ached. The sun was already sinking behind a tree and still no Elisha was to be seen.

"Perhaps he has passed me," thought Efim, "or perhaps some one gave him a lift and he drove by while I slept, and did not see me. But how could he help seeing me? One can see so far here in the steppe. Shall I go back? Suppose he is on in front we shall then miss each other completely and it will be still worse. I had better go on, and we shall be sure to meet where we put up for the night."

He came to a village, and told the watchman, if an old man of a certain description came along to bring him to the hut where Efim stopped. But Elisha did not turn up that night. Efim went on, asking all he met whether they had not seen a little, bald-headed old man. No one had seen such a traveller. Efim wondered, but went on alone, saying:

"We shall be sure to meet in Odessa, or on board the ship," and he did not trouble more about it.

On the way he came across a pilgrim wearing a cassock, with long hair and a skull-cap such as priests wear. This pilgrim had been to Mount Athos, and was now going to Jerusalem for the second time. They both stopped at the same place one night and, having met, they travelled on together.

They got safely to Odessa and there had to wait three days for a ship. Many pilgrims from many different parts were in the same case. Again Efim asked about Elisha, but no one had seen him.

Efim got himself a foreign passport, which cost him five rubles. He paid forty rubles for a return ticket to Jerusalem, and bought a supply of bread and herrings for the voyage.

The pilgrim began explaining to Efim how he might get on to the ship without paying his fare, but Efim would not listen. "No, I came prepared to pay, and I shall pay," said he.

The ship was freighted and the pilgrims went on board, Efim and his new comrade among them. The anchors were weighed and the ship put out to sea.

All day they sailed smoothly, but towards night a wind arose, rain came on, and the vessel tossed about and shipped water. The people were frightened: the women wailed and screamed and some of the weaker men ran about the ship looking for shelter. Efim too was frightened, but he would not show it, and remained at the place on deck where he had settled down when first he came on board, beside some old men from Tambov. There they sat silent, all night and all next day, holding on to their sacks. On the third day it grew calm, and on the fifth day they anchored at Constantinople. Some of the pilgrims went on shore to visit the Church of St. Sophia, now held by the Turks. Efim remained on the ship, and only bought some white bread. They lay there for twenty-four hours and then put to sea again. At Smyrna they stopped again, and at Alexandretta; but at last they arrived safely at Jaffa, where all the pilgrims had to disembark. From there still it was more than forty miles by road to Jerusalem. When disembarking the people were again much frightened. The ship was high, and the people were dropped into boats, which rocked so much that it was easy to miss them and fall into the water. A couple of men did get a wetting, but at last all were safely landed.

They went on on foot, and at noon on the third day reached Jerusalem. They stopped outside the city, at the Russian hostel, where their passports were endorsed. Then, after dinner, Efim visited the Holy Places with his companion, the pilgrim. It was not the time when they could be admitted to the Holy

Sepulchre, but they went to the Patriarchate. All the pilgrims assembled there. The women were separated from the men, who were all told to sit in a circle, barefoot. Then a monk came in with a towel to wash their feet. He washed, wiped, and then kissed their feet, and did this to every one in the circle. Efim's feet were washed and kissed, with the rest. He stood through vespers and matins, prayed, placed candles at the shrines, handed in booklets inscribed with his parents' names, that they might be mentioned in the church prayers. Here at the Patriarchate food and wine were given them. Next morning they went to the cell of Mary of Egypt, where she had lived doing penance. Here too they placed candles and had prayers read. From there they went to the Monastery of Abraham, and saw the place where Abraham intended to slay his son as an offering to God.

Then they visited the spot where Christ appeared to Mary Magdalene, and the Church of James, the Lord's brother. The pilgrim showed Efim all these places, and told him how much money to give at each place. At mid-day they returned to the hostel and had dinner. As they were preparing to lie down and rest, the pilgrim cried out, and began to search his clothes, feeling them all over.

"My purse has been stolen, there were twenty-three rubles in it," said he, "two ten-ruble notes and the rest in change."

He sighed and lamented a great deal, but as there was no help for it, they lay down to sleep.

IX

As Efim lay there he was assailed by temptation.

"No one has stolen any money from this pilgrim," thought he, "I do not believe he had any. He gave none away anywhere, though he made me give and even borrowed a ruble of me."

This thought had no sooner crossed his mind than Efim rebuked himself, saying: "What right have I to judge a man? It is a sin. I will think no more about it." But as soon as his thoughts began to wander, they turned again to the pilgrim: how interested he seemed to be in money, and how unlikely it sounded when he declared that his purse had been stolen.

"He never had any money," thought Efim. "It's all an invention."

Towards evening they got up, and went to midnight Mass at the great Church of the Resurrection, where the Lord's Sepulchre is. The pilgrim kept close to Efim and went everywhere with him. They came to the Church; a great many pilgrims were there, some Russians and some of other nationalities: Greeks, Armenians, Turks, and Syrians. Efim entered the Holy Gates with the crowd. A monk led them past the Turkish sentinels, to the place where the Saviour was taken down from the cross and anointed, and where candles were burning in nine great candlesticks. The monk showed and explained everything. Efim offered a candle there. Then the monk led Efim to the right, up the steps to Golgotha, to the place where the cross had stood. Efim prayed there. Then they showed him the cleft where the ground had been rent asunder to its nethermost depths; then the place where Christ's hands and feet were nailed to the cross; then Adam's tomb, where the blood of Christ had dripped on to Adam's bones. Then they showed him the stone on which Christ sat when the crown of thorns was placed on His head; then the post to which Christ was bound when He was scourged. Then Efim saw the stone with two holes for Christ's feet. They were going to show him something else, but there was a stir in the crowd and the people all hurried to the Church of the Lord's Sepulchre itself. The Latin Mass had just finished there and the Russian liturgy was beginning. And Efim went with the crowd to the tomb cut in the rock.

He tried to get rid of the pilgrim, against whom he was still sinning in his mind, but the pilgrim would not leave him, but went with him to the Mass at the Holy Sepulchre. They tried to get to the front, but were too late. There was such a crowd that it was impossible to move either backwards or forwards.

Efim stood looking in front of him, praying, and every now and then feeling for his purse. He was in two minds: sometimes he thought that the pilgrim was deceiving him, and then again he thought that if the pilgrim spoke the truth and his purse had really been stolen, the same thing might happen to himself. Efim stood there gazing into the little chapel in which was the Holy Sepulchre itself with thirty-six lamps burning above it. As he stood looking over the people's heads, he saw something that surprised him. Just beneath the lamps in which the sacred fire burns, and in front of every one, Efim saw an old man in a grey coat, whose bald, shining head was just like Elisha Bodrov.

"It's like him," thought Efim, "but it cannot be Elisha. He could not have got ahead of me. The ship before ours started a week earlier. He could not have caught that; and he was not on ours, for I saw every pilgrim on board."

Hardly had Efim thought this, when the little old man began to pray, and bowed three times: once forward to God, then once on each side—to the brethren. And as he turned his head to the right, Efim recognized him. It was Elisha Bodrov himself, with his dark, curly beard turning grey at the cheeks,

Efim stood looking in front of him, praying, and every now and then feeling for his purse.

with his brows, his eyes and nose, and his expression of face. Yes, it was he!

Efim was very pleased to have found his comrade again and wondered how Elisha had got ahead of him.

"Well done, Elisha!" thought he. "See how he has pushed ahead. He must have come across some one who showed him the way. When we get out I will find him, get rid of this fellow in the skull-cap, and keep to Elisha. Perhaps he will show me how to get to the front also."

Efim kept looking out, so as not to lose sight of Elisha. But when the Mass was over the crowd began to sway, pushing forward to kiss the tomb, and pushed Efim aside. He was again seized with fear lest his purse should be stolen. Pressing it with his hand, he began elbowing through the crowd, anxious only to get out. When he reached the open he went about for a long time searching for Elisha both outside and in the Church itself. In the chapels of the Church he saw many people of all kinds, eating and drinking wine, and reading and sleeping there. But Elisha was nowhere to be seen. So Efim returned to the inn without having found his comrade. That evening the pilgrim in the skull-cap did not turn up. He had gone off without repaying the ruble, and Efim was left alone.

X

The next day Efim went to the Holy Sepulchre again, with an old man from Tambov, whom he had met on the ship. He tried to get to the front, but was again pressed back; so he stood by a pillar and prayed. He looked before him, and there in the foremost place under the lamps, close to the very Sepulchre of the Lord, stood Elisha, with his arms spread out like a priest at the altar, and with his bald head all shining.

"Well, now," thought Efim, "I won't lose him!"

He pushed forward to the front, but when he got there, there was no Elisha: he had evidently gone away.

Again on the third day Efim looked, and saw at the Sepulchre, in the holiest place, Elisha standing in the sight of all men, his arms outspread and his eyes gazing upwards as if he saw something above. And his bald head was all shining.

"Well, this time," thought Efim, "he shall not escape me! I will go and stand at the door, then we can't miss one another!"

Efim went out and stood by the door till past noon. Every one had passed out, but still Elisha did not appear.

Efim remained six weeks in Jerusalem, and went everywhere: to Bethlehem, and to Bethany, and to the Jordan. He had a new shroud stamped at the Holy Sepulchre for his burial, and he took a bottle of water from the Jordan and some holy earth, and bought candles that had been lit at the sacred flame. In eight places he inscribed names to be prayed for, and he spent all his money except just enough to get home with. Then he started homeward. He walked to Jaffa, sailed thence to Odessa, and walked home from there on foot.

XI

Efim traveled the same road he had come by; and as he drew nearer home his former anxiety returned as to how affairs were getting on in his absence. "Much water flows away in a year," the proverb says. It takes a lifetime to build up a homestead but not long to ruin it, thought he. And he wondered how his son had managed without him, what sort of spring they were having, how the cattle had wintered, and whether the cottage was well finished. When Efim came to the district where he had parted from Elisha the summer before, he could hardly believe that the people living there were the same. The year before they had been starving, but now they were living in comfort. The harvest had been good, and the people had recovered and had forgotten their former misery.

One evening Efim reached the very place where Elisha had remained behind; and as he entered the village a little girl in a white smock ran out of a hut.

"Daddy, daddy, come to our house!"

Efim meant to pass on, but the little girl would not let him. She took hold of his coat, laughing, and pulled him towards the hut, where a woman with a small boy came out into the porch and beckoned to him.

"Come in, grandfather," she said. "Have supper and spend the night with us." So Efim went in.

"I may as well ask about Elisha," he thought. "I fancy this is the very hut he went to for a drink of water."

The woman helped him off with the bag he carried, and gave him water to wash his face. Then she made him sit down to table, and set milk, curd-cakes, and porridge, before him. Efim thanked her, and praised her for her kindness to a pilgrim. The woman shook her head.

"We have good reason to welcome pilgrims," she said. "It was a pilgrim who showed us what life is."

"We have good reason to welcome pilgrims," she said. "It was a pilgrim who showed us what life is. We were living forgetful of God and God punished us almost to death. We reached such a pass last summer that we all lay ill and helpless with nothing to eat. And we should have died, but that God sent an old man to help us—just such a one as you. He came in one day to ask for a drink of water, saw the state we were in, took pity on us, and remained with us. He gave us food and drink and set us on our feet again; and he redeemed our land, and bought a cart and horse and gave them to us."

Here the old woman, entering the hut, interrupted the younger one and said:

"We don't know whether it was a man or an angel from God. He loved us all, pitied us all, and went away without telling us his name, so that we don't even know whom to pray for. I can see it all before me now! There I lay waiting for death, when in comes a bald-headed old man. He was not anything much to look at, and he asked for a drink of water. I, sinner that I am, thought to myself: 'What does he come prowling about here for?' And just think what he did! As soon as he saw us he let down his bag, on this very spot, and untied it."

Here the little girl joined in.

"No, Granny," said she, "first he put it down here in the middle of the hut, and then he lifted it on to the bench."

And they began discussing and recalling all he had said and done, where he sat and slept, and what he had said to each of them.

At night the peasant himself came home on his horse, and he too began to tell about Elisha and how he had lived with them.

"Had he not come we should all have died in our sins. We were dying in despair, murmuring against God and man. But he set us on our feet again; and through him we learned to know God and to believe that there is good in man. May the Lord bless him! We used to live like animals, he made human beings of us."

After giving Efim food and drink, they showed him where he was to sleep; and lay down to sleep themselves.

But though Efim lay down, he could not sleep. He could not get Elisha out of his mind, but remembered how he had seen him three times at Jerusalem, standing in the foremost place.

"So that is how he got ahead of me," thought Efim. "God may or may not have accepted my pilgrimage, but He has certainly accepted his!"

"So that is how he got ahead of me," thought Efim. "God may or may not have accepted my pilgrimage, but He has certainly accepted his!"

Next morning Efim bade farewell to the people, who put some patties in his sack before they went to their work, and he continued his journey.

XII

Efim had been away just a year and it was spring again when he reached home one evening. His son was not at home, but had gone to the public house, and when he came back he had had a drop too much. Efim began questioning him. Everything showed that the young fellow had been unsteady during his father's absence. The money had all been wrongly spent and the work had been neglected. The father began to upbraid the son, and the son answered rudely.

"Why didn't you stay and look after it yourself?" he said. "You go off, taking the money with you, and now you demand it of me!"

The old man grew angry and struck his son.

In the morning Efim went to the village elder to complain of his son's conduct. As he was passing Elisha's house his friend's wife greeted him from the porch.

"How do you do, neighbor?" she said. "How do you do, dear friend? Did you get to Jerusalem safely?"

Efim stopped.

"Yes, thank God," he said. "I have been there. I lost sight of your old man, but I hear he got home safely."

The old woman was fond of talking:

"Yes, neighbor, he has come back," said she. "He's been back a long time. Soon after Assumption, I think it was, he returned. And we were glad the Lord had sent him back to us! We were dull without him. We can't expect much work from him any more, his years for work are past; but still he is the head of the household and it's more cheerful when he's at home. And how glad our lad was! He said, 'It's like being without sunlight, when father's away!' It was dull without him, dear friend. We're fond of him, and take good care of him."

"Is he at home now?"

"He is, dear friend. He is with his bees. He is hiving the swarms. He says they are swarming well this year. The Lord has given such strength to the bees that my husband doesn't remember the like. 'The Lord is not rewarding us according to our sins,' he says. Come in, dear neighbor, he will be so glad to see you again."

Efim passed through the passage into the yard and to the apiary, to see Elisha. There was Elisha in his grey coat, without any face-net or gloves, standing under the birch trees, looking upwards, his arms stretched out and his bald head shining as Efim had seen him at the Holy Sepulchre in Jerusalem; and above him the sunlight shone through the birches as the flames of fire had done in the Holy Place, and the golden bees flew round his head like a halo, and did not sting him.

Efim stopped. The old woman called to her husband.

"Here's your friend come," she cried.

Elisha looked round with a pleased face, and came towards Efim, gently picking bees out of his own beard.

"Good-day, neighbor, good-day, dear friend. Did you get there safely?"

"My feet walked there and I have brought you some water from the river Jordan. You must come to my house for it. But whether the Lord accepted my efforts. . . ."

"Well, the Lord be thanked! May Christ bless you!" said Elisha.

"My feet have been there, but whether my soul or another's has been there more truly . . ."
—EFIM

Efim was silent for a while, and then added: "My feet have been there, but whether my soul or another's has been there more truly . . ."

"That's God's business, neighbor, God's business," interrupted Elisha.

"On my return journey I stopped at the hut where you remained behind . . ."

Elisha was alarmed, and said hurriedly:

"God's business, neighbor, God's business! Come into the cottage, I'll give you some of our honey." And Elisha changed the conversation, and talked of home affairs.

But he now understood that the best way to keep one's vows to God and to do His will, is for each man while he lives to show love and do good to others.

Efim sighed, and did not speak to Elisha of the people in the hut, nor of how he had seen him in Jerusalem. But he now understood that the best way to keep one's vows to God and to do His will, is for each man while he lives to show love and do good to others.

First published in 1885. Translated by Louise and Aylmer Maude.

GAUGING THE GAP

"Let him who cannot do the thing he would
Will to do that he can. To will is foolish
Where there's no power to do. That man is wise
Who, if he cannot, does not wish he could."

—a verse that the young Leonardo da Vinci copied into his notebook

"One pushes down the other. By these little blocks are meant the life and the efforts of men."

—Leonardo da Vinci, describing a doodle he drew
near the end of his life, comprised of a series of rectangles
representing his life's great ambitions and endeavors,
but drawn tipping each other over like collapsing dominoes

"We should not desire the impossible."

—Leonardo da Vinci, written in his
notebook shortly before he died at the palace of Cloux

"My soul is heavy."

—Leo Tolstoy, to his daughter, after a particularly
lavish and splendid eightieth birthday party

"What a man writes after he is sixty is worth little more than tea continually remade with the same leaves."

—art historian Bernard Berenson

"You suppose that I contemplate my life's work with calm satisfaction. But seen close up the whole thing has quite a different look. There is not one single notion that I am convinced will hold its ground and broadly speaking I am not certain of being on the right path. Our contemporaries look at me both as a heretic and as a reactionary who has, as it were, outlived himself. To be sure, this is a question of fashion and of a shortsighted view; but the feeling of inadequacy comes from within."

—Albert Einstein, age 70, in a letter to a colleague, March 1949

"Though we would like to live without regrets, and sometimes proudly insist that we have none, this is not really possible, if only because we are mortal. When more time stretches behind than stretches before one, some assessments, however reluctantly and incompletely, begin to be made. Between what one wishes to become and what one *has* become there is a momentous gap, which will now never be closed. And this gap seems to operate as one's final margin, one's last opportunity, for creation. And between the self as it is and the self as one sees it, there is also a distance, even harder to gauge. Some of us are compelled, around the middle of our lives, to make a study of this baffling geography, less in the hope of conquering these distances than in the determination that the distance shall not become any greater."

—James Baldwin, *New York Review of Books*, 1967

QUESTIONS FOR THOUGHT AND DISCUSSION

1. In what ways is a pilgrimage different from tourist travel? What makes it such an ideal form of spiritual discipline?

2. How would you describe Efim and Elisha in terms of class, wealth, and status within their community? In terms of virtues and vices? Why do you think Tolstoy emphasized Elisha taking snuff?

3. In discussing a pilgrimage to Jerusalem, what are the possible barriers to going for the two men? How are their approaches to the problems and the possibility of the trip different? What does this say about their attitudes toward family, money, and responsibilities?

4. How did each man get ready for the pilgrimage? What did they take with them? What were their moods in setting out? What were they thinking of as they left?

5. Part VI is the turning point in Elisha's journey. What is Elisha saying in the paragraph, "There seems to be no end to it . . . "? What does he mean by, "You've slipped your cables and lost your reckoning"?

6. How does Elisha decide what to do about the family? What does he mean by, "or else while I go seek the Lord beyond the sea I may lose Him in myself"? What are the consequences of this decision for him? How would Efim have handled this situation, do you think? What would you have done and why?

7. Do you think Efim's assessment of the pilgrim's money being stolen is fair or unfair? Why? How did Efim's thoughts affect how he interacted with the pilgrim from then on? What do you think Elisha would have thought and done had he been in Efim's shoes?

8. How would you describe Efim's experience in Jerusalem? What are some of the things that absorbed his attention? What do you make of all the "Elisha sightings"? Later, when Efim is on his way home and has met the family Elisha helped, he says, "'So that is how he got ahead of me . . . God may or may not have accepted my pilgrimage, but He has certainly accepted his!'" What does he mean?

9. Why do most people *identify* with one of the two old men but *appreciate* the other? What does that say? Who would you say had the most successful pilgrimage?

10. What lessons and considerations about the journey of life do you take away from this story for your own situation?

Questions for Reflection and Appraisal

At this point in the study, we invite you to take some time by yourself to go through the questionnaire on the following pages.

PLEASE NOTE: This questionnaire is designed exclusively as an aid and stimulus for personal reflection on the topics raised in this study. It is not intended either for group discussion or as a response to a public opinion survey.

INTRODUCTORY QUESTIONS

1. How would you describe the season of life in which you are now? What are its major opportunities and challenges?
2. Looking back over your life, what have been the main chapters in your story so far?
3. Who are the most influential people and what are the defining events of your life?
4. What do you consider your foremost
   - satisfactions and accomplishments?
   - failures?
   - regrets?
   - uncompleted projects or dreams?

ACTION:

Plan a longer "time out" with sufficient opportunity for solitude, reflection, and appraisal.

FAITH

1. How would you identify yourself in terms of your core faith, view of life, moral standards, and believing community?
2. Would you describe your faith as a private part of your life or as decisive for the whole? Something which has stayed much the same or grown and matured with you over the years? Something purely formal or something as emotionally and intellectually deep as you are?

3. Who are the people and what are the resources through which your faith is regularly challenged to deepen and grow?
4. Do you make a practice of taking "time out" to review your journey and reorient your life in light of your faith? What does this mean to you?

ACTION:

Consider one single step that would most help to revitalize and deepen your faith.

GIFTEDNESS

1. What do you consider the core of your God-given talents?
2. How would you describe the moments in your childhood or in later years when you first realized the satisfaction of expressing your own unique gifts?
3. Do you feel your gifts are recognized and fruitfully employed—or neglected, even wasted—at home? At work? In your community? In your faith community?
4. What are the chief goals you would like to serve with your gifts?

ACTION:

From your talents that have not so far come into play as much as others, consider which one you would like to emphasize at this stage of your life.

RELATIONSHIPS

1. How would you describe the depth, intimacy, and richness of your closest relationships—with your family, friends, neighbors, and colleagues?
2. Who are your heroes and mentors in life? What example, inspiration, and challenge do you gain from each? Who are those younger than you for whom you play a mentor/hero role?
3. What regular, practical form do close friends play in your life in terms of fellowship, encouragement, and accountability?
4. If your family and friends were asked to describe you in five words, what would those words be? What do you think they would miss?

ACTION:

Put down one thing (for example, an expression of gratitude or an apology) which would most improve one of your closest relationships.

WORK

1. Describe how your daily work contributes to a sense of "personal mission" and "life task." What are the satisfactions and what are the frustrations you experience in your daily activities?
2. What gifts that are truly "you" are not brought into play in your job?
3. How much is your sense of identity, status, and satisfaction derived from your position and salary? What would be the effect of losing all this tomorrow?
4. What do you see as your sense of calling that links your working life and your life outside work, including retirement, however far in the future?

ACTION:

Identify one initiative that could improve your work satisfaction, including a possible alternative career track.

WIDER COMMUNITY

1. What part does the wider community (neighborhood, city, nation, world) play in your thinking?
2. Trace the story revealed to you by the ways you spend your time and money. Does this confirm or contradict what you say above?
3. Do you feel a sense of connection and involvement with your faith community and your neighborhood? Why or why not?
4. Describe the part played by your faith community in giving you a sense of the times in which we live and helping you to participate in wider community affairs.

ACTION:

Consider how you could take your entrepreneurial gifts and use them to contribute to some worthwhile community or nonprofit initiative.

CONCLUDING QUESTIONS

1. What would you say you have accomplished with your life so far?
2. Think back over the dreams, ambitions, and hopes of your youth. How does your present position in life measure up to these?
3. Where are the main imbalances in your life that you would like to address?
4. What is the principal legacy you would like to pass on at the end of your life?

ACTION:

Focus on one thing in your life that is missing, wrong, or confused, and decide what to do to improve it.

ADDING IT ALL UP

"For some months now I have lived with my own youth and childhood, not always writing indeed but thinking of it almost every day, and I am sorrowful and disturbed. It is not that I have accomplished too few of my plans, for I am not ambitious; but when I think of all the books I have read, and of the wise words I have heard spoken, and of the anxiety I have given to parents and grandparents, and of the hopes that I have had, all life weighed in the scales of my own life seems to me a preparation for something that never happens."

—W. B. Yeats, *Autobiographies*

HEBREW

  5 years is the age for reading (Scripture);
10 for Mishnah (the laws);
13 for the Commandments (Bar Mitzvah, moral responsibility);
15 for Gemara (Talmudic discussions; abstract reasoning);
18 for Hupa (wedding canopy);
20 for seeking a livelihood (pursuing an occupation);
30 for attaining full strength ("Koah");
40 for understanding;
50 for giving counsel;
60 for becoming an elder (wisdom, old age);
70 for white hair;
80 for Gevurah (new, special strength of age);
90 for being bent under the weight of the years;
100 for being as if already dead and passed away from the world

—The Talmud

GREEK

0–7 A boy at first is the man; unripe, then he casts his teeth; milk-teeth befitting the child he sheds in his seventh year.

7–14 Then to his seven years God adding another seven, signs of approaching manhood show in the bud.

14–21 Still, in the third of the sevens his limbs are growing; his chin touched with a fleecy down, the bloom of the cheek gone.

21–28 Now, in the fourth of the sevens ripen to greatest completeness the powers of the man, and his worth becomes plain to see.

28–35 In the fifth he bethinks him that this is the season for courting, bethinks him that sons will preserve and continue his line.

35–42 Now in the sixth his mind, ever open to virtue, broadens, and never inspires him to profitless deeds;

42–56 Seven times seven, and eight; the tongue and the mind for fourteen years together are now at their best.

56–63 Still in the ninth is he able, but never so nimble in speech and in wit as he was in the days of his prime.

63–70 Who to the tenth has attained, and has lived to complete it, has come to the time to depart on the ebb-tide of Death.

—Solon, 6th century B.C

CHINESE

The Master said,

At 15, I set my heart upon learning.

At 30, I had planted my feet firm upon the ground.

At 40, I no longer suffered from perplexities.

At 50, I knew what were the biddings of heaven.

At 60, I heard them with a docile ear.

At 70, I could follow the dictates of my own heart; for what
    I desired no longer overstepped the boundaries of right.

—Confucius, 5th century B.C.

RENAISSANCE

"All the world's a stage,
And all the men and women merely players:
They have their exits and their entrances;
And one man in his time plays many parts,
His acts being seven ages. At first the infant,
Mewling and puking in the nurse's arms.
And then the whining school-boy, with his satchel
And shining morning face, creeping like snail
Unwillingly to school. And then the lover,
Sighing like furnace, with a woeful ballad
Made to his mistress' eyebrow. Then a soldier,
Full of strange oaths and bearded like the pard,
Jealous in honour, sudden and quick in quarrel,
Seeking the bubble reputation
Even in the cannon's mouth. And then the justice,
In fair round belly with good capon lined,
With eyes severe and beard of formal cut,
Full of wise saws and modern instances;
And so he plays his part. The sixth age shifts
Into the lean and slipper'd pantaloon,
With spectacles on nose and pouch on side,
His youthful hose, well saved, a world too wide
For his shrunk shank; and his big manly voice,
Turning again toward childish treble, pipes
And whistles in his sound. Last scene of all,
That ends this strange eventful history,
Is second childishness and mere oblivion,
Sans teeth, sans eyes, sans taste, sans everything."

—William Shakespeare, *As You Like It*, Act II

FIVE
FINISHING WELL

WHAT DO MOSES, SOPHOCLES, MICHELANGELO, FRANKLIN, TOLSTOY, VERDI, HUGO, *Yeats, Freud, Churchill, and Picasso have in common? Many of their greatest works were accomplished in their sixties, seventies, and eighties. The point is important because it focuses the spotlight on the last great productive period of life—the late adult years—which, for a number of reasons, have become a renewed focus of attention. "Gentlemen," Victor Hugo said to his friends one evening, "I am seventy-four and I am beginning my career."*

But, of course, all the people above were exceptions. In almost every field of human endeavor the most important work has been done by far younger men and women. Conventional wisdom tends to avert its gaze from these later years, and with good reason. Sometimes the diversion is expressed popularly in "over the hill" jokes and toasts. Sometimes it is put more sophisticatedly in statistics about the early deaths of such geniuses as Mozart and Pascal ("Those whom the gods love die young"). Sometimes it simply reflects the realism that all too often "the golden years" are anything but. Physical decline, sickness, financial hardships, increasing deaths of friends, and a retirement loss of purpose can all be devastating whether or not one has ample time to play golf and sit in the sun. A few cultures, such as China, have given almost unqualified veneration to old age. But the vast majority of humankind has looked on old age with sorrow or rebellion.

For all the handy stock of euphemisms—such as "golden years," "senior citizens," and "elders of the tribe"—the outcome is plain. "Over the hill" may generate fears and anxieties for twentysomethings turning thirty or fortysomethings turning fifty, but the outcome in the late adult years is not loss of youth or loss of vitality or loss of power but loss of life itself. The end is death, and the old age that marks the last stretch of the road is often a terrible burden.

Modern society, in fact, gives to the old with one hand and takes away with

189

the other. With its open hand it increases our life expectancy and offers, through such things as plastic surgery and genetics, fresh prospects of the ancient dream of rejuvenating youth. With its other hand, though, it discounts experience, which is forever being rendered obsolete through innovation, and therefore disqualifies the old from using the main treasure they have won—the wisdom gained from their life journey.

Is the only option to heed Dylan Thomas's advice to his aging father, "Do not go gentle into that good night"? As science continues to lengthen our life expectancy and the "graying" of the modern world swells the number of people living longer and more healthily, the challenge mounted becomes political as well as personal. A British minister described the aging of the world as "the Mount Everest of social problems."

But as history and experience show clearly, any solutions offered must move beyond issues of higher pensions, better health care, and greater leisure opportunities. Two things have constantly been seen to affect retirement and old age: continuity of life before and after retirement and, supremely, the presence of a project to work on. Simone de Beauvoir writes, "There is only one solution if old age is not to be an absurd parody of our former life, and that is to go on pursuing ends that give our existence a meaning—devotion to individuals, to groups or to causes, social, political, intellectual, or creative work."

Once again the truth of calling makes the difference. First, calling is the life-project that spurs us to keep journeying purposefully—and thus growing and maturing—to the very end of our lives. We have not arrived, but nor are we traveling aimlessly. Followers of Christ are wayfarers, not wanderers. They have found the way, but they have not yet come to their destination. They may retire from their jobs, but there is no retiring from their callings. As Henri Nouwen wrote, "He who thinks he has finished is finished. Those who think they have arrived have lost their way."

Second, calling helps us finish well because it prevents us from confusing the termination of our occupations with the termination of our vocations. If we ever limit our calling to what we do, and that task is taken away from us—we suddenly find ourselves unemployed, fired, retired, or pronounced terminally ill—then we are tempted to depression or doubt. What has happened? We have let our occupation become so intertwined with our vocation that losing the occupation means losing the sense of vocation too.

Third, calling helps us finish well because it encourages us to leave the entire outcome of our lives to God. We modern people talk glibly of "discovering our identities" and "fulfilling our passions" as if we could sustain our own significance

Two things have constantly been seen to affect retirement and old age: continuity of life before and after retirement and, supremely, the presence of a project to work on.

Followers of Christ are wayfarers, not wanderers.

"He who thinks he has finished is finished. Those who think they have arrived have lost their way."
—Henri Nouwen

and crown our own accomplishments by ourselves. But, as always, there is mystery and incompletion at the heart of life. For all his herculean labors, Michelangelo never lived to see the dome of St. Peter's and neither may we see the fruit of all our endeavors. God calls, and, just as we hear him but don't see him on this earth, so we grow to become what he calls even though we don't see until heaven what he is calling us to accomplish and become.

In summary, as the readings in part 5 explore, there are many pitfalls in the later years of life, such as the drivenness of workaholism and the paralysis of perfectionism. For followers of the call for whom life is an entrepreneurial venture to the end, the challenge is plain: to break the "conspiracy of silence" about aging, to confront the cultural contradictions of disqualifying the old as obsolete, and to finish strong and well.

God calls, and, just as we hear him but don't see him on this earth, so we grow to become what he calls even though we don't see until heaven what he is calling us to accomplish and become.

THE DISQUALIFYING PROCESS

"I have learnt a great deal since I was twenty, but year by year I become relatively more ignorant because there are more and more discoveries; the sciences grow richer, and in spite of my efforts to keep abreast at least in some fields, the number of things I do not know increases."

—Simone de Beauvoir, *The Coming of Age*

"At present the aged man can no longer reckon upon an eternity of this kind: the pace of history has increased. Tomorrow it will destroy what was built yesterday. The trees the old man has planted will be cut down. Almost everywhere the family unit has fallen apart. Small firms are either taken over by monopolies or they fail. The son will not re-live his father's life, and the father knows it. Once he has gone, the estate will be abandoned, the shop sold, the business wound up. All that he has achieved and all that gave a meaning to his life lies under the same threat that menaces him. If he has a generous love for his children and if he approves of the course they have chosen he may be happy to think that he lives on in them. But because of the chasm that usually divides the generations, this does not happen very often. Generally speaking, the father does not see himself in his son. The void swallows him entirely.

"Modern society, far from providing the aged man with an appeal against his biological fate, tosses him into an outdated past, and it does so while he is still living."

—Simone de Beauvoir, *The Coming of Age*

Evelyn Waugh

Evelyn Waugh (1903–1966) was a writer and novelist, best known as the author of Brideshead Revisited (1945), which was made into a successful television series. Born in London, he studied at Oxford and made a reputation with such social satirical novels as Decline and Fall. He became a Roman Catholic in 1930 and his later novels show a more serious attitude toward life.

Brideshead Revisited is a nostalgic evocation of student days at Oxford. The following passage is a gentle description of the last days of Sebastian Flyte, typical of those who fail to overcome their problems—in this case, alcohol—and end up becoming caricatures of themselves. Indulgent on themselves, such people are indulged by others, at a cost. As Simone de Beauvoir writes, "They pay a high price for the indulgence they enjoy—their individual inferiorities are forgiven because they are looked upon as definitively inferior beings; they no longer have anything to lose because they have already lost everything."

"They pay a high price for the indulgence they enjoy—their individual inferiorities are forgiven because they are looked upon as definitively inferior beings; they no longer have anything to lose because they have already lost everything."
—SIMONE DE BEAUVOIR

TIME AND TIDE WAIT FOR NO ONE

"Never-resting time leads summer on/To hideous winter."

—William Shakespeare, "Sonnet V"

"Luck does not serve men of our age, Monsieur le Maréchal."

—Louis XIV,
to the Marshal de Villeroy after the defeat of Romilly

"I never wake up in the morning without finding life a little more devoid of interest than it was the day before. But what saddens me most is remembering my life as it was twenty years ago and then suddenly coming back into the present."

—Jonathan Swift, in a letter, 1729

"I wake in such a state of indifference to everything that may happen in the world and in my own narrow circle that . . . I should certainly stay in bed all day if decency and the fear of illness did not rouse me out of it."

—Jonathan Swift

"Already my imagination is less vivid, and it no longer glows as once it did at the view of an object that stirs it into life; dreaming is less of an intoxicating rapture and there is more of recollection than of creation in what it gives me now. A lukewarm weariness drains my faculties of all their strength; little by little the spirit of life is going out; and it is only with pain that my soul leaps from its now decrepit frame."

—Jean-Jacques Rousseau, in his sixties

"Age takes hold of us by surprise."

—Johann Wolfgang von Goethe

"Death, Oh cruel death! Death is a monster that expels the intent spectator from the great theatre before the end of a play that interests him beyond measure. This alone is reason enough to make it hated."

—Giovanni Giacomo Casanova, age 70

"When I used to dream in former times my youth lay before me; I could advance towards the unknown that I was looking for. Now I can no longer take a single step without coming up against the boundary-stone."

—Vicomte de Chateaubriand

"We harden in some places and rot in others: we never ripen."

—Charles-Augustin Sainte-Beuve

Brideshead Revisited

"Poor Sebastian!" I said. "It's too pitiful. How will it end?"

"I think I can tell you exactly, Charles. I've seen others like him, and I believe they are very near and dear to God. He'll live on, half in, half out of the community, a familiar figure pottering round with his broom and his bunch of keys. He'll be a great favourite with the old fathers, something of a joke to the novices. Everyone will know about his drinking; he'll disappear for two or three days every month or so, and they'll all nod and smile and say in their various accents, 'Old Sebastian's on the spree again,' and then he'll come back dishevelled and shamefaced and be more devout for a day or two in the chapel. He'll probably have little hiding places about the garden where he keeps a bottle and takes a swig now and then on the sly. They'll bring him forward to act as guide, whenever they have an English-speaking visitor; and he will be completely charming, so that before they go they'll ask about him and perhaps be given a hint that he has high connections at home. If he lives long enough, generations of missionaries in all kinds of remote places will think of him as a queer old character who was somehow part of the Hope of their student days, and remember him in their masses. He'll develop little eccentricities of devotion, intense personal cults of his own; he'll be found in the chapel at odd times and missed when he's expected. Then one morning, after one of his drinking bouts, he'll be picked up at the gate dying, and show by a mere flicker of the eyelid that he is conscious when they give him the last sacraments. It's not such a bad way of getting through one's life."

From Evelyn Waugh, *Brideshead Revisited* (Boston: Little, Brown and Co., 1945), pp. 308–309.

TIME AND TIDE WAIT FOR NO ONE, CONTINUED

"The future holds nothing for me, and I am being devoured by the past. Mark of old age and decay."
—Gustave Flaubert, age 54

"The notion of life as a grant in perpetuity—the illusion in which most men live—is one that I possess no more."
—Edmond de Goncourt, in his journal, 1889

"Do you know the worst of all vices? It is being over fifty-five."
—Ivan Sergeyevich Turgenev (often quoted by Lenin)

"Being old makes me tired and furious; I am everything that I was and indeed more, but an enemy has bound and twisted me so that although I can make plans and think better than ever, I can no longer carry out what I plan and think."
—W. B. Yeats, age 57

"I have not the least wish to put my toys away. I hate the idea of going."
—H. G. Wells, 1940, age 70,
likening himself to a child sent to bed
just after having been given some wonderful toys

"I loathe the hardness of old age. I feel it coming. I creak. I am embittered."
—Virginia Woolf, 1940, age 58

"I fall back on themes I have handled again and again, themes that no longer seem capable of yielding me anything."
—André Gide

"I have said, more or less well, all I thought I had to say, and I am afraid of repeating myself."
—André Gide, *Ainsi soit-il*

"It is an extraordinary business, Charles, growing old."
—Winston Churchill, to his doctor

"It's not being forty that bothers me, but the impossibility of holding up time."
—Albert Camus, on his fortieth birthday

"In this way every artist has deep within him a unique spring which flows during his life, feeding what he is and what he says. When the spring dries up, we see his work gradually shrivel and crack."
—Albert Camus,
preface to *L'Envers et l'endroit*

"But as the years go by, and as our time to come grows shorter, and when the stakes are down, the book finished and in the printers' hands, and when the human adventure is nearing its end, then the characters of a novel no longer have room to move about in us: they are caught between the hardened, impenetrable mass of our past, into which nothing can now make its way, and that death, near at hand or farther off, which is now present."
—François Mauriac

"Yes, autumn is really the best of the seasons: and I'm not sure that old age isn't the best part of life. But, of course, like autumn it doesn't last."
—C. S. Lewis,
in a letter to George Sayer

"Why, what has happened? It is life that has happened; and I am old."
—Simon Aragon

"Die early or grow old: there is no other alternative."
—Simone de Beauvoir

QUESTIONS FOR THOUGHT AND DISCUSSION

1. What do you think of the speaker's final comment, "It's not such a bad way of getting through one's life"? What does this say of the speaker's sense of life purpose? What is your view?
2. What sort of developments lie behind someone becoming like Sebastian? What do the phrases "great favorite," "something of a joke," and "queer old character" have to do with the reality of dying an alcoholic?

3. What does Waugh's description tell us of the community's role in Sebastian's condition? Or earlier, of his friends' role? Why do you think people are willing to let him go on the way he is?

4. Why does the speaker say, "They are very near and dear to God"? Do you think this is so? Why?

5. Sebastian's downfall is obviously the bottle. What other flaws have you seen harden into problems that, left unchecked, lead people to finish badly?

6. What are the best safeguards to prevent any of us finishing life in this sad way?

❈ Henry James ❈

Henry James (1843–1916) was an eminent American novelist, short-story writer, and critic. Born in New York City, he spent a roving youth in America and Europe. His first novels were on the impact of American life on the older European civilization. From 1876, he himself lived in England. The acknowledged master of the psychological novel, he wrote his masterpieces Portrait of a Lady *in 1881 and* The Ambassadors *in 1903. The story from which the following reading is taken was written in 1873 after his second trip to Europe as an adult. It is the story of an American artist in Italy who never manages to paint the perfect madonna because of his perfectionism. In the passages below he is visited by a friend from the United States who breaks into his delusion.*

PERFECTIONISM SPELLS PARALYSIS

"If a thing is worth doing, it's worth doing badly."

—G. K. Chesterton

"The maxim, 'nothing avails but perfection,' spells paralysis."

—Winston Churchill

The Madonna of the Future ❧

"And what do you think of the divine Serafina?" he cried with fervor.

"It's certainly good solid beauty!"

He eyed me an instant askance, and then seemed hurried along by the current of remembrance. "You should have seen the mother and the child together, seen them as I first saw them—the mother with her head draped in a shawl, a divine trouble in her face, and the *bambino* pressed to her bosom. You would have said, I think, that Raphael had found his match in common chance. I was coming in, one summer night, from a long walk in the country, when I met this apparition at the city gate. The woman held out her hand. I hardly knew whether to say, 'What do you want?' or to fall down and worship. She asked for a little money. I saw that she was beautiful and pale. She might have stepped out of the stable of Bethlehem! I gave her money and helped her on her way into the town. I had guessed her story. She, too, was a maiden mother, and she had been turned out into the world in her shame. I felt in all my pulses that here was my subject marvelously realized. I felt like one of the old convent artists who had had a vision. I rescued them, cherished them, watched them as I would have done some precious work of art, some lovely fragment of fresco discovered in a moldering cloister. In a month—as if to deepen and consecrate the pathos of it all—the poor little child died. When she felt that he was going, she held him up to me for ten minutes, and I made that sketch. You saw a feverish haste in it, I suppose; I wanted to spare the poor little mortal the pain of his position. After that, I doubly valued the mother. She is the simplest, sweetest, most natural creature that ever bloomed in this brave old land of Italy. She lives in the memory of her child, in her gratitude for the scanty kindness I have been able to show her, and in her simple religion! She's not even conscious of her beauty; my admiration has never made her vain. Heaven knows I've made no secret of it. You must have observed the singular transparency of her expression, the lovely modesty of her glance. And was there ever such a truly virginal brow, such a natural classic elegance in the wave of the hair and the arch of the forehead? I've studied her; I may say I know her. I've absorbed her little by little; my mind is stamped and imbued, and I have determined now to clinch the impression; I shall at last invite her to sit for me!"

"'At last—at last'?" I repeated, in much amazement. "Do you mean that she has never done so yet?"

"I've not really had—a—a sitting," said Theobald, speaking very slowly. "I've taken notes, you know; I've got my grand fundamental impression. That's the great thing! But I've not actually had her as a model, posed and draped and lighted, before my easel."

What had become for the moment of my perception and my tact I am at a loss to say; in their absence, I was unable to repress a piece of *brusquerie* which I was destined to regret. We had stopped at a turning, beneath a lamp. "My poor friend," I exclaimed, laying my hand on his shoulder, "you've *dawdled*! She's an old, old woman—for a Madonna!"

It was as if I had brutally struck him; I shall never forget the long, slow, almost ghastly look of pain with which he answered me. "Dawdled—old, old!" he stammered. "Are you joking?"

"Why my dear fellow, I suppose you don't take the woman for twenty?"

He drew a long breath and leaned against a house, looking at me with

"I rescued them, cherished them, watched them as I would have done some precious work of art, some lovely fragment of fresco discovered in a moldering cloister."
—THEOBALD

questioning, protesting, reproachful eyes. At last, starting forward, and grasping my arm: "Answer me solemnly: does she seem to you truly old? Is she wrinkled, is she faded, am I blind?"

Then at last I understood the immensity of his illusion; how, one by one, the noiseless years had ebbed away and left him brooding in charmed inaction, forever preparing for a work forever deferred. It seemed to me almost a kindness now to tell him the plain truth. "I should be sorry to say you're blind," I answered, "but I think you're deceived. You've lost time in effortless contemplation. Your friend was once young and fresh and virginal; but, I protest, that was some years ago. Still, she has *beaux restes*. By all means make her sit for you!" I broke down; his face was too horribly reproachful.

He took off his hat and stood passing his handkerchief mechanically over his forehead. "*De beaux restes*? I thank you for sparing me the plain English. I must make up my Madonna out of *beaux restes*! What a masterpiece she'll be! Old—old! Old—old!" he murmured.

"Never mind her age," I cried, revolted at what I had done, "never mind my impression of her! You have your memory, your notes, your genius. Finish your picture in a month. I proclaim it beforehand a masterpiece, and I hereby offer you for it any sum you may choose to ask."

He stared, but he seemed scarcely to understand me. "Old—old!" he kept stupidly repeating. "If she is old, what am I? If her beauty has faded, where— where is my strength? Has life been a dream? Have I worshiped too long—have I loved too well?" The charm, in truth, was broken. That the chord of illusion should have snapped at my light, accidental touch showed how it had been weakened by excessive tension. The poor fellow's sense of wasted time, of vanished opportunity, seemed to roll in upon his soul in waves of darkness. He suddenly dropped his head and burst into tears.

I led him homeward with all possible tenderness, but I attempted neither to check his grief, to restore his equanimity, nor to unsay the hard truth. When we reached my hotel, I tried to induce him to come in. "We'll drink a glass of wine," I said, smiling, "to the completion of the Madonna!"

With a violent effort he held up his head, mused for a moment with a formidably somber frown, and then giving me his hand, "I'll finish it," he cried, "in a month! No, in a fortnight! After all, I have it *here*!" and he tapped his forehead. "Of course she's old! She can afford to have it said of her—a woman who has made twenty years pass like a twelvemonth! Old—old! Why, sir, she shall be eternal!"

I wished to see him safely to his own door, but he waved me back and walked away with an air of resolution, whistling and swinging his cane. I waited

Then at last I understood the immensity of his illusion; how, one by one, the noiseless years had ebbed away and left him brooding in charmed inaction, forever preparing for a work forever deferred.

"If she is old, what am I? If her beauty has faded, where—where is my strength? Has life been a dream? Have I worshiped too long— have I loved too well?"
—THEOBALD

a moment and then followed him at a distance and saw him proceed to cross the Santa Trinità Bridge. When he reached the middle, he suddenly paused, as if his strength had deserted him, and leaned upon the parapet, gazing over into the river. I was careful to keep him in sight; I confess that I passed ten very nervous minutes. He recovered himself at last, and went his way, slowly and with hanging head. . . .

[After not seeing the artist Theobald for a month, the narrator finally finds out where he lives and goes to visit him.]

It was in an obscure corner of the opposite side of the town, and presented a sombre and squalid appearance. An old woman in the doorway, on my inquiring for Theobald, ushered me in with a mumbled blessing and an expression of relief that the poor gentleman had a friend. His lodging seemed to consist of a single room at the top of the house. On getting no answer to my knock, I opened the door, supposing that he was absent; so that it gave me a certain shock to find him sitting there helpless and dumb. He was seated near the single window, facing an easel which supported a large canvas. On my entering, he looked up at me blankly, without changing his position, which was that of absolute lassitude and dejection, his arms loosely folded, his legs stretched before him, his head hanging on his breast. Advancing into the room, I perceived that his face vividly corresponded with his attitude. He was pale, haggard, and unshaven, and his dull and sunken eye gazed at me without a spark of recognition. I had been afraid that he would greet me with fierce reproaches, as the cruelly officious friend who had turned his peace to bitterness, and I was relieved to find that my appearance awakened no visible resentment. "Don't you know me?" I asked as I put out my hand. "Have you already forgotten me?"

He made no response, kept his position stupidly, and left me staring about the room. It spoke most plaintively for itself. Shabby, sordid, naked, it contained, beyond the wretched bed, but the scantiest provision for personal comfort. It was bedroom at once and studio—a grim ghost of a studio. A few dusty casts and prints on the walls, three or four old canvases turned face inward, and a rusty-looking color box formed, with the easel at the window, the sum of its appurtenances. The place savored horribly of poverty. Its only wealth was the picture on the easel, presumably the famous Madonna. Averted as this was from the door, I was unable to see its face; but at last, sickened by the vacant misery of the spot, I passed behind Theobald, eagerly and tenderly, and yet I can hardly say that I was surprised at what I found—a canvas that was a mere dead blank, cracked and discolored by time. This was his immortal work! But though not surprised, I confess I was powerfully moved, and I think that for five minutes

I could not have trusted myself to speak. At last, my silent nearness affected him; he stirred and turned, and then rose and looked at me with a slowly kindling eye. I murmured some kind, ineffective nothings about his being ill and needing advice and care, but he seemed absorbed in the effort to recall distinctly what had last passed between us. "You were right," he said with a pitiful smile, "I'm a dawdler! I'm a failure! I shall do nothing more in this world. You opened my eyes; and, though the truth is bitter, I bear you no grudge. Amen! I've been sitting here for a week, face to face with the truth, with the past, with my weakness and poverty and nullity. I shall never touch a brush! I believe I've neither eaten nor slept. Look at that canvas!" he went on, as I relieved my emotion in the urgent request that he would come home with me and dine. "That was to have contained my masterpiece! Isn't it a promising foundation? The elements of it are all here." And he tapped his forehead with that mystic confidence which had marked the gesture before. "If I could only transpose them into some brain that had the hand, the will! Since I've been sitting here taking stock of my intellects, I've come to believe that I have the material for a hundred masterpieces. But my hand is paralyzed now, and they'll never be painted. I never began! I waited and waited to be worthier to begin, and wasted my life in preparation. While I fancied my creation was growing, it was dying. I've taken it all too hard! Michelangelo didn't, when he went at the Lorenzo! He did his best at a venture, and his venture is immortal. *That's* mine!" And he pointed with a gesture I shall never forget at the empty canvas. "I suppose we're a genus by ourselves in the providential scheme—we talents that can't act, that can't do or dare! We take it out in talk, in plans and promises, in study, in visions! But our visions, let me tell you," he cried, with a toss of his head, "have a way of being brilliant, and a man hasn't lived in vain who has seen the things I have! Of course, you'll not believe in them when that bit of worm-eaten cloth is all I have to show for them, but to convince you, to enchant and astound the world, I need only the hand of Raphael. I have his brain. A pity, you'll say, I haven't his modesty. Ah, let me babble now; it's all I have left! I'm the half of a genius! Where in the wide world is my other half? Lodged perhaps in the vulgar soul, the cunning, ready fingers of some dull copyist or some trivial artisan who turns out by the dozen his easy prodigies of touch! But it's not for me to sneer at him; he at least does something. He's not a dawdler! Well for me if I had been vulgar and clever and reckless, if I could have shut my eyes and dealt my stroke!"

"I never began! I waited and waited to be worthier to begin, and wasted my life in preparation. While I fancied my creation was growing, it was dying."
—THEOBALD

From Henry James, "The Madonna of the Future," (London, MacMillian & Co., 1873).

COMING TO TERMS

"During the case nothing could stop him saying 'the King' and, on addressing him, 'Sire.' A member of the Convention said to Malesherbes, 'What makes you so bold?' 'Contempt for life,' he replied."

—Simone de Beauvoir, on Malesherbes,
age 72, the defender of King Louis XVI
at his trial during the French Revolution, 1792

"George Simmel records that one day Rodin had seen Rilke, who was in Paris for a visit, and had confessed, 'haltingly and in a tone of embarrassment, that today he had thought for the first time about death. And he spoke about dying, in the most primal and almost childish terms; dying as something incomprehensible: "*Pour-quoi laisser tout ça*—Why leave all this?"'"

—Frederic V. Grunfeld, *Rodin*

"No longer in Lethean foliage caught
Begin the preparation for your death
And from the fortieth winter by that thought
Test every work of intellect or faith,
And everything that your own hands have wrought,
And call those works extravagance of breath
That are not suited for such men as come
Proud, open-eyed and laughing to the tomb."

—W. B. Yeats, "Vacillation,"
written at age 67

"Old, am I? In absolute terms, yes, if I am to believe the registry office, long-sightedness, greying at the temples, and grown-up children. Last week, for the first time, somebody gave up their seat for me in a tram, and that felt really funny. Subjectively, I don't feel old. I haven't lost my curiosity in the world around me, or my interest in my family and friends, or my taste for fighting, playing, and problem-solving. I still enjoy nature; it brings perceptible pleasures to my five senses, and I love to study it, and describe it with words. My organs, limbs, and memory still serve me well, although I am very aware of the grave implications of that word that I have just written but that I have uttered twice: 'still.'"

—Primo Levi, after celebrating his sixtieth birthday, in *La Stampa*

"It's a long, long while from May to December
And the days grow short when you reach September."

—"September Song," Maxwell Anderson and Kurt Weill, 1938

"At my age, why should I be afraid to make public protests along with Stokely Carmichael?"

—pediatrician Dr. Benjamin Spock, age 80,
on his indictment for protesting the Vietnam war, 1968

QUESTIONS FOR THOUGHT AND DISCUSSION

1. In his retelling of his meeting Serafina, how does Theobold describe his reaction in first seeing the young mother and child?

2. What strikes you about his comments, "I've studied her; I may say I know her. I've absorbed her little by little; my mind is stamped and imbued"? What do you think held Theobald back from attempting to paint "The Madonna"?

3. What does Theobald mean when he asks, "Have I worshiped too long—have I loved too well?"

4. How is it that someone can live in a dream world for years, but one "light accidental touch" can shatter the spell? What does this say about the power of others in our lives? About the strength of our illusions? Do you think Theobald really had no idea that he had "dawdled" and that his revered subject was now "old, old"? Why or why not?

5. How does the narrator find Theobald next? Why is it that, even now, he cannot paint from memory?

6. What does Theobald mean by "I waited and waited to be worthier to begin"? Why couldn't he transfer what was in his brain to his hand? Do you think he did not have the talent? What was he missing? Do you think it would be better to be "vulgar and reckless" or to have a head full of masterpieces? Why?

7. What do you find most compelling in James's description of this pathetic man paralyzed by his illusions?

8. How can you tell the difference in practice between the constructive inspiration of an ideal and the destructiveness of perfectionism?

THE GREATEST BOOK NEVER WRITTEN

"O, that is the painter who scrapes out every day what he painted the day before."
—a stranger to W. B. Yeats, talking of his father, John Butler Yeats

"He is never satisfied and can never make himself say that any picture is finished."
—W. B. Yeats, writing of his artist father

"Lord Acton would poignantly refer to his unfinished lifework—a history of liberty—as 'The Madonna of the Future'"
—Gertrude Himmelfarb, *Lord Acton*

"His history of liberty has been described as 'the greatest book never written'"
—Gertrude Himmelfarb, *Lord Acton*

❧ *Arianna Huffington* ❧

Arianna Stassinopoulos Huffington (born 1950) is a writer, biographer, journalist, and society hostess. Born in Greece, she was educated at Cambridge before coming to live in the United States. The passage below is from her best-selling biography, Picasso: Creator and Destroyer. *It captures well the drivenness of a man unable to rest, even in his nineties.*

I WORK, THEREFORE I AM

"All old people cling to life more than children and they leave it with less good will, a poorer grace. The reason is that all their labor has been directed towards this same life of theirs, and at its end they see that theirs was labor lost."

—Jean-Jacques Rousseau, *Rêveries*

A friend once said to Winston Churchill that there was something to be said for being a *retired* Roman Emperor. "Why retired?" Churchill growled. "There's nothing to be said for retiring from anything."

"The spirit falls into boredom when it has no goal left, when it is a prey to leisure."

—André Gide, 1941

"The future is the only transcendence known to an atheist."

—philosopher Roger Garaudy

"He was a very conscious genius. He had a compelling drive to be a genius all the time, and as far as he was concerned, nothing compared in importance to what he had to do."

—Françoise Gilot, Picasso's mistress, on Picasso

"Picasso was like a conqueror, marching through life, accumulating power, women, wealth, glory, but none of that was very satisfying anymore."

—Françoise Gilot

"A guard at the bank where he stored many of his paintings had once told him how enviably different he was from so many other customers he had observed year in, year out, with the same woman, only older, while he was always with a new woman, each younger than the last. Picasso liked that. It was a way, he thought, of fooling destiny and death."

—Arianna Huffington, *Picasso*

"Life is but a struggle for existence fought with the certainty of being vanquished."
—Schopenhauer, quoted to Picasso by his mistress Marie-Thérèse

"When a man knows how to do something he ceases being a man when he stops doing it."
—Pablo Picasso, to a friend

"You know, you must never equate age with death. The one has nothing to do with the other."
—Pablo Picasso, repeated whenever he heard news
of another friend's death

"It is by the light of our projects that the world reveals itself; if they diminish so it grows poorer. Giving up our occupations does not mean reaching idle pleasures that they have deprived us of; it means depopulating the world by sterilizing the future."
—Simone de Beauvoir, *The Coming of Age*

"The reason why death fills us with anxiety is that it is the inescapable reverse of our projects: when a man is no longer active in any way, when he has ceased all undertakings, all plans, then there remains nothing that death can destroy."
—Simone de Beauvoir, *The Coming of Age*

"'I do worse every day,' he said in a rare moment of self-awareness. But he did not let that stand in his way: 'I have to work. . . . I have to keep going.'"
—Arianna Huffington, *Picasso*

"Few men have dared confront the spiritual void of living in an alien universe as starkly as he did. And in that void, all that was left was a relentless, demonic productivity. Occasionally, through falling 'in love,' through being a father, through camaraderie, there was a temporary reconciliation with life, but ultimately only in work was there release."
—Arianna Huffington, *Picasso*

Pablo Picasso ℞

On the day of the opening he was greatly amused by the thought of all the *other* painters flocking to the show instead of doing their own work, and of all the unpainted canvases he must have on his conscience as a result. And musing on the exhibition, he wondered what was the point of it all: "I really don't know why I let it happen. Basically, I'm against exhibitions and homages, as you know. Moreover, it is of no use to anyone. Painting, exhibiting—what's it all about?"

It was the question that set the tone of the last years of Picasso's life. He felt more and more like Sisyphus, condemned to roll his heavy stone up a hill, only to have it roll back as he reached the top—day after day. "Worst of all," he said, "is that he never finishes. There's never a moment when you can say, 'I've worked well and tomorrow is Sunday.' As soon as you stop, it's because you've started again. You can put a picture aside and say you won't touch it again. But you can never write THE END."

Against his growing sense of futility and waste he could only pit more work, more and more frenzied, faster and faster, coarser and coarser. He was still recovering from an attack of hepatitis when, in December 1966, he started painting again. His work was suddenly invaded by soldiers—seventeenth-century soldiers that he named musketeers and that had come to him when, during his fallow period, he spent a lot of time studying Rembrandt. "When things were going well," Jacqueline said, "he would come down from the studio saying, 'They're still coming! They're still coming!'"

"You would think," someone was quoted as saying, "he is trying to do a few more centuries of work in what he has left to live." He had already enclosed the terrace and turned it into an additional studio, having complained that he no longer had enough room to paint in: "The house is full of paintings, everywhere. They breed like rabbits!" Zervos kept arriving to photograph whatever he produced—paintings, drawings, etchings. "It's like going to the movies—or to a bullfight," he said. Jacqueline and the rest of the court seemed convinced that there was greatness in numbers.

But what did *he* think? "The more time passed," Parmelin said, "the more concerned he was to protect his work and to achieve finally the painting he dreamed of—*the* painting of which he had been dreaming all his life." And Otero wrote later, "Picasso has been painting at the rate of two canvases a day." But quantity and speed and ingenuity and prodigiousness and all the other easy yardsticks of achievement were of no relevance to the ultimate painting he longed for. That he knew. Perhaps he hoped that the more he painted, the greater the chances that he might stumble on it. White canvases had become a source of reproach to him. "What could I do?" he said once after he had turned away a party of Andalusians from Malaga who had come to visit him. "I would have liked to see them—but how? You know, two months ago Jacqueline bought sixty canvases from a paint supplier who was going out of

"Worst of all," he said, "is that he never finishes. There's never a moment when you can say, 'I've worked well and tomorrow is Sunday.'"

"The more time passed," Parmelin said, "the more concerned he was to protect his work and to achieve finally the painting he dreamed of— the painting of which he had been dreaming all his life."

business. Well, there are still eleven canvases unpainted, absolutely blank!"

Famished for real nourishment, he voraciously devoured the canvases Jacqueline kept feeding him. Work had become his only source of satisfaction, and the more unsatisfactory it was, the more, like an addict, he went back for bigger and bigger doses. "I have only one thought: work," he said. "I paint just as I breathe. When I work, I relax; not doing anything or entertaining visitors makes me tired." Sartre had said, "Hell is other people," and Picasso paraphrased his wartime friend: "I suffer from people's presence, not from their absence." And later, "I despise wasting my time with people. Not only now, but ever since I can remember."

As work gradually took over his whole being and everything else was starved out, he seemed further away both from humanity and from the ultimate painting, which he even tried to describe: "The extraordinary would be to make with absolutely no constraints a picture that would incorporate itself into reality. . . . The opposite of a photograph. . . . A painting that contained everything of a particular woman and yet would not look like anything known about her." The closest he would ever come during his last years to capturing the invisible in painting was in words. . . .

> *"The extraordinary would be to make with absolutely no constraints a picture that would incorporate itself into reality."*
> —PABLO PICASSO

Picasso mourned his old studio, in which he had not set foot for twelve years, longer and more volubly than he had ever mourned a friend. His need to feel and express affection sought refuge in the past, and not in the people of his past but in the places. "What one *will* do is more interesting than what one has already done," he had said in the rue des Grands-Augustins days. He tried frantically to act as though that were still true, but the urgency was born of futility rather than passion. . . .

Picasso was sick. And the couples that filled his work in 1969, kissing, copulating, and suffocating each other, bore the stamp of his sickness. His body was a sack of ills and frustrated desires. The body that had for so long served him so well had turned against him. He could not see well, he could not hear well, his lungs fought for breath, his limbs fought for the strength to sustain him, and he fought for the unconsciousness of sleep. But a sickness much more frightening than the inevitable sicknesses of a man close to ninety was the soul-sickness of a man close to death and utterly disconnected from the source of life, a man staring at death and seeing his own fearful imaginings.

> *But a sickness much more frightening than the inevitable sicknesses of a man close to ninety was the soul-sickness of a man close to death and utterly disconnected from the source of life, a man staring at death and seeing his own fearful imaginings.*

From Arianna Stassinopoulos Huffington, *Picasso: Creator and Destroyer* (New York: Simon & Schuster, 1988), pp. 453–457. © Arianna Huffington 1988. Reprinted with permission of Simon & Schuster.

NO TIME TO SMELL THE ROSES

"Nobody running at full speed has either a head or a heart."

—W. B. Yeats, *Autobiographies*

"To accomplish what I had set out to do, I had to put blinders on. My life's dream was at stake! And I was determined to stop at nothing to turn that dream into a reality. Nothing. Only later, much later, did I come to see how my tunnel vision, my steamrolling personality, and my total commitment to wine, wine, wine, ended up inflicting terrible pain on Marge, the children, and some of the people working closest to me. The truth is, I was oblivious to the impact of my ways until it was too late to undo the damage. . . .

". . . So even by the time I was in my fifties and early sixties, I knew next to nothing about art or music, literature or medicine. Philosophy, spirituality, the inner life: these too were alien to me. I rarely read books; I didn't have the time or inclination. I was too busy building my business and pursuing my quest. That's one price, among many, that I paid for being so single-minded."

—Robert Mondavi, *Harvests of Joy*

QUESTIONS FOR THOUGHT AND DISCUSSION

1. What do you see as the components making up Picasso's drivenness? What areas of his life was it consuming?

2. What strikes you about the great painter's attitude toward his exhibition and other painters flocking to see it and not painting themselves?

3. What is the significance of the comparison to Sisyphus? What does Picasso mean by "There's never a moment when you can say, 'I've worked well and tomorrow is Sunday'"?

4. Why do you suppose Picasso's "growing sense of futility and waste" fed such a working frenzy? How did this affect his painting? What was he hoping to create?

5. What do you think was Picasso's "yardstick of achievement" at this point in his life?

6. Why do you think Picasso mourned his old studio and places of the past? Why were people not part of the memories? How would you describe the way he related to the world around him?

7. In what ways did his art of 1969 reflect both his physical illnesses and "soul-sickness"? Of what do you think he was afraid?

8. How would you compare the work of Picasso's final days to Theobald's Madonna?

9. What are the differences between being "called" and being "driven"?

John Pollock

William Wilberforce was introduced earlier in part 2. John Pollock, his most eminent biographer, describes here his final months when the theme of finishing well is clear and strong.

"LITTLE LIBERATOR" TO THE END

"His last surviving great-grandson, who was then over a hundred and blind, told me how his father as a small boy was walking with Wilberforce on a hill near Bath when they saw a poor carthorse being cruelly whipped by the carter as he struggled to pull a load of stone up the hill. The little liberator expostulated with the carter who began to swear at him and tell him to mind his own business, and so forth. Suddenly the carter stopped and said, 'Are you Mr. Wilberforce? . . . Then I will never beat my horse again!'"

—John Pollock,
A Man Who Changed His Times

"I had never thought to appear in public again, but it shall never be said that William Wilberforce is silent while the slaves require his help."

—opening words of his last public speech,
three months before his death in 1833, aged 73

William Wilberforce: The Path to the Abbey ❧

Sydney Smith, whose writings in the *Edinburgh Review* had often attacked the "patient Christians of Clapham," wrote to Lady Holland: "Little Wilberforce is here, and we are great friends. He looks like a little spirit running about without a body, or in a kind of undress with only half a body." . . .

"In truth I have entirely done with politics," Wilberforce replied to [Lord Chancellor] Brougham on 28 April 1831. He could not read a newspaper. Joseph his amanuensis had insisted on staying at half salary, though eventually agreeing to go to Stephen when Wilberforce cut down yet further, but the tedium of being read the news was often too much. His general sympathy at this time of crisis lay with Reform, partly because "it is my decided opinion that if Lord John Russell's Bill should pass without any great alteration it will, *Deo volente* [God willing], produce a House of Commons far more favourable than we now have, to the cause of West Indian reform."

Only Slavery and the Slave Trade could excite him to "internal heat," as he expressed it to Buxton. When unable to attend the Anti-Slavery Society's 1831 meeting he sent his best wishes and fervent prayers. "Our Motto must continue to be *perseverance*. And ultimately I trust the Almighty will crown our efforts with success." A year later he urged [Thomas Fowell] Buxton not to allow another delaying enquiry which the West India lobby demanded. The Anti-Slavery cause now split between the cautious, led by ancients such as Macaulay and [James] Stephen, "our worthy efficient, indefatigable old labourer or warrior shall I term him"; and impatients, led by Stephen's youngest son George. Wilberforce and Stephen senior shook their heads sadly and feared the youngsters would ruin the cause which, in fact, they hustled to its triumph.

Stephen now lay dying at his country house in Chilterns. "Our poor friend is a very great sufferer," Wilberforce told Macaulay in August 1832. "Entre nous, his spirits are greatly affected." The Wilberforces persuaded him to try Bath. He died there in October. Wilberforce, whose imminent decease had been expected again and again since 1788, lived on.

. . . On 1 January 1833 Wilberforce wrote a letter in a rather unsteady hand at [his son] Robert's vicarage in East Farleigh, only a mile from Barham Court where, so long ago, he had discussed with the Middletons their insistence that he should take up the cause of Africa. The Admiral's grandson, one of Wilberforce's most devoted disciples, now lived there.

The letter, to Samuel Roberts in Sheffield, ended: "I must not lay down my pen without informing you at length after all our disappointments, I am confidently looking forward to the fulfillment of our long offered prayers for the oppressed and much injured sons and daughters of Africa." He had been looking at the printed evidence of a Commons Committee on the subject and considered it irresistible; every fair-minded man must agree "that the danger of refusing or even of delaying the Emancipation of the Slaves is far greater than that which is to be apprehended from granting—" He broke off in mid sentence as his man entered to say the letter must go at once to the post office.

Wilberforce saw as a wonderful providence the probability that he would live long enough to see the slaves set free. And he reflected in wonder too at the providence which had led him in his last years to live at east Farleigh and

"Our Motto must continue to be perseverance. *And ultimately I trust the Almighty will crown our efforts with success."*
—WILLIAM WILBERFORCE

Brightstone. Far from whining at his losses, he found more cause for praise than ever. . . .

During the spring of 1833 a wave of popular agitation pushed Anti-Slavery forward. Wilberforce signed the local petition and insisted on attending Maidstone's public meeting and even made a short speech, his last. He sent private encouragement to Buxton, though "my mind is in such a state of bustle and confusion that I scarcely know what I am writing." On the night that Buxton moved for immediate Emancipation someone at the East Farleigh dinner table casually mentioned that the debate must now be starting. Wilberforce sprang from his chair and in a voice loud enough to startle, cried "Hear, hear, hear."

He had been weakened by a bout of influenza that winter, and his chest still gave trouble when he and Barbara moved to Sam's in late April. In mid-May, therefore, they went to Bath for the waters. Henry joined them. One week later the new Colonial Secretary, Lord Stanley, introduced the Government's resolutions for ending Slavery. Wilberforce heard from Macaulay: "Last night its death blow was struck. Stanley's allusion to you was quite overpowering and electrified the House."

To Wilberforce it was far away in the dimness of his fading sight, but vivid to his imagination. He objected especially to Stanley's Apprenticeship proposal, whereby the emancipated slaves would work for nothing for a number of years. "Get rid of the Apprenticeship system," he wrote to Buxton on 11 June. Buxton came under severe pressure in the House, as old William Smith described, to whom Wilberforce replied on 25 June: "I cannot bear remaining silent when you touch on a string which vibrates in my inmost soul. . . . Do go to Buxton and say from me all that is affectionate. Future ages will justly regard the work as a grand national victory over wickedness and cruelty." He added after the signature: "You will be sorry to hear I am seriously ill. But thank God suffering very little pain."

. . . The Wilberforces reached London with Henry on 19 July and stayed at the house of cousin Lucy Smith, 44 Cadogan Place off Sloane Street. Parliament still sat, to dispose of the Abolition of Slavery Bill. The Commons were debating the second reading.

Dr. Chambers considered Wilberforce less ill than was feared and hoped to get him into the country after a short rest. Each morning Wilberforce took the air in a wheelchair for ten minutes before family prayers and breakfast at ten, and then received friends on a sofa in a back room while Barbara fussed complainingly, keeping some of them out and shooing others away when he began to tire. On 25 July young William Ewart Gladstone, M.P. "went to breakfast with old Mr. Wilberforce—heard him pray with his family. Blessing and honour are upon his head." Gladstone then went down to the House to speak and vote on the planter side.

Wilberforce remained alert and full of talk about things in heaven and things on earth. He seemed to be getting better. Late on Friday, 26 July he heard that the Abolition of Slavery had passed its Third Reading in the Commons. Passage through the Lords being not in doubt, Slavery as a legal state was to all intents dead—at a price. "Thank God," said Wilberforce "that I have lived to witness a day in which England is willing to give twenty millions sterling for the Abolition of Slavery." Tom Macaulay, fresh from the house, saw how he "excelled in the success which we obtained . . . as much as the youngest and most ardent partisan could have done."

Macaulay found him lively and cheerful. On the Saturday he suddenly tired, though when his mind worked it was tranquil and contented. On the Sunday he suffered fainting fits and sank rapidly.

Late that night he stirred, and Barbara and Henry heard him murmur, with apparent reference to his body, "I am in a very distressed state." "Yes," said Henry, "but you have your feet on the Rock." The old humility asserted itself. "I do not venture to speak so positively. But I hope I have."

At 3 a.m. on Monday morning, 29 July 1833, he knew.

Within hours of the announcement of Wilberforce's death two letters signed by the Duke of Gloucester, the Lord Chancellor, and as many peers and Members of the House of Commons as could be reached hurriedly, asked the family to permit burial in Westminster Abbey. On Saturday, 3 August while thousands of Londoners wore mourning, Wilberforce's coffin entered the Abbey. Two royal dukes, the Lord Chancellor, the Speaker, and four peers supported the Pall. Members of both Houses walked in the procession.

"The attendance was very great," recorded a Member of Parliament in his diary that night. "The funeral itself with the exception of the Choir of the Abbey perfectly plain. The noblest and most fitting testimony to the estimation of the man."

From John Pollock, *William Wilberforce* (Kingsway, 1977). Reprinted by permission of the author.

TERMINATION DAY

"It is a singular fact that on the very night on which we were successfully engaged in the House of Commons, in passing the clause of the Act of Emancipation—one of the most important clauses ever enacted . . . the spirit of our friend left the world. The day which was the termination of his labours was the termination of his life."

—Thomas Fowell Buxton,
Wilberforce's successor in leading the campaign

QUESTIONS FOR THOUGHT AND DISCUSSION

1. Wilberforce told Brougham, "In truth I have entirely done with politics." What effect did being "entirely done" have on his sense of calling? How was he involved in the battle against slavery?

2. How does Wilberforce's motto explain the "ancients'" cautious stance toward anti-slavery? What does this say about their desire for success— both personal and corporate?

3. Why was Wilberforce—a sick, old man who was expected to die soon—so confident he would see slavery abolished? What was his attitude toward his sickness and the end of life? Do you think he could have died satisfied if abolition had not happened in his lifetime? Why or why not?

4. What were his relationships like at this point in his life?

5. Compare Wilberforce's "perseverance" with Picasso's drivenness. How would you describe their outlook on their respective goals?

6. What do you find most moving in this description of Wilberforce's last months?

7. How would you like your life and accomplishments to be summed up?

On the next page is the text of the epitaph on Wilberforce's memorial in Westminster Abbey, London.

TO THE MEMORY OF

WILLIAM WILBERFORCE

(BORN IN HULL AUGUST 24TH 1759,
DIED IN LONDON JULY 29TH 1833;)
FOR NEARLY HALF A CENTURY A MEMBER OF THE HOUSE OF COMMONS,
AND, FOR SIX PARLIAMENTS DURING THAT PERIOD,
ONE OF THE TWO REPRESENTATIVES FOR YORKSHIRE.

IN AN AGE AND COUNTRY FERTILE IN GREAT AND GOOD MEN,
HE WAS AMONG THE FOREMOST OF THOSE WHO FIXED THE CHARACTER OF THEIR TIMES
BECAUSE TO HIGH AND VARIOUS TALENTS
TO WARM BENEVOLENCE, AND TO UNIVERSAL CANDOUR,
HE ADDED THE ABIDING ELOQUENCE OF A CHRISTIAN LIFE.

EMINENT AS HE WAS IN EVERY DEPARTMENT OF PUBLIC LABOUR,
AND A LEADER IN EVERY WORK OF CHARITY,
WHETHER TO RELIEVE THE TEMPORAL OR THE SPIRITUAL WANTS OF HIS FELLOW MEN
HIS NAME WILL EVER BE SPECIALLY IDENTIFIED
WITH THOSE EXERTIONS
WHICH, BY THE BLESSING OF GOD, REMOVED FROM ENGLAND
THE GUILT OF THE AFRICAN SLAVE TRADE,
AND PREPARED THE WAY FOR THE ABOLITION OF SLAVERY
IN EVERY COLONY OF THE EMPIRE:

IN THE PROSECUTION OF THESE OBJECTS,
HE RELIED, NOT IN VAIN, ON GOD;
BUT IN THE PROGRESS, HE WAS CALLED TO ENDURE
GREAT OBLOQUY AND GREAT OPPOSITION:
HE OUTLIVED, HOWEVER, ALL ENMITY:
AND, IN THE EVENING OF HIS DAYS,
WITHDREW FROM PUBLIC LIFE AND PUBLIC OBSERVATION
TO THE BOSOM OF HIS FAMILY.
YET HE DIED NOT UNNOTICED OR FORGOTTEN BY HIS COUNTRY:
THE PEERS AND COMMONS OF ENGLAND,
WITH THE LORD CHANCELLOR, AND THE SPEAKER, AT THEIR HEAD,
CARRIED HIM TO HIS FITTING PLACE
AMONG THE MIGHTY DEAD AROUND,
HERE TO REPOSE:
TILL, THROUGH THE MERITS OF JESUS CHRIST,
HIS ONLY REDEEMER AND SAVIOUR,
(WHOM, IN HIS LIFE AND IN HIS WRITINGS HE HAD DESIRED TO GLORIFY,)
HE SHALL RISE IN THE RESURRECTION OF THE JUST.

George MacDonald

George MacDonald (1824–1905) is among the world's greatest writers of fantasy. He is deeply influential on the world of English-speaking faith because, through his writing, he became mentor to C. S. Lewis and G. K. Chesterton, among several others. Born in Huntly, Scotland, he was a graduate of King's College, Aberdeen, and became the minister of a small dissenting chapel in Arundel, Sussex in 1850. Resigning two years later after disagreements with the deacons, he embarked on a precarious life of lecturing, tutoring, occasional preaching, writing, and "odd jobs"—often fighting lung disease and living on the verge of starvation.

George MacDonald is not usually reckoned to be in the first rank of writers, except in his fantasies and myth-making. (C. S. Lewis: "MacDonald is the greatest genius of this kind whom I know.") But though an average novelist, he was not only a master fantasist but a superb preacher whose Unspoken Sermons have had an extraordinary impact on Lewis and many others.

The following passage comes from his sermon "The New Name" (on Revelation 2:17). It makes a piercing and somewhat haunting point that stands in stark contrast to the fashionable modern notion that discerning our "giftedness and calling" and fulfilling "the real you" is a simple and straightforward matter. As with our identities themselves, our callings will always be partly a mystery until God himself gives us our names and we realize what he has had in mind for us all along.

As with our identities themselves, our callings will always be partly a mystery until God himself gives us our names and we realize what he has had in mind for us all along.

TRUE IDENTITY

"He who has an ear, let him hear what the Spirit says to the churches. To him who overcomes, I will give some of the hidden manna. I will also give him a white stone with a new name written on it, known only to him who receives it."

—Jesus, in Revelation 2:17

"When a person is having a fainting fit and is in danger of wasting away, it is advisable to whisper his name into his ear, because his name has the power to call a person back to life."

—Abraham J. Heschel, *A Passion for Truth*

The New Name ❧

The giving of the white stone with the new name is the communication of what God thinks about the man to the man. It is the divine judgment, the solemn holy doom of the righteous man, the "Come, thou blessed," spoken to the individual. . . .

The true name is one which expresses the character, the nature, the *meaning* of the person who bears it. It is the man's own symbol—his soul's picture, in a word—the sign which belongs to him and to no one else. Who can give a man this, his own name? God alone. For no one but God sees what the man is. . . .

It is only when the man has become his name that God gives him the stone with the name upon it, for then first can he understand what his name signifies. It is the blossom, the perfection, the completeness, that determines the name: and God foresees that from the first because He made it so: but the tree of the soul, before its blossom comes, cannot understand what blossom it is to bear and could not know what the word meant, which, in representing its own unarrived completeness, named itself. Such a name cannot be given until the man is the name. God's name for a man must be the expression of His own idea of the man, that being whom He had in His thought when he began to make the child, and whom He kept in His thought through the long process of creation that went to realise the idea. To tell the name is to seal the success—to say "In thee also I am well pleased."

> *The true name is one which expresses the character, the nature, the* meaning *of the person who bears it.*

> *It is only when the man has become his name that God gives him the stone with the name upon it, for then first can he understand what his name signifies.*

From *George MacDonald: Unspoken Sermons: Series One* (London: Alexander Strachan, 1889).

LAST CALL

"The voyage of my life at last has reached,
across tempestuous sea, in fragile boat
the common port all must pass through to give
cause and account of every evil, every pious deed."

—Michelangelo,
one of his last "Sonnets of Renunciation"

"After this, it was noised abroad, that Mr. *Valiant-for-Truth* was taken with a summons by the same post as the other; and had this for a token that the summons was true, *That his pitcher was broken at the fountain.* When he understood it, he called for his friends, and told them of it. Then, said he, I am going to my Father's, and tho' with great difficulty I am got hither, yet now I do not repent me of all the trouble I have been at to arrive where I am. *My Sword* I give to him that shall succeed me in my Pilgrimage, and my *Courage* and *Skill* to him that can get it. My *marks* and *scars* I carry with me, to be a witness for me, that I have fought His battles, who now will be my Rewarder. When the day that he must go hence was come, many accompany'd him to the River-side, into which as he went, he said, *Death, where is thy Sting?* And as he went down deeper, he said, *Grave, where is thy Victory?* So he passed over, and all the Trumpets sounded for him on the other side."

—John Bunyan, *The Pilgrim's Progress*

"Nothing that is worth doing can be achieved in our lifetime; therefore, we must be saved by hope. Nothing which is true or beautiful or good makes complete sense in any immediate context of history; therefore, we must be saved by faith. Nothing we do, however virtuous, can be accomplished alone; therefore, we are saved by love. No virtuous act is quite as virtuous from the standpoint of our friend or foe as it is from our standpoint. Therefore we must be saved by the final form of love, which is forgiveness."

—Reinhold Niebuhr

QUESTIONS FOR THOUGHT AND DISCUSSION

1. How does George MacDonald view the link between one's "true name" and one's nature? How does God's naming a person give him or her meaning?

2. What does he mean by "the solemn holy doom of the righteous man"? How would this be on par with "Come, thou blessed"?

3. Read the sentence, "It is only when the man has become his name. . ." What is MacDonald saying? What do you think? When would this be in a person's life?

4. What is the connection between God naming us—"the communication of what God thinks about man to man"—and one's calling? Why is it that only God can crown our callings with his name for us?

5. In the light of this passage, what do you think of the modern notion that gifts and calling can be specified and assessed easily?

6. What does this view of "becoming our names" mean for our sense of our own "giftedness" and "leaving a legacy"?

FOR FURTHER READING

For those who desire to read further on the foundational concepts introduced here, the following is a short list of books that are both helpful and accessible.

Dietrich Bonhoeffer, *The Cost of Discipleship* (New York: Simon & Schuster, 1995).

Os Guinness, *The Call: Finding and Fulfilling the Central Purpose for Your Life* (Nashville: Word, 1998).

Garth Lean, *God's Politician* (Colorado Springs: Helmers & Howard, 1987). This is a gripping account of William Wilberforce's struggle to abolish the slave trade and reform morality in Britain.

Arthur F. Miller and Ralph T. Mattson, *The Truth About You* (Berkeley, California: Ten Speed Press, 1989). This book is designed to help people discover what motivates them and, from there, what they do best.

Aleksandr Solzhenitsyn, *The Oak and the Calf: Sketches of Literary Life in the Soviet Union* (London: HarperCollins, 1975).

Dallas Willard, *The Divine Conspiracy: Rediscovering Our Hidden Life in God* (San Francisco: HarperCollins, 1998).

For a catalog of our publications, please contact The Trinity Forum, 7902 Westpark Drive, Suite A, McLean, VA 22102. We also accept orders online at www.ttf.org.

READER'S GUIDE:

Using This Book in a Discussion Group

THE FOLLOWING SMALL GROUP GUIDE OFFERS A FORMAT FOR LEADING EIGHT NINETY-minute discussions of *Entrepreneurs of Life*. Ideally, participants will read about thirty pages of the book before each group meeting. However, it's possible for people to participate even if they have not had time to read the material beforehand.

The goals of this discussion group are to help participants:

- Understand the Jewish and Christian concept of calling and how it differs from other views of a life purpose
- Appreciate the ups and downs of life as a journey, with a sense of calling providing unique benefits and challenges
- See examples of people whose sense of calling led them to make an enormous difference in the world
- Begin to assess where they are in life, identify the central purpose of their lives, and take some first steps toward fulfilling that purpose
- Know how to live as to finish life well

The eight group sessions break down as follows. The names listed are those of either the author of a reading or the person discussed in a biographical reading. In addition to the main readings marked here, you will sometimes discuss the short quotations that are scattered throughout the book.

1. The Ultimate Why: Buddhism and Secular Materialism (Introduction, Hesse, Rand)
2. The Ultimate Why, continued: The Jewish and Christian Tradition of Calling (Steiner, Bonhoeffer, Eusebius, Luther)

221

The Leader's Role

You don't need any special background in order to lead this discussion group effectively. The readings in this book include background information about the writers and their ideas. This reader's guide offers help in small-group leadership. The format of the group will be discussion, not lecture, so you will not be expected to teach or answer questions. Any background you have (in history, philosophy, political science, and so on) will enrich the group, but your knowledge will not be the group's focus.

Your role is:

- To begin and end the meeting on time
- To introduce each reading
- To ask people to read aloud key portions of each reading
- To keep the group moving from reading to reading at a reasonable pace
- To select the questions that are most important for the group to discuss
- To ask questions
- To listen closely to answers and ask follow-up questions as appropriate
- To express your opinions at appropriate moments
- To set a tone of respect and free exchange of ideas
- To make sure that everyone who wants to speak gets adequate air time
- To help the group keep track of the big picture that the readings are sketching

Beginning and ending on time is a way of respecting participants. Latecomers won't mind if you start without them, and doing so rewards those who come on time. Likewise, even if you're in the middle of a great discussion, people will thank you if you cut it off when the time is up. Those who need to leave can leave, and if your host permits, others can stay and continue the conversation informally.

Each reading is preceded by a brief introduction about the author and the context. As you come to each reading, begin by summarizing this introduction in a few sentences. Then, ask someone to read aloud a portion of the reading that relates to the first question you want to ask. (This guide will suggest portions to be read aloud.) Reading aloud and asking questions will set the rhythm of the discussion. Reading aloud refreshes everyone's memory and involves people who may not have read the material ahead of time. (However, be aware that some people are uncomfortable reading aloud. You may want to ask people ahead of time how they feel about doing so.)

After twenty minutes or so, summarize the discussion about that reading and introduce the next one.

Most groups function better with two cofacilitators than with one. It's helpful to take turns guiding discussions on the different readings, or to let one person guide the discussion while the other keeps track of the time.

The Group's Emphasis

Some small groups emphasize the sharing of personal experiences and feelings. Many don't challenge people to think deeply. This series addresses whole people, the understanding as well as the feeling parts of them. Your task is to help the group think, understand, and draw conclusions together. However, the conversation will not be banter about airy notions. The questions are designed to be practical. The issues raised are relevant to the nitty-gritty lives of each person in your group. Ideally, people will leave each meeting with new thoughts about what they do all day: conduct business, raise children, vote for lawmakers, relate to neighbors, spend money. And you may be surprised at how emotional these thoughtful discussions become as people's hearts are pierced with new perspectives on their lives.

The questions typically progress along the following lines:

- What's being said?
- Is it true?
- So what?

That is, you'll begin by identifying exactly what the writer of the given selection is trying to say. Then you'll have a chance to react to it. Some people like to jump to expressing their opinions before taking the time to understand clearly what the author is saying. If this happens, it will be your job to slow participants down and ask them to look first at the text. An essential group skill is *listening*—listening both to the other members of the group and to the author of the selection being discussed. To speak one's own opinion without listening to others long enough to understand them is to shortchange oneself and the whole group.

Each session is designed to take about ninety minutes. During that time you will discuss three or four readings from *Entrepreneurs of Life,* so you may have just twenty or thirty minutes for each one. Therefore, you won't have time to discuss all the questions listed in the book. It's not necessary to have an exhaustive discussion about any reading. Instead, you'll draw out the main points of each one so that group members can follow the inner logic that flows through the progression of readings. You won't have time to get bogged down in one reading because if you did, you would lose the thread of the big picture. Another benefit of keeping up the momentum is that in any given session, everyone is likely to find at least one of the readings especially meaningful to him or her personally. It is always better to cut off a good discussion than to drag it out until it dies.

This reader's guide will point out the questions for each reading that will be most helpful for group discussion. It will also trace the big picture from reading to reading so that you will have no trouble seeing where you're going. This guidance is meant to simplify your job. Nevertheless, you are still the group leader, so if you think your group will benefit most from questions other than those suggested here, follow your intuition. Instead of the pointed questions that follow each reading, you may prefer to use open-ended questions, such as, "What is your perspective, feeling, or reaction to this reading?"

The reader's guide contains no suggestions for worship, such as prayer or the singing of hymns. This format makes the group open to everyone, regardless of faith convictions.

Guiding the Discussion

Most groups depend heavily on the leader in the beginning. The leader asks a question, and someone answers. The leader asks another question, and someone answers. People direct their responses to the leader. However, an effective leader nudges participants toward talking to each other. The leader plays referee and timekeeper so that the group stays on track.

One tool for nudging people to talk to each other is the follow-up question. For instance, one type of follow-up question invites others' input: "What do others of you think about Terry's view?" Other kinds of follow-up questions include:

- Rephrasing the question
- Probing gently for more information ("Can you say more about that?")
- Asking for clarification ("So are you saying that . . . ?")
- Summarizing a portion of the discussion

You will probably want to summarize (or ask someone else to do so) at the end of your discussion of each reading. This will help people keep track of where each reading fits into the big picture.

Maintain eye contact with all participants, particularly those on your immediate left and right, so that everyone feels included in the discussion. It's a good idea to arrange the room in a circle before the meeting so that people will be able to see one another's faces.

Avoid answering your own questions. Allow silence, especially when people are looking at the readings to refresh their memories. If people seem not to understand your question, it's best to rephrase it, rather than answering it.

Also, avoid commenting on each participant's response. Instead, ask a follow-up question to draw out others' comments.

Encourage participants to ask questions about one another's comments. Your ultimate goal is to foster a lively discussion among participants about the point under discussion. However, if you sense that the conversation is drifting off the main point of the reading, summarize the comments that have been made and move on to a new question that builds toward the focus of the reading.

Dealing with Talkative and Quiet People

In any small group, some people are naturally more talkative than others. While it's desirable for everyone to participate aloud, it's not essential for this group. One of the ground rules (see page 232) is that everyone is welcome to speak, but no one is obliged to speak. There are several reasons why a person might be quiet during the meeting, and you'll want to assess which reasons apply to each of your quiet people. Reasons for quietness include the following:

- A person may be overwhelmed by the material and not be following the discussion. This person needs you to listen to his or her concerns outside the group meeting.
- A person may be processing the discussion internally. Some people prefer to digest ideas and feelings inside and speak only when they have thought through what they want to say. By contrast, other people think out loud. They often don't know what they think until it comes out of their mouths. It's possible that both the talkative and the quiet people are getting what they need in your group. Don't assume that silence equals nonparticipation.
- A person may strongly disagree with what is being said but may be uncomfortable with overt conflict. There are ways of handling covert conflict that strengthen the group (see page 227).
- A person may want to speak but feel intimidated by groups. It's usually best to draw such people out in conversation outside the formal discussion, but not to call attention to them during the meeting.

This is not an exhaustive list of reasons for quietness. The important thing is to gauge each person individually and ask yourself, "What might this person need?"

With people whom you think talk too much, knowing why they're talking is less important than assessing their effect on the group. Are the quieter people getting something out of what the talker is saying? Or are they wishing they were somewhere else? If you think someone's talking is excessive, there are several subtle ways to discourage it. You can sit next to the person rather than facing him or her. You can avoid making eye contact or nodding, since these are signals that the speaker should continue. In extreme cases, you can take the person aside after the meeting and enlist his or her help in drawing out the quieter group members.

Above all, take care that you are not the group member who talks too much. Keep the group focused on the readings, not on you. Resist the temptation to fill silence with your observations. Silence can be productive if people are thinking.

Disagreement and Conflict

In a discussion group of this kind, disagreement is good. *Tough-minded discussion* occurs when one person's ideas, conclusions, or opinions are incompatible with another's, and the two seek a deeper understanding of truth or wisdom together. Views are aired openly, and everyone has a chance to evaluate the merits of each position. Someone might even change his or her mind.

Debate occurs when people's ideas, conclusions, or opinions are incompatible; each person argues for his or her position; and a winner is declared. Debate is not necessarily bad in a group either. People may feel strongly that they are right and someone else is wrong. A strenuous defense of one's position is fair play.

Some ground rules can make tough-minded discussion and debate constructive:

- Genuine disagreement is an achievement because it enables people to learn. We assume that a disagreement is valuable until proven otherwise.
- Deepening our understanding of truth or wisdom is more important in this group than winning an argument.
- Respect is important in this group. The merits of a position may be debated, but persons may not be attacked.
- If people feel attacked, they will say so respectfully, and the group will assess the situation together.

Many people fear all forms of conflict, including tough-minded discussion and debate. If you have group members who are uncomfortable with conflict in the group, you may want to have a discussion about constructive conflict. Explain that while quarreling is unproductive, disagreement is not. Emphasize that *concurrence-seeking* is less productive than open controversy. Concurrence-seeking happens when group members inhibit discussion in order to avoid disagreement. Concurrence-seeking can lead to *groupthink,* in which everyone feels obliged to think alike and people cease to think for themselves. Religious versions of political correctness are not uncommon.

A certain amount of concurrence-seeking is natural in a group of people who don't know each other well. However, the more you can draw covert conflict out into the open, the less likely people are to withdraw from the group because of unvoiced dissatisfaction. If you sense people simmering but not speaking, the best course may be to give a short speech about the value of healthy disagreement and to state some ground rules for tough-minded discussion.

The Roadmap

Because you'll cover a lot of ground in each group session, you'll find it helpful to keep in mind the book's "roadmap." The readings have been arranged as a journey leading logically from point to point. Each reading contains many more interesting ideas than you have time to discuss, so you can avoid time-consuming side trips if you keep the roadmap or big picture in mind. The section entitled "For All Who Seek Significance" in the introduction (pages 18-20) summarizes the roadmap. Here is a more detailed summary that you might use to orient the group as you begin each session:

Entrepreneurs of Life is about finding and fulfilling our ultimate purpose in life. It's about responding to the call of God. God calls us to himself so decisively that everything we are, everything we do, and everything we have is invested with a special devotion and dynamism lived out in response to his summons. As philosopher Dallas Willard states, all of us have "a unique eternal calling to count for good in this great universe." The entrepreneur of life is the person who answers this call—who takes responsibility for a creative task as a venture of faith, including risk and danger, to count for good. Regardless of age or disability, and despite the many things we can't control, every living human has the capacity to count for good. *Entrepreneurs of Life* motivates us to find and do that good.

The notion of purpose through calling is rooted in Jewish and Christian ideas. Part 1 of this book contrasts this biblical view with the two alternate views that have been most influential historically. First, the novel *Siddhartha* by Hermann Hesse expresses the Eastern ideas that the search for purpose in an individual life is wrong-headed, that there is no personal God who calls, that our feeling of being individuals with personal purpose is an illusion, and that the proper response to life's illusions is renunciation and withdrawal. Second, the novel *Atlas Shrugged* by Ayn Rand asserts the Western secular view that there is no God outside one's self who can call us, that each individual chooses his or her own purpose, and that self-assertion is the highest good. With those two perspectives as a backdrop, a series of ancient and modern writers express the Jewish and Christian ideas about calling as they have developed over the centuries. Part 1 concludes with three contemporary readings that reflect Western society's present confusion over work, calling, purpose, and fulfillment. This confusion results as Judeo-Christian ideas collide with those of the East and the secular West.

Part 2 makes the case that individuals can make a difference and change their times. The selection by historian Arthur Schlesinger presents the argument. Then, writings by and about two heroes—William Wilberforce and Aleksandr Solzhenitsyn—illustrate the case.

Part 3 explores some of the tests and trials of living life as an entrepreneurial calling. The story of musician Yehudi Menuhin raises the question of whether we become whatever genes and fate make us, or whether we can become what we are not yet by re-creation. The seventeenth-century priest François de Fénelon shows that the deepest elements of our calling cannot be taught in words, but must be learned by experience under the authority of a Master. Florence Nightingale represents a woman who persevered through social barriers in order to answer a call from God. The Inklings, a group of writers and thinkers that included C. S. Lewis and J. R. R. Tolkien, illustrate the role of community and friendship in nurturing a call. Ludwig van Beethoven's letters reveal a man who achieved his noblest work in the face of severe handicap: increasing deafness. And Ferdinand Magellan, the first European to sail around the world, exemplifies how success can be the worst enemy of a called person who allows pride to swell.

Part 4 challenges us to appraise our character and priorities. Tolstoy's much-loved story of "Two Old Men" lays out the issues. Then a questionnaire allows readers to assess their faith, giftedness, relationships, work, and community involvement, as well as to consider what steps they'd like to take next.

Part 5 discusses "finishing well" in life's journey. The aging Picasso is revealed as driven rather than called. A Henry James short story depicts a man who, at the end of his life, has produced nothing because he feared to start. And William Wilberforce exemplifies one who perseveres in his call to the end and with confidence and serenity goes to his Maker.

The trajectory of the book, then, is this:

- What is calling? How does it differ from other ways of dealing with my longing for purpose in life?
- Can I as an individual really make a difference?
- If I answer a call, what challenges can I expect?

- What do I need to address in my unique life in order to hear and respond to a call from God?
- What will my final days look like if I accept the trials of a call and respond until the end? What will my final days look like if I don't?

You may want to refer the group to this roadmap at the beginning of each session. This reader's guide will help you orient each session within the roadmap.

SESSION 1

Unless yours is an ongoing group, people will usually treat the first meeting as an opportunity to decide whether they want to participate. They will decide what they think about one another, the material, and the discussion format. Therefore, you'll want to do a few extra things in the first meeting that will help people feel comfortable with each other, have a sense of where the group is going, and become excited enough about the group to return.

Perhaps the best way to break the ice in a new group is to share a meal. Plan a simple enough meal that the focus will be on conversation. Schedule the meal so that people don't feel rushed as they eat, yet you still have ninety minutes for a full discussion session. You'll want the full ninety minutes in order to give people a realistic taste of what the group will be like. If sharing a full meal is impractical, consider planning a two-hour session in which the first half-hour is devoted to light refreshments and informal chatting.

Overview and Introductions   (25 minutes)

When the food is set aside and the group gathers formally, welcome everyone. Then take ten minutes to give people an overview of what to expect. Explain:

- *What the* Trinity Forum Study Series *is:* It makes the forum curricula available to study groups. It helps thoughtful people examine the foundational issues through which faith acts upon the public good of modern society. It is Christian in commitment but open to all who are interested in its vision. Issues are discussed in the context of faith and the sweep of Western civilization.
- *The theme of this particular study:* What is a calling, and what might our lives look like if we committed ourselves to respond to a call.
- *The goals of this study:* See page 221.
- *The big picture of this study:* You may want to walk the group through "The Roadmap" on page 228.
- *The format of the group:* Your discussions will take about ninety minutes. In each session, you will cover about thirty pages from the book. Ideally, everyone will have read the material ahead of time, but it is possible to participate without having done so. As the leader, you'll

select questions that you think are most helpful for the group to discuss. Your goal is an open give-and-take, and you will not be lecturing. Differing opinions are welcome.

Ground Rules:

Here is a list of suggested ground rules for your group. You may want to add to this list the ones about disagreement on page 227:

- *Leadership:* The leader is not an expert or an authority, merely a facilitator and fellow-seeker. All in the group are teachers; all are students.
- *Confidentiality:* All discussion is free, frank, and *off-the-record.* Nothing will be repeated outside the group without permission.
- *Voluntary participation:* Everyone is free to speak; no one is required to take part. The only exception will be in the final session, when everyone will be asked to share two or three things he or she has found helpful or striking.
- *Non-denominational, non-partisan spirit:* Many people have strong beliefs and allegiances, both denominational and political. However, the desire here is to go deeper, so it will be important to transcend political advocacy and denominational differences. The book comes from the perspective of what C. S. Lewis called "mere Christianity" and reflects no particular denomination. Participants are welcome to express their own views and even to disagree with the readings.
- *Punctuality:* In order to get to all of the readings, the leader will keep the discussion moving. The formal meeting will begin and end on time.
- *Logistics:* Tell people anything they need to know about the location and schedule of the meetings. Explain that the group will finish promptly at the official ending time. That is the "soft" ending. However, if the host permits, you can also set a "hard" ending time thirty, sixty, or more minutes later. In that case, people are free to stay after the soft ending and talk informally until the hard ending time. (Setting a hard ending is a courtesy to the host if you are meeting in a home.)

Next, ask participants to go around and introduce themselves briefly. You'll go first to model the length and type of response you're looking for. That is, if your answer is one sentence, the others will usually give one sentence. If you take one minute, or three minutes, others will follow suit. The same is true for the content of your answer: if you say something brief and substantive, others will tend to do the same. Therefore, it will be a good idea to think ahead of time about how you can introduce yourself in a minute or less. In this way, you won't shortchange time for discussing the book. By way of introduction, ask each person to state his or her name and answer the following questions briefly:

- When you were about ten years old, what did you want to be when you grew up?
- Who was one of your heroes when you were about that age?

Introduction: Entrepreneurs of Life   (10 minutes)

Find the section, "Visionaries Who Add Value" in the introduction. Ask some-one to read aloud three paragraphs from this section, starting with the paragraph that begins, "One place where the confusion is lifting. . ." (p. 17) Ask participants where they would place themselves with regard to these ideas of calling and entrepreneurship. For example:

- I don't understand what this writer means by "calling."
- I understand what the writer means, but I question whether there is any God who calls humans in this way.
- I'm open to the possibility that there may be a God who calls, but I'm not yet convinced.
- I would like to believe there are answers to questions like, "What shall we do and how shall we live?"
- I believe I am called to a unique purpose, but I don't know what it is.
- I believe I am called to a unique purpose, and I have some idea about what it is.
- I'm convinced I am called to a unique purpose, and I have a fairly clear sense of what it is.
- My current challenge is whether and how to respond to the calling I believe I have.
- I have been following a call for some time; my challenge is to stay true to it.
- Other: _____

Hermann Hesse   (20 minutes)

The two readings you will cover in the rest of this first session represent schools of thought that reject the Jewish and Christian notion of calling. Although written by a Western European, Hermann Hesse, the novel *Siddhartha* briefly and effectively expresses the Eastern response to the human longing for purpose in life. The character named Siddhartha is the prince who, at the end of his search, becomes known as the Buddha, the enlightened one. Your main goal in examining this reading is to understand the Eastern view of the search for purpose in an individual life.

Read aloud question 1 and the first three sentences of the reading. Ask participants to scan the first paragraph and identify the issues troubling Siddhartha.

Next, focus on the central portion of that first paragraph, the portion that deals with Atman. Have someone read aloud from "Was it really Prajapati . . ." through ". . . was there another way that was worth seeking?" Discuss question 2. Note especially that Atman, the creator, the Only One, is said to dwell in the innermost Self within each person. In what ways is this understanding of Atman like and unlike the Judeo-Christian view of God?

Siddhartha believes that "to press towards the Self, toward Atman" is "the one important thing" to do in life. How would a person live if he or she treated this as his or her first priority? How would this life differ from that of a person who thinks "the one important thing" is:

- To make money
- To serve a God who is beyond the Self
- To care for the earth and its inhabitants

The first paragraph under "With the Samanas" answers the question in the previous paragraph. Ask someone to read it aloud. Discuss question 3. In practice, how does a person live a life of pressing toward the inner Self?

Read aloud the next paragraph, which begins, "Siddhartha had one single goal. . ." Read also the final paragraph of the reading. Discuss question 4. Discuss questions 5 through 7 to the extent that you have time, but be sure to save enough time for the Ayn Rand reading.

Ayn Rand   (20 minutes)

Summarize the introduction to Ayn Rand and her book, *Atlas Shrugged* on page 32. Underscore the statement in its first paragraph, "The central tenet of objectivism is that selfishness and self-assertion is the highest good to which human beings can attain." Set up the scene about the "reverse strike" by the industrialists.

The "moral code" that Francisco disparages in the first full paragraph is the code of the Jewish and Christian faiths: the rightness of loving one's neighbor and caring for the weak, the wrongness of theft and murder, and so on. Dagny says she and the other industrialists have always rejected that code and lived by their own. Francisco replies, "Yes—and paid ransoms for it!" Read aloud Francisco's account of the ransom in that paragraph and discuss question 2.

In their strike, the entrepreneurs are going to walk away from their industries and prove that the workers are utterly dependent upon the entrepreneurs, that the workers will starve without their masters' leadership abilities. How does this plan echo the "renounce and withdraw" worldview of the East?

Try to save a few minutes to look at questions 5 and 6. Your group may well contain the kinds of people Rand's philosophy has traditionally appealed to: educated, strong-minded people with the kinds of gifts that enable them to get ahead in a competitive world.

You have just looked at two arguments against calling that are very much alive today. One states that the longing for a calling and purpose is an illusion to be fought through withdrawal from the world. The other states that one creates one's own purpose by asserting one's own interests against those of everyone else. As you close your session, invite participants to bring to your next meeting any news items or recent literature that reflects these ideas. Also, ask them to read the selections by Steiner, Bonhoeffer, Eusebius, and Luther for next time. In session 2 you will compare the ideas you have discussed this time with Judeo-Christian ideas about calling.

SESSION 2

Now that you have looked at the two main philosophies that oppose the idea of calling, you are going to see how ancient and modern writers express Jewish and Christian ideas about calling as they have developed over the centuries.

George Steiner   (20 minutes)

In this selection, Steiner, who is Jewish, depicts what he thinks Hitler would say in defense of the Holocaust if he were alive to state his views. Steiner's Hitler hates but understands how profoundly Jewish ideas about God and God's call have affected our world.

Hitler cites three ways in which the Jew has "pressed on us the blackmail of transcendence": the moral demands of the transcendent God; the even more radical expectations of Jesus; and the secular utopia of Marxism (Karl Marx was Jewish). Read the first paragraph on page 41 and discuss question 2. Read the second paragraph and discuss question 3. Read the third paragraph and discuss question 4.

The paragraph that begins, "'Sacrifice yourself . . . '" parodies the teachings of Marx. In Hitler's view, how does communism—even without God—continue in the Jewish tradition?

Question 7 asks where you see the idea of God's calling behind Judaism, the Christian faith, and even Marxism. How does calling underlie the moral demands that Hitler despises?

Dietrich Bonhoeffer   (30 minutes)

Bonhoeffer wrote *The Cost of Discipleship* in the years after Hitler became Chancellor of Germany but before World War II broke out. Those were the years when the evils of Nazism were spreading, but when a concerted opposition by German Christians might have prevented the war and the Holocaust. However, most German Christians were either too afraid of the Nazis or too enchanted by the myth of Aryan supremacy to pay the cost of discipleship. Bonhoeffer was one of the exceptions, and he paid the supreme price. Thus, this selection from *The Cost of Discipleship* is neither the idle theory of an academic nor the pious sermon of a comfortable preacher. Bonhoeffer was living what he was writing, and his words were directed to a specific and dire situation. In fact, historians agree that the failure of the European churches to do what Bonhoeffer describes was one powerful reason why post-war Europeans became disillusioned with the Christian faith and now leave Europe's grandest churches largely empty.

Read aloud the quotation from Mark 2:14 that begins this selection on page 45, as well as the first paragraph. Discuss question 1.

The second paragraph addresses "the content of discipleship." Read it aloud and discuss question 2.

In contrast to Levi, Bonhoeffer examines three disciples who attempt "discipleship without Jesus Christ," that is, discipleship according to their own rules. Read aloud the quotation of Luke 9:57-62 and the paragraph that follows it. Discuss question 4 about the first of these three disciples.

The second disciple wants to obey Jesus' call after he obeys the Jewish commandment to honor his father. His father is either dying or dead and needs to be cared for throughout that process, however long it takes. The law requires this, and the man's community expects it of him. Read the paragraph that begins, "But where Jesus calls. . ." What does Bonhoeffer think about laws and community expectations when they conflict with Jesus' call? How might Bonhoeffer's words have applied to the situation German Christians were facing under Nazism? Can you imagine any situations today in which the call of Jesus conflicts with laws or community expectations? What are the potential abuses of a statement like, "Now, if never before, the law must be broken for the sake of Jesus"? (You don't have time to digress into a discussion of Bonhoeffer's choices, but it's worth recalling that he eventually decided to join a plot to assassinate Hitler, and breaking the law for the sake of Jesus was part of his rationale.)

Like the others, the third disciple tries to set the terms of his discipleship, but then he is in charge, not Jesus. You may need to skip question 6 in order to invite some summary thoughts: What do participants think of such an uncompromising call from Jesus? How is this different from just saying one believes in Jesus?

Eusebius   (10 minutes)

You may deal with Eusebius briefly. He was bishop in a century when the
Christian faith was spreading throughout the Roman Empire. In order to
accommodate masses of converts, leaders like Eusebius deemed it realistic to
have a two-tiered system in which less was required of the "average"
Christian. The uncompromising call of Jesus you just discussed could not, in
Eusebius's view, be imposed upon everyone. For such people, the church was
a hospital for sinners and required little from them. Because his view dominated the medieval world until the Reformation and still lives today, it is worth
examining here, at its root. The important thing is to understand what
Eusebius believed about calling and how it differs from what you just read in
Bonhoeffer and what you will read next in Martin Luther.

"The one" in the first paragraph of this reading refers to God when he
inscribed the Ten Commandments on stone; "the Other" refers to Jesus. Read
aloud the first paragraph on page 50. Discuss question 2. What's the difference
between the two groups of people, in Eusebius's view? Read the second and
third paragraphs and discuss question 1.

Eusebius set celibate monks, priests, and nuns apart from persons who
married and pursued secular work. The former had callings from God to their
religious life; the latter had none. Both the Reformation among Protestants and
post-Vatican II papal encyclicals among Roman Catholics have tried to break
down this notion that "secular" people don't have callings. Still, where do you
see examples of this kind of thinking today? Discuss questions 5 through 7 to
the degree you have time.

Those who are interested in question 8 might begin with Genesis 2;
Matthew 28:18-20 ("teaching them to obey *everything* I have commanded you"
[emphasis added]); Ephesians 6:5-8; 1 Corinthians 7:17-35; Colossians
3:17,22-24; 4:1.

Martin Luther   (20 minutes)

In this reading, Luther spoke out against both Eusebius's teaching and the
twelve hundred years of bad habits that grew from it. Luther opposed joining
religious orders for several reasons. Most notably, he thought religious orders
gave people the impression that works like prayer, fasting, and celibacy earned
God's favor and put the religious on a higher spiritual plane than everyone else.

This impression obscured the truth that only faith in Christ alone put a person right with God. Luther exalted faith over works, but he should not be misunderstood as supporting the kind of belief-without-discipleship that Bonhoeffer criticized.

Read aloud the second paragraph of this selection on page 54 and discuss questions 2 through 5. Close by inviting the group to summarize what they learned from the brief journey through history in this session. Ask participants to read the rest of part 1 for next time.

SESSION 3

In session 2 you traced the idea of calling from the Jews, through Jesus, and into the early church and the Middle Ages. You saw that the medieval view was a two-tiered system in which professional religious people had a higher calling than those who raised family and had "secular" or "worldly" jobs. Then you observed how Martin Luther reacted against this two-tiered system during the Reformation. In this session you will finish your historical tour by sampling the concept of calling among the Puritans a century after Luther. Then you will jump to the twentieth century to see how the concept has fared in the modern world. What happens when a culture is founded on faith in a God who calls but then loses faith in God? What happens when Judeo-Christian ideas collide with those of the East and the secular West?

John Cotton　　　　　　　　　　　　　　(30 minutes)

Cotton was the father of New England congregationalism. The views on Christian calling he espoused sank deep roots into the soil of Anglo-America. In later readings you will see how secularism later distorted these views, but here you have them in their original form. Plan to spend more time on this reading than on the others in this session.

Eusebius wrote of a two-tiered system in which some people lived the "religious" life and others the "secular" life. Cotton described a twofold life. Read aloud the first three paragraphs of this selection on page 57 and discuss questions 1 and 2. Read the fourth paragraph and discuss question 3. Read the fifth paragraph and discuss question 4. For question 5, look at the sixth paragraph. For question 6, look at the paragraphs that begin, "Fourthly . . . ", "Fifthly . . . ", and "Sixthly. . ." For question 7, see the paragraph that begins, "A man that in his calling hath. . ." Discuss questions 8 and 9 to the degree that you have time. The important thing here is to digest what Cotton meant when he spoke of a "calling" or "vocation" (the latter is the Latin word for the former).

Marilyn Ferguson   (15 minutes)

In Ferguson's words on vocation you will see what three centuries of secular-ization, along with influence from Eastern thought, did to Cotton's ideas. Read aloud this brief selection on page 63. Discuss at least questions 1 through 3. Be aware that some in your group may be sympathetic to Ferguson's views. She represents a strong strain in modern thought. Many people have not stopped to think whether it makes sense to speak of calling without a God who calls. Also, the idea that we create our own meaning is a truism in our culture—the suggestion that we *don't* create our own meaning is what is radical today. You may have to go slowly to examine what Ferguson is actually saying. Is there really a difference between finding meaning by working and finding mean-ingful work if the meaning in work comes from nowhere but our personal opinion? Putting the question this way may confuse some participants, but the confusion is embedded in Ferguson's own words.

Ernest Becker   (15 minutes)

Becker did not believe in the existence of a transcendent God, but in this selec-tion he describes an idea by Kierkegaard, who did believe in such a God. The selection on page 65 is short; read it aloud and discuss questions 2 through 5. Help the group hear the old Jewish and Christian idea that Becker describes wistfully as a thing now out of reach for the modern secularist.

Václav Havel   (20 minutes)

When he wrote this selection, Havel was an atheist raised in a society where faith in a personal God was considered hopelessly backward. But he was also in prison for opposing the communist regime. Havel's thinking is sophisticated, and you may not have time for all the questions, but the central thing to get out of this reading is a sense of an intelligent, modern person wrestling with whether there is anyone out there, beyond the Self, who is calling. Ferguson and Becker both assume there isn't, and that assumption affects their thoughts about calling. Havel is astute enough to see the philosophical problems he encounters when he dismisses the idea of a Caller.

Havel observes that it makes sense not to pay for his tram ride from a strictly self-interested, Ayn Rand point of view: he gains nothing by paying and loses nothing by not paying. Not even a concern for society compels him to pay because society loses little if he withholds his one coin. But something rebukes his thought of not paying. Read aloud the paragraph that begins, "Let us examine . . ." Discuss questions 2 and 3. Read the paragraph that begins, "Who, then, is in fact . . ." and discuss question 4.

In the last three paragraphs of his July 17 letter, Havel moves from the theory that the "partner" is his "inner voice" to the possibility that the "partner" is "God." See if you can follow his train of thought. Then discuss question 5.

Look at the first paragraph of his July 31 letter. Here he describes not just theoretical guilt, but real guilt over a real situation. Discuss question 6. Read the last paragraph and discuss question 7.

By now you have a sense of what a "calling" is. You have probably begun to consider whether you believe it is possible to have a calling and whether there is anyone beyond the Self who calls us. Perhaps you have learned from Havel that this is no theoretical exercise, but a practical issue that confronts you daily. At this point, someone might raise the objection, "This talk of a calling is all very well, but isn't it rather grandiose? Or perhaps simply 'pious'? In today's global society, can one person make a difference?" Part 2 addresses that question by pointing to two individuals who altered history. Ask participants to read all of part 2 for your next meeting—it is much shorter than part 1.

SESSION 4

Part 2 makes the case that individuals can make a difference and change their times. The selection by historian Arthur Schlesinger Jr. presents the argument. Then, writings by and about two heroes—William Wilberforce and Aleksandr Solzhenitsyn—illustrate the case. Your goal in this session is to discover what enabled these men to make a difference—is there anything in their example that we could ourselves practice?

Arthur M. Schlesinger Jr.   (20 minutes)

What do you think about Schlesinger's definition of leadership: "the capacity to inspire and mobilize masses of people"? Why does this definition require that individuals matter? (One might also ask whether the capacity to inspire and mobilize groups of people smaller than masses also qualifies as valuable leadership.)

Read aloud the second paragraph of this selection, which begins, "Now the very concept . . . ," and the one that begins, "Determinism may or may not be true. . ." Discuss questions 2 and 4. Read the last paragraph and discuss questions 5 and 6.

William Wilberforce   (30 minutes)

Summarize who Wilberforce was and what he did. Then read the letter by Rev. Thomas Scott (p. 80). Discuss question 1. If necessary, refer the group back to the words of Eusebius (pp. 50-51).

Read the "Advice from his Friend, Prime Minister William Pitt (the Younger)." Discuss question 3.

Read Wilberforce's mission statement on page 82: "God Almighty has set before me two great objects. . ." The phrase "reformation of manners" included moral reform and social reform: education and voting rights for common people; religious liberty for Roman Catholics: campaigns against political corruption, drunkenness, Sabbath-breaking, and prostitution; and many other causes. "Manners" in this sense meant morals, not table etiquette. Discuss question 4. Read Wesley's letter on page 84 and discuss question 5.

Questions 6 through 8 can be dealt with quickly. For question 6, read the first two paragraphs under "People of Character and Integrity," as well as the indented paragraph that begins, "Confidence and respect. . ." For question 7, have the group scan the whole section entitled, "Networking." For question 8, look at the first two paragraphs under, "Prerequisites of an Effective Reformer." Save time for question 9.

Aleksandr Solzhenitsyn (30 minutes)

Summarize the biographical introduction about Solzhenitsyn. His most famous works deal with life inside Soviet prison camps: *The Gulag Archipelago* and *One Day in the Life of Ivan Denisovich.* Then read aloud the third and fourth paragraphs of the selection (p.96), beginning with, "I drifted into literature," and discuss question 1.

His statement that "no one [would] ever publish me" comes in the fourth paragraph. Read also the fifth, where he speaks of "the surety that my work would not be in vain," and discuss question 2. Then ask the group to review the next six paragraphs to discuss question 3.

In the section entitled, "An Urgent Mission," Solzhenitsyn speaks of "one careless move" that led to KGB confiscation of his archives of source material. His entire life's work was at risk. Read the first paragraph in that section and discuss question 4. Read the paragraph that begins, "They could take my children hostage . . . " and discuss question 5. For question 6, read the two paragraphs under, "The Word as Weapon." For question 7, read the first paragraph under, "Calling and Conscience." For question 8, read the paragraph that begins, "The one worrying thing. . ." Invite participants to respond to question 9. Allow some silence for thinking. Avoid pressure for anyone to respond because some participants will feel acutely a lack of this sense of purpose. Perhaps question 10 will be easier for people to answer.

These questions are personal and will work best if your group has reached a level of trust in which participants feel they can disclose their sense of calling or their lack of one. It will be important not to give the impression that a "real" calling must be as grand as Wilberforce's or Solzhenitsyn's—not everyone is called to lead a movement or bring down a regime. On the other hand, most of us tend to think too small. You may want to leave questions 9 and 10 hanging in the air and give the group an open invitation to revisit them whenever someone wants to share something he or she is thinking about his or her life.

In session 5 you will change gears again. Part 3 explores some of the challenges of living life as an entrepreneurial calling. Neither Wilberforce nor Solzhenitsyn had an easy life. Ask the group to read the selections by and about Menuhin, Fénelon, and Nightingale — three stories that inspire us to face the challenges.

SESSION 5

Part 3 addresses six challenges we face when we choose an entrepreneurial life. In this session you will look at three of these: genes and fate; the limits of learning through books and lectures alone; and social pressure.

Yehudi Menuhin   (30 minutes)

Summarize who Menuhin was. Then read through the second and third paragraphs of the introduction to this excerpt from his book (p. 105). Make sure everyone understands the two views on fate. One view (held equally by Eastern philosophers and Western secularists) says birth is destiny. We are what we are born to be, what our genes, environment, or *karma* determine us to be. The Jewish and Christian tradition agrees that creation tells part of the story but insists that more is possible. When God calls us and we respond, we can become more than our genes and our socio-economic status. For the called, re-creation is destiny. The central question you will bring to Menuhin's autobiography is, "Was Menuhin simply born to be a brilliant violinist and conductor, or were calling and response involved?"

Begin with the box of quotations entitled, "Fated to Be." It expresses the idea that birth is destiny. Ask someone to read the quotations aloud. What are the main features of this theory of destiny?

Next, read the third and fourth paragraphs of the selection from Menuhin's book and discuss questions 1 and 2. Read the next paragraph and discuss question 3. Go back to the first two paragraphs of the selection for questions 6 and 7. Finish with question 5. Menuhin speaks of "vocation" but describes it as demanding nothing more than compliance with a happy accident. Do you think Wilberforce would have spoken of his vocation in the same terms?

François de Fénelon   (30 minutes)

Summarize who Fénelon was. Then read aloud these sentences from the fourth paragraph of the introduction: "The deepest things in life cannot be taught in words (or books, lectures, seminars, and sermons). They must be learned in experience under the authority of a Master." This is the theme of *Telemachus*.

Set the scene: Telemachus's father, Odysseus (Ulysses), has not been seen for years, not since he left Troy. Telemachus has gone searching for his father and is guided by what he thinks is his father's counselor and friend, the old man Mentor. (Our word "mentor" comes from the name of this Homeric character.) But his Mentor is the goddess of wisdom in disguise.

Read the first paragraph on page 113 and discuss question 1. Read the second paragraph and discuss question 2. According to Mentor, what should be the role of experience and guidance by "mentors," as opposed to book-learning, in a leader's education?

Read the paragraph that begins, "At last Minerva addressed him. . ." Discuss question 3. Select among questions 5 through 7 according to the amount of time you have. Save time for question 8.

Florence Nightingale   (30 minutes)

Florence Nightingale suffers from idealized treatment in children's books and little serious attention in adult histories. Today nursing is underpaid and undervalued as a "women's profession," but in Nightingale's day it had a far lower status. Moreover, Nightingale practiced her vocation not in a clean, modern hospital, but in war zones. She founded the "Doctors Without Borders" of her day and offers an example of a person who put her calling ahead of comfort, physical safety, social convention, and pressure from the people who controlled her livelihood.

Summarize the introduction to this reading. Read the first, third, and fourth paragraphs and discuss question 1. Read the paragraphs that begin, ". . . While Florence inwardly longed . . . " (p. 122) and "Mrs. Nightingale had no idea . . . " and discuss question 2. From the paragraph that begins, "One morning . . . ," read Florence's question and Dr. Howe's response, and discuss question 3. For question 4, read the paragraphs that begin, "The plans of the two . . . " and "It wasn't just the field of nursing. . ." Skip to question 7 and read the letter to Hilary, which begins, "I have always found. . ."

Ask the group to scan Florence's diary entries from Egypt (beginning with "[March] 7. Thursday . . . ") to discuss question 8. Look at her diary entry further down for question 9 and her last two entries for questions 10 and 11. Be sure to save time for question 12.

Think back to the ideas of fate versus calling you discussed under the Menuhin reading. Which of those two views of destiny do you think best fits

Florence Nightingale? What do you think she would have said about Menuhin's sense that he simply complied with the way he was made and the longings of his family?

Ask participants to read the selections by Sayer, Beethoven, and Manchester for next time.

SESSION 6

This session continues with more lessons from people who have lived entrepreneurial lives. The Inklings were a group of intellectuals who achieved great work partly because of the support they had from each other. Beethoven achieved his great work while struggling with a disability. By way of warning, Ferdinand Magellan offers an example of a man who let his success breed pride and so, defeat him.

George Sayer   (30 minutes)

Sayer writes about the Inklings, an informal group of intellectuals that included C. S. Lewis, J. R. R. Tolkien, Dorothy Sayers, Charles Williams, and others. The point of this reading is to observe how the support of likeminded comrades is of infinite help to the person on a quest through life. Summarize the background information. Then begin with question 2. Read the paragraphs that begin, "It was always utterly informal . . . (p. 132)," "Although Jack studied Icelandic literature . . . ," "This discussion was the germ . . . ," and further on, "After the arrival of Charles Williams . . . " and "The ritual never varied." Discuss questions 2, 4, and 5. For question 3, go back to the paragraph that begins, "Dr. Havard (always called Humphrey). . ."

Read aloud the last paragraph to discuss question 7. Save time for question 8. Can you think of any other influential groups, such as Wilberforce's Clapham Circle? Positive examples include Jesus' twelve apostles. Terrorist groups and violent gangs offer negative examples of the power of a dedicated team.

Ludwig van Beethoven   (30 minutes)

Summarize the introduction to this reading. Read aloud the first paragraph on page 139 and discuss questions 1 and 2. Direct the group to the second and third paragraphs for question 4. For question 5, read the first half of the paragraph that begins, "Such experiences. . ." Read the second, short letter and discuss question 7. Read the Steiner quotation and discuss question 8.

William Manchester (30 minutes)

Magellan was the first European to sail around the world. A man who would attempt such a feat in a wooden ship and without modern equipment had to be a lover of risk and a luster for glory. Kept within bounds, such determination and courage are noble qualities, but Manchester's essay traces how success fed a cancerous pride that eventually proved lethal.

The challenge of reading aloud from this essay is pronouncing the many Spanish and Portuguese names and phrases. You might want to say something about that so that people won't feel embarrassed to read. Have someone read the third paragraph on page 147 and discuss question 1. Read the paragraph, "It was good advice . . . " for question 2. For question 3, look at the paragraph that begins, "His resolution was strengthened. . ."

The paragraphs, "The expedition had left . . . " and "The serenity of the Pacific . . . " may be too disgusting to read aloud; ask the group to scan them for question 4. Read the paragraph that begins, "Now in late April of 1521 . . . " for questions 5 through 7.

For question 8 you might think of Napoleon and Hitler, both of whom overreached when they attacked Russia. If your group is not historically minded, perhaps they can think of business leaders who have fallen into a similar trap.

Close by asking the group to read part 4 for your next meeting, as well as the introduction to part 5 and the selection by Waugh and James in part 5. When you meet you will discuss the readings by Tolstoy (part 4) and Waugh and James (part 5)—all fictional works by premier storytellers.

You will not discuss the questions for reflection and self-appraisal at the end of part 4. These are for individuals to use on their own. You might suggest that participants schedule several hours or even a whole day of solitude to use these questions to take stock of their lives. They might need to schedule this time of solitude several weeks or even months away, but it will be worthwhile to calendar the time. If you set the example of scheduling even a two-hour block of time, others will do likewise. Let participants know that the many people who have taken the time to use these questions have found them invaluable. Part 4 is designed to help you take stock of where your lives are now, while part 5 looks ahead to where you want your lives to end up.

SESSION 7

Part 4 offers a chance to take stock of your priorities. What do you value most? Are those the things you are actually pursuing with the most zeal? The personal questions at the end of part 4 are for participants to use on their own, but the Tolstoy story will spark more general reflections. Part 5 raises the question of finishing well—who do you want to be at the end of your life? It is rarely too late to make a mid-course correction if we realize we have been questing toward the wrong goal. The two stories by Waugh and James show what can happen when people don't make wise choices about where they're heading.

Leo Tolstoy   **(35 minutes)**

This fascinating story will require extra time. Read the first three paragraphs and discuss questions 1 and 2. (Regarding the snuff, you may want to look down at part III of the story, where Efim asks, "How is it you don't give up that nasty habit?" and Elisha replies, "The evil habit is stronger than I.")

Ask for two readers to take the roles of Efim and Elisha for the rest of the reading. Have them read six paragraphs, beginning with Efim's line, "'The time's right enough . . .'" (p. 162). Discuss question 3.

Have someone else read two paragraphs, beginning with, "Elisha left home in a cheerful mood. . ." (p. 164). Discuss question 4.

Summarize the story down to part VI. Then have your Elisha read his lines in the paragraph that begins, "'There seems to be no end to it. . .'" Discuss question 5. Have Elisha read the paragraph that begins, "'To-morrow I will redeem their cornfield . . .'" (p. 170) for question 6. Summarize part VII.

Part VIII picks up Efim's story. Summarize part VIII, then have your Efim read the first four paragraphs in part IX. Discuss question 7.

Have someone else read the paragraph that begins, "Efim stood looking in front of him. . ." Then summarize parts X and XI. In part XI, have Efim read the paragraph that begins, "'So that is how he got ahead of me. . .'" Discuss question 8.

Summarize part XII until the two men's final lines. Have your Efim and Elisha read from "Efim was silent for a while . . . " to the end. Discuss questions 9 and 10.

Evelyn Waugh   (25 minutes)

Begin by reading from the introduction to part 5, the paragraph that begins, "But as history and experience show clearly . . ." (p. 190). Note the three points made about calling in that introduction: that calling gives us a life-project that keeps us growing until the end; that calling enables us to continue to live a purpose-full life even if circumstances limit our activities; and that calling helps us finish well by taking away the pressure to guarantee the outcome of our efforts.

Summarize the context of the excerpt from *Brideshead Revisited*. The main character of the novel, Charles, was a close friend of Sebastian Flyte when the two were students at Oxford. They remained friends for years thereafter until Sebastian fled to North Africa, hoping to escape his family, their Catholic faith, and his guilt over his sins. He was a confirmed alcoholic and resisted all attempts to force him into sobriety. In the passage you are reading, Charles (who is by now in his mid-thirties) is discussing his old friend with Sebastian's sister Cordelia, who has recently managed to track down her brother in Morocco. Ask someone to read the selection. Discuss as many of questions 1 through 6 as you have time for.

Henry James   (30 minutes)

Set up the scene: the narrator has just met the woman who is modeling for the painter Theobald's masterpiece. Ask someone to read the third paragraph ("He eyed me an instant askance . . . ") down to ". . . and I made that sketch." Discuss question 1. Read the rest of that paragraph for question 2.

For question 4, read "Then at last I understood . . . " (p. 199) and further down, "He stared, but he seemed scarcely. . ." For question 5, have the group review the two paragraphs, "It was in an obscure corner . . . " and "He made no response. . ." From the middle of that last long paragraph, have someone read beginning with, "'I never began!'" to the end. Discuss as much as you can of questions 6 through 8.

These stories can be unnerving as they shine harsh light on our own illusions. Assure the group that the final two readings include more encouragement than warning.

SESSION 8

Arianna Huffington   (20 minutes)

It's not necessary to work exhaustively through these last three readings. The first is about the last years of the great painter, Pablo Picasso. A stronger contrast with Theobald in Henry James's story, "The Madonna of the Future" could seemingly not be found. While Theobald feared to begin working, Picasso feared to stop. Yet both were driven by the illusion of the ultimate masterpiece that would give meaning to their lives. Both were driven rather than called and so, in the end, knew their lives lacked meaning.

Read aloud the second paragraph on page 206 and discuss question 3. You might explain that Sisyphus is a character from a Greek myth, a man whom the gods punished with the task of forever rolling a stone uphill. Read the third and fourth paragraphs for question 4. Read the last paragraph for question 7. Save time for question 9.

John Pollock   (20 minutes)

How different were Wilberforce's last years from Picasso's! When his body no longer allowed him to participate actively in politics, his sense of calling about the battle against slavery continued to animate but not frustrate him. Read the third paragraph on page 210 and discuss question 1. For question 3, read the paragraph that begins, "Wilberforce saw as a wonderful providence. . ." Read, "Dr. Chambers considered . . . " for question 4. Then read the four paragraphs that begin, "Wilberforce remained alert. . ." Discuss questions 5 through 7 to the degree you have time.

Note: In 1833, Parliament paid £20 million to the plantation owners to compensate them for freeing their slaves. In today's currency, that is roughly equivalent to £1.2 billion or $1.8 billion.

George MacDonald   (15 minutes)

From the introduction to this selection on page 215, read the last paragraph aloud. Then read the selection. Discuss questions 1, 3, and 6.

Closing Thoughts (30 minutes)

To close the session, let each person respond to this question: "What key thoughts, ideas, and comments struck you personally during our study? What stands out to you?" Think carefully ahead of time whom you will ask to answer this question first, since that person's answer will set the tone for the other responses. Choose someone who you think is reflective and has been taking the readings to heart.

Thank everyone for participating. Some light refreshments and informal time to talk would be a fitting way to end the meeting.

AUTHORS

Os Guinness is a Senior Fellow at The Trinity Forum in McLean, Virginia. Born in China and educated in England, he earned his D.Phil from Oxford University. He is the author or editor of numerous books, including *The Call, The American Hour, Invitation to the Classics,* and *Long Journey Home.*

Karen Lee-Thorp (author of the reader's guide) is the senior editor of Bible studies and small group resources at NavPress and the author of more than fifty study guides. Karen has spent almost two decades studying, speaking on, and writing about the learning process. A graduate of Yale University, she speaks at women's groups and writes from her home in Brea, California.

For a catalog of The Trinity Forum's publications, including others in this series, please write: The Trinity Forum, 7902 Westpark Drive, Suite A, McLean, VA 22102. The catalog is also online at The Trinity Forum's website, www.ttf.org.

OTHER BOOKS IN THE TRINITY FORUM STUDY SERIES.

The Journey

Chart your own path toward faith. This compilation of views about life's meaning is perfect for reflecting seriously on why you believe what you believe.

The Journey (Os Guinness) $16

The Great Experiment

Discover the critical role faith played in the formation of America and why it's essential to freedom in society today.

The Great Experiment (Os Guinness) $16

Doing Well and Doing Good

What does the way we make and dispose of money say about us as a nation? Discover the connection between a society's character and its view of money, giving, and caring.

Doing Well and Doing Good (Os Guinness) $16

Steering Through Chaos

There is a huge difference between knowing about good and becoming a good person. This thoughtful, probing study examines the seven deadly vices and contrasts them with the beatitudes from Jesus' Sermon on the Mount.

Steering Through Chaos (Os Guinness) $16

When No One Sees

True character is demonstrated by what you do when no one else is around. This compelling book illustrates how character is built and tested, and offers practical help for bringing about radical change in your own character.

When No One Sees (Os Guinness) $16

Get your copies today at your local bookstore, visit our website at www.navpress.com, or call (800) 366-7788. Ask for offer **#6180** or a FREE catalog of NavPress products.

NAVPRESS
BRINGING TRUTH TO LIFE
www.navpress.com

Prices subject to change.